apparel
concepts and practical applications

BEVERLY KEMP-GATTERSON
Art Institute of Houston

BARBARA L. STEWART
The University of Houston

FAIRCHILD BOOKS, INC.

NEW YORK

Director of Sales and Acquisitions: Dana Meltzer-Berkowitz

Executive Editor: Olga T. Kontzias

Acquisitions Editor: Joe Miranda

Senior Development Editor: Jennifer Crane

Development Editor: Michelle Levy

Art Director: Adam B. Bohannon

Production Director: Ginger Hillman

Associate Production Editor: Jessica Rozler

Cover and text design: Erin Fitzsimmons

Copyeditor: Jennifer Sammartino

Photo Research: Beth Cohen

Illustrator: Jenny Green, shu shu design

Associate Art Director: Erin Fitzsimmons

Library of Congress Catalog Card Number: 200792850

ISBN-13: 978-1-56367-481-5

GST R 13304424

Printed in the United States of America

TP12

Contents

v

Extended Contents

Preface

Changes in the past three decades have profoundly affected the field of retailing. The wealth of data now available through the computer, advances in technology for designing and producing apparel, global markets, and the changing face of management in retail organizations provide only a few examples. Consumers have become more discerning with regard to the quality of the apparel they purchase and while price is no longer the sole determining factor for a purchase, quality remains high on the list.

Thirty years ago, the majority of formally educated retail buyers and managers were required to take courses in textiles, apparel design, apparel history, consumer behavior, and clothing construction. That requirement is no longer the norm as those courses vie for curriculum space with other contemporary subjects. Hence, apparel retailers and manufacturers may find themselves with merchants who have very little knowledge of how apparel is designed and produced.

Knowledge of apparel, however, continues to play a major role in the execution of apparel buying functions. Given the variety of ways in which merchandise is designed and produced for today's dynamic world market, it is essential for merchants to develop and maintain a solid foundation of current apparel knowledge. Technological advances and societal changes fuel the need for up-to-date information and understanding among merchandising and management executives in the retailing industry. While detailed, specialized manufacturing specifications are not required and are not included in this text, a broadly based understanding of design, manufacturing, and marketing processes is needed. *Apparel: Concepts and Practical Applications* is designed to fill that need by examining the many components involved in becoming knowledgeable about apparel.

This text is divided into five units beginning with Unit I, *Foundations of Apparel*, which provides a broad overview of the evolution of apparel and summarizes the sociological and psychological foundations that influence consumer demand.

Unit II, *The Creative Processes and Design*, focuses on multiple aspects of the creative process as well as on introducing the student to the world of haute couture by using brief summaries of selected fashion designers.

Unit III is titled *Apparel Factors* and allows the student to understand design by examining design principles. This unit also introduces the student to the world of textiles and the importance that they play in apparel development. The manufacturing process from conception and design to assembly of garments is a fundamental part of this unit. Industry standards for sizing, labeling, and quality control are also discussed. Then, the origin of footwear and handbags is explored and the role these play in the apparel industry is investigated.

Unit IV is titled *Coordination and Marketing*. This unit can be used as practical application for the preceding units in that it provides tools to assist the student in selecting apparel either for personal use or resale. The fundamentals of apparel marketing are introduced and allow the student to think strategically about influencing consumer trends.

Unit V, *Decision Making*, focuses on the decision-making processes used by individual consumers and by buyers and merchants in selecting apparel for the various companies in the retailing industry. Throughout each unit, the material is enhanced with illustrations as well as key terms and concepts.

The authors have deliberately geared the presentation of the subject matter to be of direct value to both undergraduate students and seasoned merchants and merchandising executives who may require guidance in selecting and evaluating quality apparel. Even advanced merchants in apparel businesses of all sizes will find that a study of this text will enable them to increase their understanding of the broad foundations of apparel without having to devote an entire semester of study on specific topics such as history of fashion and textiles.

The mission of this text is to provide a broad conceptual and practical perspective of apparel including the production processes and consumer marketing involved while making it an enjoyable learning experience. As a basis for the preparation of future as well as current professionals in all segments of the apparel industry, its goal is to assist textile and apparel students to better understand garment manufacturing and the complex decision-making involved in producing apparel to meet the needs of the target customer.

Acknowledgments

From Beverly: With thanks to the many friends and family members who have encouraged me during this journey. A special thanks to my beloved mother-aunt, Ima Jean Tigner, who has been my biggest cheerleader; and to friends, Mazella Boulden, George Holloway, Justine Richardson, Deborah Perkins, and Linda Burnett; and to my wonderful sons, Greg and Michael. I must give special thanks to my Lord and Savior, Jesus, who guided me and sustained me, physically, financially, and spiritually throughout the writing of this book.

From Barbara: Students, first, have been the inspiration for investing the energy needed to write this book. Thank you for sharing your lives and expectations with me through the years. Second,

I express appreciation to my colleagues, especially those at the University of Houston, with whom for more than 20 years I have shared friendship and camaraderie in creating academic programs and tools to meet student needs. Among those colleagues I extend special recognition to my current department chair, Carole Goodson, for her support of me as I teach and write from my temporary assignment in Australia. Finally, most gratefully, I express appreciation to my husband, Quentin, and youngest daughter, Juliana, for their contributions to my ability to complete this project. Quentin, for more than 35 years, has recognized and supported my need to learn and serve as an academic. Juliana, now 14, contributes to my love of apparel by reminding me daily of the fun and excitement of shopping and wearing apparel fashions.

Together we acknowledge the contributions of the editors and staff at Fairchild Books. Michelle Levy, Development Editor for her diligence and editorial support; Jennifer Crane, Senior Development Editor; Jessica Rozler, Associate Production Editor; Erin Fitzsimmons, Associate Art Director; Adam Bohannon, Art Director; and Olga Kontzias, Executive Editor, for her generous attention and guidance throughout this project.

unit
> one

foundations of apparel

>> *chapter one*

FIGURE 1.7 A pioneer in her time, Queen Elizabeth of England (1533–1603) was known for wearing elaborate gowns that were adorned with stiff lace collars and covered with pearls, gems, and ribbons.

FIGURE 1.8 Henry VIII (1491–1547) was another leader in fashion. He stands in a doublet, jerkin, and codpiece, all of which he made famous during his reign.

of masculinity and tights were only worn by the rich. The most favored materials were velvet, satin, and cloth made from gold.

Clothing of the upper classes was made in bright colors and often encrusted with diamonds, rubies, and pearls. Reds and purples were favorite colors. Because of the explorations of Mexico and Peru, Spain became wealthy from the influx of gold and silver (Tortora, 2005). As the Spanish influence was felt in the economy, it also began to dominate fashion, as colors became darker and more somber.

The Baroque Period

The Baroque period during the 1600s was dominated by the French influence. Women's dresses featured two skirts and included the bodice, petticoat, and gown. The over skirt was gathered up to reveal the skirt underneath and usually ended in a train made of heavy fabric. Another element, the **ruff**, became popular and was created on upper garments by use of a drawstring on the upper side of the shirt. The ruff forced the wearer to hold their head higher since it stood up around the neck. The ruff became a mark of aristocratic privilege (Laver, 1969). Women also wore the ruff, but adjusted it so that the front of the bodice was open to expose the top of the bosom.

Women's clothing was more natural, yet still elaborate. The body was not as deformed as it had been by the tight lacing and farthingale. There was also a transition from the ruff to a falling collar. Billowing layers of petticoats replaced hoop skirts and instead of starched, stiff materials, softer satins and silks were used. Sleeves were large, slashed, and puffed out with stuffing.

FIGURE 1.9 (top) Example of a gown with a farthingale and lace ruff

FIGURE 1.10 (left) Women's dresses showing the outer skirts

FIGURE 1.11 Prior to King Louis XIV's reign (1543–1715), affluent French men dressed incredibly flamboyantly. This lavish clothing consisted of short-waisted doublets and breeches. Louis XIV's reign, however, was marked by a royal mandate to give up extravagance in dress.

FIGURE 1.12 (top left) Marie Antoinette (1755–1793), or "Queen of Fashion," wearing an extravagant dress that distends sideways by means of a pannier

FIGURE 1.13 (bottom left) Madame de Pompadour wearing a robe a la Francaise trimmed with flowers, lace, and ribbons

FIGURE 1.14 (above) Example of casual men's wear

Elizabethan era with puffed or slashed sleeves. Leg 'o mutton sleeves were oversized gathered sleeves and narrowed at the elbows.

Josephine Bonaparte was the "trophy wife" of Napoleon. She became the leader of French fashion. Her private tailor's name was Leroy, who became the last word in fashion during that time. Leroy designed dresses in an empire line, featuring deep décolleté and puffed sleeves. Josephine set several fashion trends. She made the color white popular again in ball gowns. Other trends included fur trims on dresses and the wearing of shawls or pashminas. It is reported that Josephine owned 676 dresses (Cosgrave, 2001).

During the second half of the nineteenth century, women's dress changed and the layers of petticoats were replaced by the crinoline or hooped petticoat (Laver, 1969). The Empress Eugenie, who was Napolean III's Spanish wife, had a great influence on fashion trends, especially the wearing of crinolines. She was considered the leader of French fashion in her time (Cosgrave, 2001). The crinoline eventually evolved into the bustle by the late 1800s. The bustle also disappeared and day dresses were shown with fullness at the back toward the hemline and sometimes flowing into a train.

Prince Albert, also known as the Prince of Wales, is considered an innovator in men's fashion. Savile Row resulted from a tailor, Henry Poole, joining with other tailors to transform this street into the center of influence for men's fashions. Savile Row dressed the Prince of Wales. He became the model of masculine dressing. Americans started buying clothing **"off-the-peg."** Brooks Brothers opened in New York in 1818, selling high quality ready-made suits for men. Due to the superior skill of English tailors, the French readily adopted the style of the English for the male costume. Ordinary male costume changed very little from the previous years. The basic items were cut-away coats worn in the evening and frock coats for daytime.

FIGURE 1.15 Josephine Bonaparte wearing a chemise dress with a high waist typical of the period

FIGURE 1.16 Prince Albert, also called the Prince of Wales, set the standard for men's costume.

The Twentieth Century

The S-shape silhouette was popular at the beginning of the twentieth century. The skirt was smooth over the hips and flared out toward the floor in a bell-shape. Bodices were adorned with tucks and lots of trim. By 1910, skirts began to narrow at the hem so extremely that they were called hobble skirts. It was very difficult to take anything but very small steps in these skirts. By 1913, the V-neck was popular and replaced standing collars on dresses. Designers eventually loosened the constricted waist and relieved the pressure of the S-shape corset. The brassiere (bra) was introduced as a mainstay in the wardrobe.

All women's clothing could now be purchased ready-made. World War I caused a shortage of men, which created the demand for more alluring clothing. This resulted in short skirts and the adoption of trousers. The silhouette was long, slender, and flat with no waistline. All curves were completely gone in an attempt to give the female a boyish figure.

By 1919, the flared skirt that lasted throughout the war was replaced by the barrel line. This garment had a tubular, almost shapeless effect with a low waistline. There were many outstanding designers who emerged during this time, including Madeleine Vionnet, Coco Chanel, and Elsa Schiaparelli. During this time, skirts reached the extreme of shortness (shorter than any time in history up to that time). As the 1920s came to a close, skirts suddenly got longer with the natural waistline again being shown.

During the 1930s, the silhouette emphasized the natural form of the woman's body with clearly defined curves. The fashion industry thrived. Emphasis shifted from the legs to the back (Laver, 1969). Backs were bared to the waist. Dresses were slim and straight, sometimes wider at the shoulder line than at the hips. The shirtwaist dress also became popular. As World War II drew near, the silhouette changed with a defined waistline. Men's dress clothing remained

FIGURE 1.17 A dress from 1911 with empire style lines that narrowed at the hem. This style of skirt was sometimes called a "hobble skirt" because it was so hard to walk in.

FIGURE 1.18 At the races, 1930: Three women wearing dresses with long skirts, which was the height of fashion at the time.

FIGURE 1.19 Dior's New Look, featuring a wide skirt and slim waist-hugging top

FIGURE 1.20 In the late 1940s to the early 1950s, men's suits were cut with wide shoulders, broad lapels, and double-breasted coats.

unchanged for the most part. But there was a movement toward more casual attire for men and as a result, the double-breasted blazer waistcoat became popular, as well as knickers.

During World War II, the Limitation Orders eliminated trouser cuffs and extra pockets, and regulated the width of skirts and lengths of trousers and jackets as well as the depth of skirt hems and belts. The emphasis was on utility of clothing. The silhouettes showed broad shoulders with pads and narrow hips and skirts that ended just below the knee.

Nylon hosiery disappeared when the war broke out and women painted their legs to look like hosiery. The acute shortage of material during the war affected the look of garments.

When the war ended, styles took a marked turn. In the spring of 1947, Christian Dior, revealed his '**New Look**.' This look had narrow shoulders, a defined waist, and emphasis on the bust with a wide skirt in a longer length. Hemlines dropped to half way between the knee and the ankle. The feminine figure returned, accenting rounded bosoms, slim waistlines and molded hips. Materials used for coats, suits, dresses and skirts were used excessively in yardage.

Men's clothing had more generous cuts in suiting with wide shoulders. Broad lapels and double-breasted coats were popular with wide trousers finishing the look. French cuffs on men's dress shirts were common.

The silhouette still defined the body, but skirts were longer and fuller. Gradually, more feminine trims were added back to garments. One popular dress during this time was the chemise (formerly popular in the twenties), which had no waistline with a loose, straight body with an optional belt carried at the hipline. By 1958, this style was gone. Less fabric was used in women's costumes with a trimmer shoulder line and small, defined waists. Skirts were longer and straighter. During this time, the full, permanently pleated skirt was the trend. Two dominant skirt styles were popular: the sheath and the regular, full skirt generally gored or gathered

(Lester, 1967). Slacks, pants, and shorts received acceptance as practical wear for women. Men's suit styles of the forties remained popular during the fifties.

By 1959, fashions for women were extremely diverse because of the variety of fibers, fabrics, colors, and garment styles being made. During 1963, the defunct chemise of the fifties was resurrected as a jumper dress without sleeves intended to be worn with a blouse underneath. In 1966, Yves Saint Laurent created his legendary smoking suit known as 'Le Smoking,' which was essentially a female version of a tuxedo. Pants for women became the height of fashion. Pop art joined with fashion when Mondrian shift dresses were introduced. Other popular looks were extremely short mini dresses, safari looks, animal prints, granny dresses, and all black garments.

Denim became very popular and jeans were worn very tightly. Jeans were shown in forms of ripped, torn, and a variety of washes. By the early seventies, the hippie look was the rage with long hair, beads, and clothing with influences from London and Russia.

Extreme styles such as bell bottom pants and hip hugger pants were worn with very high platform shoes. As the hippie look waned, the new looks became punk and disco. Hot pants, popular with the younger set, were very short and tight.

By the eighties, everything went big, including hair and shoulder pads. Fashions for this period were in direct opposition to what was accepted in the seventies. Jeans, while still popular, became baggy and loose. Fashion trends were dictated by the influence of designers. As the nineties approached, activewear for women became popular and clothing was being produced with the comfort of the wearer in mind. In excess of casual, relaxed silhouettes, the grunge look took hold, consisting of baggy pants, loose flannel shirts, torn garments, and army boots.

Unlike the lavish and overdone fashions of the 1980s, the nineties represented a rejection of excess, and society embraced casual dress. Corporate America, who traditionally expected certain

FIGURE 1.21 A woman in bell bottom jeans and a denim jacket. These extreme styles were worn with very high platform shoes in the 1970s.

FIGURE 1.22 Yves Saint Laurent's power suit

FIGURE 1.23 Fashion of the twenty-first century features vibrant and energetic designs like those of Christian Lacroix.

dress requirements, relaxed its standards and implemented "casual dress" days where employees could wear sports shirts, casual slacks, and more relaxed attire for women along with the elimination of hosiery.

Major trends included the grunge look, which was a generally unkempt look of baggy jeans, often torn and worn with oversized shirts. The influence of rap music artists also reinforced the looks of baggy pants and loose, long T-shirts. Denim continues to be a staple in fashion. Variety is obtained by changing the color, finishes, washes, and fit. By the mid 1990s, jeans became a status symbol depending on what designer's label was worn.

The new twenty-first century saw economic growth in many industries. The fashion industry also began to experience new interest from consumers in fashionable clothing. As we progress well into the first decade of the new century, it is difficult to determine what particular look will surface as the one to be remembered. Currently, the trends of various designers offer functional as well as aesthetic clothing for the modern consumer who multi-tasks, has more leisure time because of technology, and is much less likely to be loyal to one brand or design. There appears to be a slow turning back to glamour and professionalism in work clothing and evening wear. Celebrities seem to contribute to this trend because of high media exposure from the Red Carpet to daily news shows. The turning back to glamour and formal dress might also be attributed to the aging of America. Baby Boomers, who are reaching mid-life, have more disposable income and greatly influence what fashion looks like by purchasing or refusing to purchase certain silhouettes, colors, materials, and styles.

One of the effects of fast-paced technology in the apparel industry is the ability of manufacturers to knock off designers' lines very quickly. It is fairly common to find garments from couture shops at discounters such as Target. Apparel consumers now have much more product knowledge and tend to make better purchase decisions about apparel.

A quote from Wilcox and Mendes sums it up well: "One of the most interesting aspects of couture and ready-to-wear design is the self-conscious manner in which the 'creative genius' of the couturier draws on references from fashion history, isolating their original meanings and context in stylistic terms, whilst also commenting on contemporary concerns. Christian LaCroix has in the past attested to the self-referential nature of much design work, stating in the March 1988 edition of Vogue 'every one of my dresses possesses a detail that can be connected with something historic, something from a past culture. We don't invent anything.'" (Wilcox, C. & Mendes, 1991.)

This chapter is important because the apparel student must understand that the events of history have a great influence on what people wear, how, and why they wear it. Understanding historical costume also aides in predicting clothing trends. It is difficult to predict what direction fashion will take in the twenty-first century. One could make an assumption that these trends will start to repeat themselves at some point. But whatever direction fashion goes, it is sure to be exciting.

Key Terms

Amictus	Breeches	Calasiris	Chiton	Codpiece	Doublet	Farthingale
Himation	Indumenta	Jabot	Jerkin	New Look	Off-the-peg	
Ruff	Sack	Schenti	Slashing	Stola	Toga	

Ideas for Discussion and Application

1. What effect, if any, do war and political unrest have on skirt lengths for women?

2. What impact did the development of buttons have on apparel? Zippers? How have closures on garments evolved over the centuries?

3. Discuss the ebb and flow of importance of linen and cotton in apparel over time.

4. Why do you think garments underwent modification during the Middle Ages?

5. What is slashing? How was it used in garments?

6. What is considered a basic ensemble for a man?

7. Discuss Dior's "New Look."

Activities

1. Research one era of costume history and find a current design that utilizes the same design lines. Compare them and discuss how they are alike.

2. Choose any current fashion silhouette and trace its development from beginning to current trends. Use pictures to illustrate your findings.

3. Bring a large sample of fabric to class. Wrap an Egyptian sheath, Grecian tunic, or Roman toga.

chapter two

social and psychological foundations of apparel

OBJECTIVES

>> *Define consumer behavior.*

>> *Recognize the multiple perspectives from which consumer behavior can be viewed.*

>> *Identify the external influences on apparel consumption.*

>> *Discuss the nature and influence of culture, social class, social group, and family on apparel consumption.*

>> *Identify the internal influences on apparel consumption.*

>> *Discuss how personality, self-concept, attitudes, involvement, motivation, and learning influence apparel consumption.*

Apparel products, including the demand by consumers for those products, inherently have physical, social, and psychological factors. While variables such as climate, geography, technological sophistication, and physical lifestyle do provide substantial physical influences on the attributes of apparel, this chapter focuses on the social and psychological roots of apparel.

The study of human behavior, the realm of inquiry by social scientists, is often divided conceptually and viewed from multiple perspectives (i.e., sociology, psychology, economics, and so forth). While **human behavior** covers the broad spectrum of the actions and activities of man, **consumer behavior** focuses more narrowly on one aspect of human behavior. Specifically, that emphasis is on the processes of individuals and groups as they select, use, and dispose of products, services, and ideas and on the impacts of these processes on consumers and society (Hawkins, Mothersbaugh, and Best, 2007). Thus, consumer behavior provides a broad framework from which to examine the specific product class—apparel—especially the consumption of apparel which, then, influences all other aspects of apparel design, creation, marketing, use, and disposal. This chapter explores the social and psychological roots of apparel.

Components of Apparel Decision Making Process

External Influences on Consumers
      Culture
      Subculture
      Social class
      Social group
      Family

Internal Influences on Consumers
      Self-concept
      Personality
      Attitudes
      Motives
      Learning and memory

Consumer Decision-Making Process
      Problem recognition
      Information search and evaluation
      Purchase
      Post Purchase Behaviors

Because consumer behavior and apparel consumption are complex processes, several models have been developed to aid consumers and practitioners in understanding them. Some of these are presented in Chapter 12. At this point, it is useful to note that many of the general models of consumer behavior, appropriately applied to apparel-related behavior, include three primary components. These three components are: (1) external influences on the consumer, (2) internal influences on the consumer, and (3) the consumer decision-making process. Important external influences include culture, subculture, social class, social group, and family. Important internal influences include self-concept, personality, attitudes, motives, and learning.

Sociological Foundations: External Influences on Apparel Consumption

External influences are those elements that are not part of the internal makeup of an individual but rather exist within the social environment. These elements can yield strong impact on apparel consumption. Culture, subculture, social class, social group, and family are examples.

Culture

Culture can be defined as a distinctive way of life for a group of people (Louden & Della Bitta, 1988), as a particular stage of advancement in civilization, and as the characteristic features of such a stage or state. From this it is evident that culture is dependent upon both place and time and will vary from place to place and over time. Indeed, in Chapter 1, evidence was seen of changes in the physical representations of culture as reflected in the historical evolution of fashion. Apparel is a strong and visible artifact of culture. Since evidence of culture is expressed in both tangible and intangible ways, it is seen as having both material and non-material components.

Material components include the physical substances used and changed by individuals who form a culture. **Non-material components** include cultural attributes such as words, ideas, customs, beliefs, and habits. Material components related to apparel include examples such as articles of clothing, accessories, and hairstyles, as well as the polymers or fibers used to create textile products. A few non-material apparel-related components include the notion of what is currently fashionable, how people think about and discuss fashion, and customs and habits that determine why individuals wear certain articles of clothing for specific occasions such as at weddings, at school, or in work environments.

Material Components of Culture Change with the Times

Did you know?

>> Canes were in vogue in eighteenth-century France for women as well as men. Women's canes were embellished with music boxes, perfume bottles, and romantic pictures. Voltaire, the French philosopher, owned eighty canes while his contemporary, Jean Jacques Rousseau, owned forty.

>> When the fashion among eighteenth-century Englishmen was to wear very tight pantaloons, the custom was to hang the pantaloons open on a peg so that the wearer could jump down into them, allowing for a fashionable fit.

>> The fashion among Egyptian women in 1400 BC was to wear a cone of scented grease on the top of their heads. During the day, the grease melted down over their bodies and clothing creating an oily, glistening sheen.

>> Blue or green silk umbrellas were the fashion for well-bred people of nineteenth-century England. Since it was considered vulgar to carry the umbrella under one's arm, the upper crust gripped their umbrellas in the middle with the handle toward the ground. Umbrellas were not affordable for the general public. Ordinary men or women could hire an umbrella for an hourly fee from a local stand (Affinity, 2007).

Because culture is a multi-dimensional concept, it is useful to examine a few of its characteristics.

>> Culture is man-made. Individuals within a society determine both consciously and unconsciously what the culture will be. In most cases, this occurs unintentionally as part of day-to-day living. However, in some cases, such as in the passage of legislation, the development or encouragement of culture is deliberate. As individuals within a society interact with ideas, technologies, and organizations specific to them, a culture emerges.

>> Culture is learned. Both formally and informally, culture is shared among individuals. Formal educational systems and intergenerational connections serve to support the continuation of culture as elders share the culture they know. Consider, for example, the experience of a small child who leaps from the safety of his bathtub out the front door of his residence without the "benefit" of clothes. It is likely that as soon as the supervising adult sees the occurrence they run to the child, wrap him in a towel, and likely provide some strong verbiage on the inappropriateness of the action. Thus, at that moment, cultural norms have been transferred or learned. Additionally, culture is learned through peer interaction. For example, a teen attending a middle school or junior high is given a copy of the campus dress code representing the cultural wisdom of elders, while at the same time observing the apparel behavior of peers. Learning culture has then occurred both formally and informally.

>> Culture is prescriptive. Its standards or norms tell the proper way to act or do something. For example, a practice such as wearing or not wearing hats for specific occasions is prescribed by culture. Indeed, the very fact that most individuals do wear clothing in public illustrates the prescriptive nature of culture. Culture tells what should and should not be done, and in some

cases it provides punishment or sanctions for the violation of the cultural norm. Sanctions can include a full range of consequences such as legal action for public immodesty or more subtle avoidance or displeasure by a peer for not adhering to a norm.

>> Culture is a group phenomenon. It is shared by the members of the society that created it and is reinforced by group pressure. Apparel norms are shared within a culture whether it is a nation or a peer group. For example, national apparel norms are seen in the emergence of national costumes. Global travel reveals that specific forms of dress have been adopted by groups, such as kimonos in Japan and sombreros in Mexico. Similarly, but on a smaller scale, members of a school group or sorority can decide to wear identical T-shirts.

>> Cultures are similar but different. Similarities and differences among societies create similarities and differences in cultures. Even when physical characteristics such as geography and weather are similar, widely diversified cultures have emerged because of the multiple attributes and nature of culture.

>> Culture satisfies a need. Norms are valuable within societies and groups because they play a vital role in identifying, simplifying, and sustaining that society. In simplest form, culture saves a group or society from continually relearning that which has already been experienced. It allows ideas and practices that have proven rewarding to its members to continue. As long as they continue to satisfy needs, cultural elements will remain in place. Once they no longer meet needs, the culture will evolve.

>> Culture changes. Culture is adaptive to the needs of those who create it. Just as societies evolve, culture, too, evolves in step. Clothing trends, for example, as artifacts of culture, change with the emergence of changes in factors such as technological advances and tastes in music, art, and entertainment.

Pantyhose: Technology Drove Cultural Change

Polymer research yielded the creation of nylon. In April, 1930, a team of researchers led by Dr. Wallace Carothers at DuPont's Experimental Station discovered the strong polymer that could be drawn into fiber, later to be known as nylon. By 1935, Dr. Carothers had experimented with more than 100 polyamides before choosing nylon as the one for development. DuPont built the first full-scale nylon plant in Seaford, Delaware and began commercial production in 1939. By 1940, nylon hosiery was introduced to the public with great success. Sixty-four million pairs were sold in the first year. By 1942, nylon production shifted to support the war effort in the form of tents and parachutes. While scarce during World War II, nylon stockings were back into production and in high demand following the war. In one case, 10,000 anxious shoppers mobbed a San Francisco store and forced the store to halt sales. Even while not readily available, ladies painted the characteristic seam down the back of their bare legs to imitate the wearing of nylons.

Pantyhose, invented by Allen Gant Senior, were the next giant step. In 1959, Glen Raven Mills of North Carolina fashioned underpants and stockings into a single garment. By the time of the miniskirt in the 1960s, the leg seam was a thing of the past, only to be reintroduced in succeeding decades for a "retro" look (Bellis, 2007).

>> Culture is integrative. Its parts fit together well to form a functioning whole. While there may be some aspects of culture that may temporarily seem out of sync, especially as part of the evolutionary process of change, the primary components of culture fit well together as an integrated whole (Louden & Della Bitta, 1988).

Culture exhibits several interesting facets, particularly those relating to apparel. First, culture has symbols. Both material and non-material artifacts of culture can have symbolic meaning. Items of clothing and accessories, for example, take on special meaning for members of a particular society. A particular hat or shirt design may indicate membership in a particular social group such as a gang or allegiance to a particular group such as a sports team. A logo printed or embroidered on a garment may show endorsement of a branded product. Wearing that same logo may, in turn, indicate membership or affiliation with a particular group that values that brand as "in." Not only do items themselves have symbolic meaning but how they are worn may also tell a story. A wedding ring is a symbol of marital status in several cultures. Yet, the hand on which it is worn differs in parts of the world.

Second, cultures develop silent languages. Hand gestures, physical movements, and preferences become communication elements. Removing one's hat may communicate respect or reverence in one situation while throwing that same hat into the air may indicate jubilation. Third, cultures develop rites of passage indicating movement from one status within the social order to another. Academic regalia worn at graduations and special dresses and suits worn for *quinceañeras* or weddings are apparel reflections of rites of passage observed within specific cultures. Fourth, cultures have taboos or prohibitions for members of that culture. Baring specific parts of the body is taboo in many cultures and, interestingly, which parts of the body are not to be bared varies from one culture to another.

FIGURE 2.1 Apparel items such as school and team uniforms may symbolically indicate membership in a social group.

FIGURE 2.2 Logos show endorsement of a brand and may have symbolic meaning.

FIGURE 2.3 Wedding rings are symbolic evidence of a rite of passage.

Cultural Myopia

Understanding key characteristics and facets of culture is useful in developing insight into apparel design, manufacturing, marketing, and consumption. Within the global, national, and regional marketplaces it is valuable to understand that multiple levels of cultural influence are in play. Astute professionals will take the time to carefully examine the cultural background of any market before making decisions. While it is natural to know and understand best the culture in which one was raised or has lived for a substantial period of time, this is not sufficient in today's economy. Most apparel marketing endeavors require a comprehensive understanding of multiple cultural environments. Failure to do so results in **cultural myopia,** which is cultural nearsightedness or making decisions as if one's culture is the only culture to be considered. Since cultures vary, and cultural consideration is important, this can be disastrous.

A solution to avoiding cultural myopia in apparel decisions is researching important key information. Three questions can be used to guide investigation: (1) What are the characteristics, symbols, and values of the culture being considered? (2) What are the marketing and distribution channels currently embedded within the culture? and (3) What are the communication systems used by the culture?

APPAREL APPLICATIONS

Since many of the concepts discussed in this section can apply to multiple product categories, the following points serve to focus on applicability to apparel products.

1. Culture provides the context in which apparel is used.
2. Apparel is a visible artifact of culture.
3. Apparel includes both material and non-material components.

4. Apparel culture is learned. Individuals learn apparel norms and behaviors from their peers and through marketing efforts.

5. Marketing efforts can substantially influence apparel culture.

6. Culture prescribes standards and norms for apparel related behavior.

7. Apparel culture is a group phenomenon created, shared, and reinforced by individuals collectively.

8. Since cultures satisfy needs, apparel can be used to satisfy cultural needs.

9. Apparel changes as the culture changes. Apparel culture is in constant evolution from week to week, season to season, and year to year.

10. Apparel is part of the integrative nature of culture. Hence, aspects of apparel culture fit well with other entities within society including social tastes in other products and services.

11. Apparel products have symbolic meaning and that meaning can change over time.

12. Apparel as part of the silent language of society can serve as a communication medium.

13. Marketers of apparel must guard against cultural myopia by learning about cultures which are not ones own.

Subculture

As soon as discussion of cultures and cultural characteristics develops, questions emerge regarding variation within predominant cultures. Indeed, this is the case. Within any major cultural unit, subcultures exist. A **subculture** can be defined as a segment within a culture which shares distinguishing values and patterns of behavior that are different from the overall culture. Within any culture, multiple types of subcultures operate. While, most commonly, marketing efforts emphasize variations in socioeconomic, ethnic, age, and geographic groups, multiple other sub-cultural groupings should also be given consideration. Religious or political affiliations, community type (rural/urban), and lifestyle elements may prove to be substantial determinants of apparel behavior. Regardless of the subculture being considered important, attributes to understand include their (1) demographic characteristics, (2) psychographic characteristics, (3) consumer behavior, and (4) media exposure.

> **African-American Consumers**
> African-Americans represent a high-potential audience with population growth projected to increase more than four times faster than the Caucasian segment in the U.S. to 26 percent by 2025. A recent Consumer Insight study reported that African-American consumers are organized, smart, aware, and vocal. They represent 12 percent of the population and their buying power is anticipated to grow 34 percent over the next four years, reaching $921 billion by 2011.

> **Subcultural Choices: Vegan Shoes**
> Subculture and lifestyle choices influence consumption. Vegetarians have vegan choices in footwear. Vegan materials include: hemp, jute, bamboo, faux leather or pleather (polyurethane), faux suede, polyester, rayon, nylon, and microfibers (Vegetarian Shoes and Bags, 2007).

APPAREL APPLICATIONS

1. Subcultures have apparel tastes and interests that vary from the predominant culture.
2. Awareness of sub-cultural differences is important to effective marketing of apparel products.
3. All individuals belong to multiple sub-cultural groups.
4. Some sub-cultural distinctions have stronger influence on apparel consumption than others.
5. Important attributes for creating effective marketing plans for apparel products based on sub-cultural differences include demographic characteristics, psychographic characteristics, consumer behavior, and media exposure.

Social Class

Within societies, some individuals acquire, by diverse means, more respect or prestige than their peers, thus creating social stratification. Rankings in compliance with society's values allow individuals to become ranked as having higher or lower social position with regard to others. Thus, **social class** emerges as a concept where a group of individuals having approximately equal position in society form a social class. While social class is most certainly a multi-faceted concept, three primary indicators are most commonly used to determine social class. These include (1) income, (2) occupation, and (3) housing, both housing type and location. While these aspects are sometimes used in isolation, an integrated approach is most likely to yield better results.

Popular outlines of social class within the United States have been developed by Coleman (1983), Gilbert (1998), and Thompson and Hickey (2005). Each description roughly divides the U.S. population into upper class (1–5%), upper middle class (12–15%), middle class (about 33%), working class (30–38%) and lower class (about 15%). Each class has their own characteristics. Important for apparel marketers is an understanding of the unique characteristics and differences among the classes with regard to lifestyle, consumer behavior patterns, and media access and use.

Occupation, Education, Income, and Wealth: Alternate Indicators of Social Class

A *NY Times* article (Scott & Leonhardt, 2005) suggested thinking of a person's position in society as being like a hand of cards. Each person is dealt four cards, one from each suit: education, income, occupation, and wealth. Relative values in each of these three areas determine position in society. Interested in your social class standing? Check it out by entering your education, income, occupation, and wealth variable at *www.nytimes.com/packages/html/national/20050515_CLASS_GRAPHIC/index_01.html.*

A couple of caveats are in order with regard to the discussion of social class, as well as the previous discussion of subculture. The first is that such discussions are based on group phenomena and aggregated characteristics. Thus, they tend to produce discussions that are stereotypical and do not adequately recognize that individuals can differ within group norms and characteristics. Second, particularly for social class, rankings are problematic in several areas. Class rankings are often, in practice, one dimensional. The most common dimension is income. In addition, even when multiple dimensions are considered, averages are used to establish categories. This ignores both high and low values on any one dimension. Individuals may be either over-privileged or under-privileged in relation to their class. Also problematic, most class rankings make the assumption that classes are stable. This practice ignores the mobility between classes, which is part of the western cultural fabric. Finally, some class ranking systems are built upon a premise of a single male wage earner per household. This is not necessarily the common state today.

Apparel products and services have both personal and social meanings. In some cases, items of apparel or services assume symbolic meaning with regard to social class. They become symbols of a particular social class. For example, a particular brand of watch or purse may be seen as symbolic evidence that one belongs to a specific social class. Additionally, ownership of that particular symbol may suggest not only that one belongs to that class but may also indicate aspirations to be like or be considered a member of the class. The phenomenon of social class symbols has given rise to the concept of conspicuous consumption. First described by Veblen in 1899, **conspicuous consumption** refers to the practice of making purchases or obtaining goods or services primarily to be seen by others for their symbolic meaning or indication of wealth and status. With this concept in mind, it is easy to see that in some cases, possessions take the place of income as a primary indicator of social class. For apparel, this means that people who dress like members of the upper-upper class may be attempting or even achieving recognition as

FIGURE 2.4 Particular accessory items can serve as social class symbols.

members of the upper-upper class, even when their income or other indicators would not place them there. It is interesting to note that social class symbols are not necessarily static. They change over periods of time. Brand names, for example, have experienced great rises and falls in popularity based on their perception as social class symbols. A brand that at one time provided social class status may soon have no positive status recognition at all, and may even be an out-dated or negative indicator.

APPAREL APPLICATIONS

1. Social class consideration is an important component in market segmentation strategies for apparel.
2. Conspicuous consumption is likely to have greater impact on apparel purchases than on many other product classes.
3. Most social classes aspire to be like members of the class or classes above them. This may be less the case for working class consumers. They may place more emphasis on achieving success and social recognition within their class.
4. Understanding the social class of the customer is likely to enable apparel marketers to increase profits by driving product design and marketing strategies geared to the needs and wants of the consumer.
5. Apparel products may be used as symbols of social class and those symbols change over time.

Social Groups and Peer Influences

As social beings, people affiliate with other individuals in a variety of contexts. Groups are formed based on a sense of relatedness that results from their interactions with one another on many different levels. In many cases, membership, affiliation, or desire for affiliation influences behavior. In these cases the group is called a reference group because it becomes a reference point for future behavior including consumption. As such, groups often exert considerable power. Four primary types of group power are evident in the adoption and purchase of apparel products. These include (1) reward power, (2) coercive power, (3) legitimate power, and (4) expert power.

First, groups exert reward power. Conformity to the norms or expectations of a group can bring rewards. For example, when a member of a teen peer group complies with the fashion direction of the members of the group and wears apparel which is similar to that adopted by the members of the group, the individual is likely to be rewarded by acceptance. Second, on the other hand, wearing apparel which is contrary to the norms of that same group may bring ostracism or coercion to change behavior in favor of a more accepted mode. This is coercive power often involving negative feedback to elicit a change in behavior. Third, groups can exert

---

Pressure to Look Good Is Escalating

Two-thirds of U.S. consumers feel that the pressure to look good is much greater than ever before. This was a finding of a global survey conducted by The Nielsen Company. Nielsen's research also indicates global approval for the "metrosexual" male, agreeing that it's OK for men to spend time and money to enhance their appearance (The Nielsen Company, 2007).

The Nielsen Company is active in more than 100 countries worldwide and serves as a global information and media resource in marketing information (ACNielsen), media information (Nielsen Media Research), online intelligence (NetRatings and BuzzMetrics), trade shows and business publication (*Billboard, The Hollywood Reporter, Adweek*) (*www.nielsen.com*).

FIGURE 2.5 A sports team has a legitimate right to prescribe the apparel of its members.

legitimate power. This occurs when the group has been given a legitimate right to influence behavior. For example, when a student enrolls in a school requiring uniforms, the student recognizes the legitimate right or authority of the school group to dictate apparel. Similarly, as individuals join various sports teams they are likely to recognize the legitimate right of the team to dictate the color and style of apparel and don the team uniform. Fourth, groups exert expert power. This can take several forms varying from cases where the expertise has been earned through special knowledge or capability to cases where the group's influence may be based only on the celebrity of the group. The influence of sports, music, and movie superstars are such examples.

Understanding the properties of groups will help in seeing how they can be influential. Groups have (1) roles, (2) status, (3) standards, and (4) socialization. First, groups not only have a function of their own but the members of the group also have behaviors that are part of their membership in that group. Sometimes, because individuals are members of multiple groups, it is possible to have role conflict when the roles relating to one group conflict with roles relating to another group. For example, time conflicts arise when family roles and work or school roles collide.

Second, groups have status. There are rights and duties related to group membership. Performance of duties brings the rewards of membership. Third, groups have standards or norms for compliance. Both punishments for violation and rewards for achievement are part of the process of maintaining cultural norms. Fourth, groups have a socialization process through which new members of the group learn the expectations, standards, and roles of the group.

Since groups can have influence on apparel consumption, it is useful to understand why individuals are willing to give up their individual power to rely on the power of a group. The benefits of allowing group influence can be briefly categorized in two ways. The first relates to the perception of the individual that the group has information or perhaps experience that will be beneficial; following the group will end in a better path or choice. Shopping at a particular store or buying a brand well accepted by the group, for example, is seen as a way to decrease the chance of making a bad purchase. The second relates to the use of the group to express one's self or bolster one's ego. Group membership allows the individual to be seen as, and to feel, a part of something judged to be worthwhile. Hence, an individual may adopt a particular style of dress (goth for example) in order to be a part of a group they view positively or to make a statement of who they are.

COMMUNICATION AND PERSONAL INFLUENCE

Just as groups exert influence, individuals working collectively or independently also have the potential to exert force. Communication—verbal, non-verbal, and visual—provides the vehicle by which individuals learn from others and is the foundation for interpersonal influence. Three classic models of communication and interpersonal influence are: (1) one-step, (2) two-step, and (3) multi-step.

In the first case, the communication is simply from one individual to a second individual through some medium such as voice or email (one-step model). When a marketer wants to send a one-step message, the sequence is the same: the message goes from the marketer via a medium (radio, TV, direct mail, etc.) to an individual. However, the introduction of an opinion leader greatly enhances the communication in many cases (two-step model). When an opinion leader is used, the message goes from the original source, via a medium, to a middle-man or opinion leader, and then to a receiver. In marketing apparel goods, this sequence can be much more influential because it is supported by an individual who is not seen as part of the marketing process. Additionally, the middle-man or opinion leader is likely to be powerful because they are viewed as "like the receiver" and reliable and because the personal contact provides social support. Thus, the use of opinion leaders in apparel marketing can be a formidable force. Certainly, a marketer who can create positive word-of-mouth communication among multiple consumers (multi-step model) will reap benefits far beyond those yielded by traditional advertising (one-step model).

Since opinion leadership plays an especially influential role in the adoption of apparel and other fashion goods, it is worthwhile to consider who opinion leaders are. Typically, opinion leaders are similar to the individuals or groups they influence, yet they may have greater interest or knowledge in the area of leadership, exposure to mass media, and be more innovative and social than the norm. They may serve as opinion leaders across a broad spectrum of product categories, in which case they are called **market mavens**, or their leadership may be specific to one product category. They may be driven to such a role by a desire to help others, gain attention,

---

One-Step, Two-Step, and Multi-Step Models of Communication

One-Step Model

Marketer → *via media* → *to consumer(s)*

Two-Step Model

Marketer → *via media* → *to opinion leader* → *to consumer(s)*

Multi-Step Model

Marketer → *via media* → *to opinion leader* → *to consumer(s)* → *to consumers*

show connoisseurship, feel like a pioneer, show status, convert others, or seek confirmation of their own decisions (Louden & Della Bitta, 1988).

On the other hand, consumers are most likely to accept the influence of an opinion leader when the product is highly visible to others, the product is complex or high risk, they are facing new experiences in life, or they are seeking membership in a group. For example, when deciding on appropriate apparel for a new job following college graduation, an individual is likely to seek the advice of one or more opinion leaders because the choice is visible, high risk, and involves a new life experience where they hope to fit in.

Marketing strategies can be designed to capitalize on the power of groups and opinion leaders. A first step is to identify existing opinion leaders. Another tactic is to create opinion leaders. This can be accomplished by the use of samples, discounts, contests, advisory boards, and demonstrations. The idea is to get the product to the public and then facilitate their talking about it. Entertaining ads and slogans, teaser or curiosity ads, fashion shows, "ask a friend" strategies, or in-store demonstrations could be used. In some cases, it is useful to simulate or make it appear that an opinion leader is providing a message. Company spokespersons, recorded testimonials, "candid camera" ads, ads including one person telling another about a product, and the use of celebrities are ways to simulate opinion leadership. In some cases, spokespersons have been created (Tony the Tiger, Michelin Man, and the Pillsbury Doughboy).

To understand and take advantage of consumer-to-consumer communication, companies such as The Nielsen Company, through their BuzzMetrics services, use data-mining technology, research, and media experience to help client companies better understand the influence and impact of consumer-generated media. Through products such as BrandPulse (that measure consumer-generated media and online word of mouth), clients can track data-driven reports and trends generated from discussion boards, blogs, forums, review sites, and Usenet newsgroups. BlogPulse.com (a property of The Nielsen Company, famous for its media tracking and ratings) is a portal that tracks and analyzes millions of blogs daily for trends, issues, news, and events (Nielsen BuzzMetrics, 2007).

Since communication plays a substantial role in individual and group influences on apparel consumers, it is wise to examine critical communication factors. While these are presented here in the context of social influences, the same principles hold true for marketer initiated communication. The simplest communication model includes the three fundamental components of sender, channel, and receiver. A "sender" sends an intended message which is encoded to become the sent message through a medium or channel. A "receiver" then decodes the received message to become the perceived message. This model is respectful not only of the major components of communication but also of the opportunity for the message to be changed or altered during the encoding and decoding processes of the sender and the receiver. For example, the sender may not actually say what he intends to say clearly or the receiver may not absorb the message as the sender intended.

At each step, multiple factors influence the effectiveness of the communication. First, the sender or source of the communication is influential. Sources can be entities like individuals

---

Communication Model
Sender (intended and sent messages) → via a Channel → Receiver (received and perceived messages)

(peer and family members); groups (social or work groups); and marketers (including retailers, advertisers, promoters, and other sales agents). Important influences on source effectiveness include such attributes as the attitude and credibility of the sender. For example, senders with a positive attitude, self confidence, and belief in the value of their product are most likely to be influential. Similarly, credible sources are more likely to be effective by exhibiting attributes such as trustworthiness or lack of intention to manipulate, expertise, likeability, status or prestige, and similarity with the receiver or audience.

Secondly, attributes of the message itself are influential. The structure of the message makes a difference. **One-sided message** structures present only the positive aspects of the product or service being promoted. This message structure is effective when it is likely that the receiver already agrees with the position of the sender. **Two-sided messages**, on the other hand, present both the positive and the negative attributes of a single product or present the positive aspects of both the promoted product and a comparable competitor. Generally, two-sided structures may be effective for receivers who already use the competing brand, are likely to disagree with the position of the sender because they like their current brand, or are likely to be exposed to information from the competitor in the future. For two-sided messages, it is critical that the communication leave the receiver with a clear understanding of the advantage of the promoted product. This can be done by overtly stating the benefits and drawing a conclusion for the receiver or by designing the message in such a clear manner that the advantage is unmistakably evident.

In addition, when two-sided structures are used to compare two products or ideas, the order of presentation can be critical. A format where the strongest point is offered in the middle of the communication is considered least effective. Climax order, with the weakest arguments building to the strongest arguments at the end, and anticlimax order, with the strongest arguments presented first and then declining to lesser arguments, are both better formats. Third, receiver factors influence the effectiveness of communication. Personal characteristics such as intelligence, self esteem, and attention make a difference.

Adoption and Diffusion Patterns

As communication proceeds, consumers are exposed to new products and services. To slow down a process that sometime occurs almost instantaneously and at other times over the course of many years, five important steps can be considered: (1) awareness, (2) evaluation, (3) attitude, (4) trial, and (5) adoption.

First, in the early stages, the potential adopter is only aware that a product or service exists. This is the introductory, or awareness, stage. The product may be new on the market or may simply be new to him. Second, the consumer begins to evaluate the new product. He begins to gather information about the product from his own experience and from the sources in his environment. Third, based on any newly acquired information and on his personal history, the potential consumer forms an opinion regarding whether the product will or will not meet his needs. Fourth, based on the outcome of the third step, the potential adopter then seeks to try the product, if possible. If not, or if the attitude formed is sufficiently positive, he proceeds to the fifth step, adoption.

DIFFUSION OF INNOVATION/PRODUCT ADOPTION

The rate at which innovations of new products are adopted by consumers varies. Five standard categories illustrate this variation through time. These categories and the percentage of the population responding at each stage are innovators (2.5%), early adopters (13.5%), early majority

(34%), late majority (34%), and laggards (16%). For example, the innovators are the first to pick up on a new trend in fashion apparel. Risks for both the buyer and the seller are high at this stage since it is unknown whether the new product or trend will prove successful. For the manufacturer, the costs of production are high because of small quantities and research, design, and set-up costs. The early adopters are those next to adopt the fashion. Early adopters tend to be role models or opinion leaders for others and are willing to assume a small but calculated risk. Production costs per unit and levels of risk for the manufacturer begin to decline slightly at this stage. The early majority waits cautiously to see if the new fashion will be popular and then adopts it before the majority of the population. Production costs per unit decline because of economies of scale. The late majority takes more time than average to adopt new products, yielding to skepticism perhaps based on peer pressure and financial constraints. Costs of production steeply decline at this stage. The laggards are the final group to adopt, and they exhibit the least amount of innovativeness. Manufacturers at this stage are clearing away existing inventory. Both manufacturers and marketers typically focus on consumers from one or two of these stages. A specialized apparel boutique, for example, may offer only new and relatively exclusive items appealing to innovators and early adopters while the mass merchandisers cater to the early and late majority segments.

The rate at which consumers move through this continuum of adopter categories varies. Some products such as **fads** move with extreme rapidity from innovators to laggards. Typically, fashion fads may involve accessory items or ways of wearing garments that can rapidly be adopted and changed. A fad may be flourishing one day and may die the next.

Fashion **classics** are at the other end of the continuum. Classics are items that move extremely slowly from one category to the next. Indeed they may remain in the majority stages for many

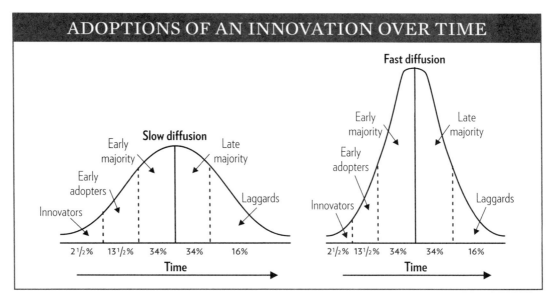

FIGURE 2.6 Early majority consumers cautiously watch to see if a new fashion will be popular before adopting it.

years. A man's oxford cloth button-down collared dress shirt is an example of a classic. Characteristics that tend to influence the speed of adoption by individuals include cost, conspicuousness, trial ability, perceived risk or advantage, and consistency with existing norms and values.

APPAREL APPLICATIONS

1. Apparel marketers can effectively use consumers' social groups to influence purchases.
2. Multi-step models of communication can be an effective tool in promoting apparel goods.
3. The cultivation or creation of opinion leaders can greatly enhance apparel marketing endeavors.
4. Cultivation of senders and attention to message factors can have substantial influence on the effectiveness of communication on receivers or potential consumers of apparel goods.
5. Understanding the five steps of the adoption process increases the opportunity to have consumers reach the adoption or purchase stage.
6. Apparel retailers can identify a niche within the stages of consumer adoption and create a marketing strategy to meet the needs of that target group.

Family Frameworks

One social group that can be particularly influential in developing consumer preferences, establishing buying habits, and making consumer choices is the family or household unit. Whether individuals form a marital or biological family unit or whether they reside together sharing a household dwelling and common resources is less important than the levels of cohesion or bonding, roles and power structures, and communication levels on consumer behavior.

FIGURE 2.7A Fads generally enter and exit the fashion marketplace quickly.

FIGURE 2.7B Classics are styles that remain fashionable over extended periods of time.

In this chapter, both family and non-family members sharing a household and resources are referred to as a family. Families form significant consumer entities because of their primary or close relationships, function as a reference group, and reciprocal relationships among family members.

Typically, individuals within families assume specific and often overlapping roles with regard to purchases. These might include (1) initiator, (2) influencer, (3) buyer, and (4) user. One family member may assume all of the roles or they may be shared among several family members. Each role has important attributes for apparel marketers and can form a specific target for promotional messages.

Family decision-making strategies are created by the specific roles and social context of the family. As families evolve through time, changes occur in family structures brought about by marriages, divorces, births, adoptions, and deaths. Each stage or condition of the family yields variation in the allocation of resources in consumer decisions. For example, certainly the presence of children in the household diverts a portion of family expenditures toward children's clothing, toys, food, and activities. The dissolution of a family by divorce often has strong economic consequences as does the decision of individuals to live together, thus forming a household or family (see Table 2.1, Stages of the Household Life Cycle).

Within family structures, consumer roles vary. Generally, consumption related tasks are distributed among family members based on perceived or assigned roles, history, interests, competence, and willingness. Men and women may assume roles traditionally held by their parents based on historical differences in gender assignments. Women, for example, may largely be responsible for the purchase of children's apparel. However, specific interests, knowledge, competence, or willingness may depart from traditional roles.

TABLE 2.1 Stages of the Household Life Cycle

Stage	Marital Status		Children at Home		
	Single	Married	None	< 6 years	> 6 years
Younger (<35)					
Single I	X		X		
Young married		X	X		
Full nest I		X		X	
Single parent I	X			X	
Middle-aged (35–64)					
Single II	X		X		
Delayed full nest I		X		X	
Full nest II		X			X
Single parent II	X				X
Empty nest I		X	X		
Older (> 64)					
Empty nest II		X	X		
Single III	X		X		

Purchasing power within family units may be characterized as **patriarchal,** where the male head of the household predominates in decision making, **matriarchal,** where the female head of household predominates in decision making, or egalitarian, the emerging form where power is shared. When an equal number of decisions are made by both the male and female household heads independently, the condition is termed **autonomic.** If, on the other hand, most decisions are made not independently but instead by both heads together, the term is **syncratic.** These are in

FIGURE 2.8 Women often assume the primary role of purchasing children's apparel.

contrast to male-dominated or female-dominated structures. Additional influences on family consumer decision-making practices include social class, culture and sub-culture, and stage in life.

Wise marketers of apparel products need to consider the implications of family structures and decision patterns. For example, when determining appropriate marketing strategies, the following issues should be considered:

>> Will family funds be used to purchase the product?

>> Will more than one member of the family use the product?

>> Do family members disagree on the value of the product?

>> Does purchase of the product restrict the purchase of other products?

>> Who within the family will influence the purchase?

>> Are there specific media or types of messages that appeal to specific family members?

Answers to these questions can guide marketers in creating product designs and promotions. For example, if more than one family member will use the product, are there alterations to the product that would be beneficial for multiple person use or that would bolster the value of the product in the eyes of additional family decision-makers? If children, for example, are likely to be influential, are there specific media placements that should be used to capture and capitalize on the influence of the children?

APPAREL APPLICATIONS

1. Roles as initiator, influencer, buyer and user are critical to understanding the apparel purchase process.

2. Influences on apparel consumption by family members include purchasing power structures, family life stage, family composition, roles, and history.
3. Apparel marketers can create informed marketing strategies by understanding family purchase patterns, roles, resource allocation, and influences by family members.

Psychological Foundations: Internal Influences on Apparel Consumption

Internal influences are elements that are part of the psychological or internal makeup within an individual. They can strongly impact apparel consumption. Personality, self-concept, attitudes, involvement, motivation, and information-processing style are examples.

Personality

With regard to apparel analysis, a suitable definition of personality is the "organization of the individual's distinguishing character traits, attitudes, or habits." Personality includes characteristic response tendencies across similar situations and the unique characteristics of individuals that make them different from one another. Hence, individuals in similar situations, by virtue of their specific personalities, are likely to behave in somewhat consistent, and thereby predictable, ways. Yet, at the same time, because personalities vary among people, behaviors will also vary. By understanding both the variation among individuals and the consistency exhibited by individuals and groups of individuals, apparel marketers can better understand potential consumers and plan to meet their needs.

Measuring personality is challenging primarily because of its multi-dimensional nature. Standardized rating methods, including interviews and observations; situational field observations; projective techniques; and inventory schemes with standardized questionnaire items have all been used in attempts to measure personality. Numerous theories have been developed to try to understand, measure, and/or use personality.

Only four theory types are described here to yield a view of the foundations and applications available in understanding the role of personality in apparel behavior. Included here are: (1) psychoanalytical theory, (2) social theories, (3) stimulus response theories, and (4) trait and factor theories.

First, psychoanalytical theory, based upon the work of Sigmund Freud, identifies the human personality as consisting of three conflicting components: the id, the ego, and the superego. The **id** drives toward immediate gratification of desires while the **superego**, representing social or individual norms, exerts a constraining force. The **ego** mediates the demands of the id and the prohibitions of the superego to find a middle ground. For example, in simple terms, during a shopping experience, the id component may desire to purchase many expensive apparel and accessory items. The superego would protest that the multiple items are too expensive and exceed the financial assets of the shopper. The ego might mediate for only one or two purchases or lower priced items. In general, **psychoanalytic theory** is based on the idea that personality is derived from the interactions of these three components which provide motivation and drive consumer action.

Second, **social theories** suggest that individuals develop personality and modes of behaving based on their social interactions with others. Three modes of operation or strategies emerge as a result of the need to succeed in social interactions: (1) compliance, stressing a need for love and approval; (2) aggression, exhibiting a need for power and strength; and (3) detachment, showing independence and self-reliance. Social theories, in the context of apparel consumption, can be used to explain how individuals might select specific garments to either please others or to show authority over them.

FIGURE 2.9 Social theories propose that consumers develop personality and behaviors on the basis of social interactions.

Third, **stimulus-response theories** focus on the relationship between behavior, consequences, and future behavior. Personality is seen as resulting from prior and often habitual behaviors reinforced by specific consequences. Positively reinforced behaviors yield positive responses and repeat behaviors, while negatively reinforced or un-reinforced behaviors yield negative responses and no repeat behavior. This type of reasoning can be applied to brand and store loyalty and brand switching.

Fourth, **trait and factor theories** use standardized inventories to identify interrelated variables. The theory is based on the concept that personality is composed of traits or ways that individuals differ from one another. The statistical technique of factor analysis allows traits to be analyzed in large numbers of individuals. Factors or traits emerge that show high levels of correlation.

By adding understanding of consumer lifestyle to understanding of personality additional insight is gained. Lifestyle refers to the way people live and patterns of living that include the spending of resources, specifically time and money. **Psychographics** is a technique to measure lifestyle by including such components as consumer activities, interests, and opinions (called AIOs). Outcomes of psychographic research have yielded systems for classifying consumer populations for both specific product applications and for general usage. Useful applications include market segmentation, target market profiling, consideration of new products, and creation of promotional strategies.

For example, Claritas, a Nielsen company, provides services that integrate demographic and psychographic information including lifestyle and purchase preferences to enable client companies to capitalize on patterns of consumer behavior. Apparel marketers armed with information about consumer preferences and lifestyles can successfully target the most lucrative market segments and reach them with messages that speak directly to them. Companies such as Claritas

Psychographics

Tools for Measuring Consumer Lifestyles: AIOs

A — Activities

I — Interests

O — Opinions

offer market research, market analysis, consulting, marketing software applications, and market segmentation systems services based on applying the benefits of psychographics (Claritas, 2007).

APPAREL APPLICATIONS

1. Because personality focuses both on the unique characteristics that make people different from one another and on the consistency of individuals' behavior across situations, it is of interest to marketers of fashion apparel.

2. Personality theories serve as tools to guide apparel marketers in understanding personality as a component in consumer apparel behavior.

3. Psychographics allows analysis of consumer apparel behavior via input of relevant activity, interest, and opinion data.

Self-Concept

Self-concept, or self image, refers to the way a consumer sees himself. It is composed of the consumer's self attitudes and is formed as a result of self evaluation including evaluation of self in

FIGURE 2.10 Self-concept is the way a consumer sees himself or herself.

the context of the social setting. Analysis of self-concept can be divided into four views: (1) the actual self, how I perceive I am; (2) the ideal self, how I would like to be; (3) the social self, how I believe others perceive me; and (4) the ideal social self, how I would like to have others see me (Louden & Della Bitta, 1988). These views and the desire to manipulate, change, or maintain these views motivate apparel purchase behaviors. Teens, for example, may wish to wear specific apparel or accessory items to influence how others perceive them. Individuals employed in business environments may purchase conservative business suits to maintain a "corporate" image. Generally, self-concept is developed by personal assessment in conjunction with social comparison. Individuals tend to label their own patterns of behavior according to socially acceptable norms and to accept the appraisal of others if it is credible, consistent with their self appraisal, and if they receive similar feedback from multiple sources.

SELF-CONCEPT/PRODUCT IMAGE CONGRUENCE

One interesting application of self-concept to apparel product design and marketing is self-concept/product image congruence. While individuals possess self-concepts and likely make purchase decisions designed either overtly or covertly to maintain their actual self-concept or to reach their ideal or ideal social self, products, too, have images. Product images are the result of a combination of innate product features and attributes as well as calculated marketing strategies. The theory of **self-concept/product image congruence** suggests that individuals purchase products and services that match or are congruent with their self-concept. Hence, self-concept serves as a guide to direct consumers toward and away from specific product classes and brands. Consumers tend to buy products that match or even enhance their self-concept. Shoppers who have seen a particular garment on display and commented to a friend, "That looks just like you," are noting this phenomenon.

Astute apparel marketers engage in research to determine the self-concept attributes of the target market and then tailor product characteristics and marketing techniques to match the self-images of the potential consumers. For example, branded lingerie such as Victoria's Secret and Bali are the result of careful attention in fabrication, design, distribution, advertising, promotion, and sales techniques to the self-concept attributes of current and potential clientele. The end result is that a bra by Fredrick's of Hollywood and one by Hanes appeal to consumers with diverse self-concepts. The goal of the seller is to offer goods that are congruent with the self-concept of the buyer.

APPAREL APPLICATIONS

1. Self-concept is a selection factor for consumers and, therefore, is useful in apparel design and marketing endeavors.
2. Self-concept/product image congruence can both consciously and unconsciously provide influence on consumer apparel choices.

Attitudes

Attitudes are important because they influence apparel consumer's intentions and buying behaviors. **Attitude** refers to the positive or negative feelings consumers have toward products. They form a learned predisposition to respond in a consistently positive or negative way. For example, consumers with a positive attitude toward a favorite brand are likely to consistently respond positively toward that brand. Fundamentally, attitudes are formed from beliefs, which are derived from personal experiences and information we get from others, including the media. The attitudes then form predispositions toward objects and/or behaviors. Hence, a consumer who has positive experiences, either personally or secondhand with a product, forms a positive belief structure. Usually, several beliefs converge to create an attitude. These positive beliefs join to create a positive attitude which, in turn, creates a positive disposition or intention toward action in the future. Such a positive predisposition may take the form of intention to purchase.

Attitudes and research on attitudes are positive tools for understanding consumer behavior and can form the basis for effective prediction of consumer preferences, product development, positioning and repositioning of products, and marketing efforts. While beneficial, attitudinal research is challenging because of the multiple components of attitudes. Attitudes have cognitive or knowledge based facets, affective or emotional facets, and cognative or behavioral facets (Hawkins, Mothersbaugh, & Best, 2007). Because of this complexity, numerous models have been developed to assist in understanding and influencing the development of attitudes. Models are explored in Chapter 12.

The ability to influence the development of attitudes and to change existing attitudes is important. One useful consideration is to understand the fundamental functions or value of attitudes for consumers. For apparel products, attitudes can perform four important functions: (1) enhancement or protection of self-concept or image, (2) expression of values, (3) filtering of knowledge needs, and (4) direction toward or away from experiences. First, by forming positive

FIGURE 2.11 Attitudes, interpreted through clothing, can provide expression of values.

or negative attitudes toward particular products, classes of products, or brands, consumers can facilitate both the development and enhancement of self-concept. In addition, attitudes can serve to defend the consumer's ego by protecting self image. Second, attitudes assist in the expression of values. Clothing items, for example, by their color, cut, style, fabrication, or design may aid in the expression of personal values.

Third, attitudes perform a knowledge selection function. They can tell the consumer what they do and do not need to know. For example, if a person has a negative attitude toward a particular brand, shopping for that brand or seeking additional information about the brand is unnecessary.

Fourth, attitudes can direct consumers away from unpleasant situations and toward pleasurable and rewarding experiences. A positive attitude toward an apparel item may create an intention to purchase the item. Unless some intervening situation prohibits the purchase, the consumer is then led toward the purchase and subsequent enjoyment of the item.

Involvement

The timing of attitude development differs based on the level of involvement the consumer has with the purchase. In cases where the consumer is highly involved with the purchase, or a high involvement situation, it is likely that the consumer will invest both time and energy in learning about the product prior to making a purchase. The consumer is interested in learning about product features and making critical evaluations. Since in high involvement situations attitude is formed prior to purchase, input from social and marketing sources is highly influential. The sequence of attitude formation in high involvement situations is: (1) thought or cognitive activity, (2) attitude development, and (3) behavior, including purchase or non-purchase.

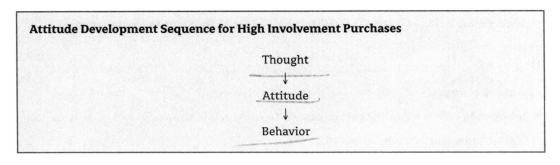

Attitude Development Sequence for High Involvement Purchases

Thought
↓
Attitude
↓
Behavior

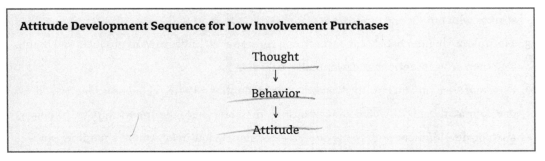

Attitude Development Sequence for Low Involvement Purchases

Thought
↓
Behavior
↓
Attitude

Contrastingly, for low involvement situations, the attitude is not formed until after the behavior occurred. There is no active search for information. Social or marketing inputs are not influential. The attitude is formed as a direct result of the behavior. True impulse buying where the consumer has little or no knowledge about the product or brand is one case where attitude is formed only after the consumer buys and tries the product. The sequence for attitude development under low involvement conditions is: (1) thought or cognitive activity, (2) behavior, including purchase or non-purchase, and (3) attitude development.

Conditions that influence whether a situation is high or low involvement include consumer variables such as values and experiences and situational variables such as product characteristics, including complexity, cost and other risk factors, and the visibility and expectations of others.

APPAREL APPLICATIONS

1. Influencing beliefs regarding apparel brands and products is a powerful tool in creating positive attitudes and consumer demand.

2. The elicitation of positive beliefs is best achieved by creating positive experiences for consumers with brands and products.

3. Multiple or singular beliefs can form strong consumer attitudes toward products and brands that then drive intentions and eventually, behaviors.

4. High involvement and low involvement conditions offer differing sequences for attitude development. In high involvement situations, marketers have the opportunity to influence attitude development prior to the purchase decision. In low involvement situations, since attitude is formed only after the purchase decision, the best strategy for apparel marketers is to create a product that meets or exceeds consumer needs.

Motivation

A **motive** is an unobservable inner force that stimulates a consumer toward action in a selective manner. It is a mechanism to arouse energy and a force that provides direction to that energy. Motives guide consumer behavior by helping consumers develop and identify basic desires and by providing guidance in developing criteria for evaluating goods and services. For example, a motive to save money or to wear the latest accessories will provide evaluative criteria for judging whether to purchase a new item. In many cases, products are viewed as the means to achieve

FIGURE 2.12 Motives such as saving money provide criteria for judging purchases.

motives. Achievement of peer acceptance, for example, may be accommodated by purchasing and wearing apparel similar to one's peers.

Motives can be of several types. They can be physiological, designed to satisfy basic biological needs, and they can be psychogenic, designed to meet psychological needs. While physiological motives may be inborn, psychogenic needs are usually learned through social interaction. Motives can be positive, providing direction toward purchases or actions, or negative, providing direction away from actions or situations. While positive motives may direct a consumer toward a new pair of jeans and acceptance by peers, negative motives may direct a consumer away from the purchase of gang related attire and thus affiliation with a particular gang or social group. In some cases, consumers are aware of their manifest motives while in other cases, they may have unconscious or latent motives. Since a single product or service can satisfy multiple motives, it is likely that purchases satisfy both manifest and latent motives simultaneously.

Many authors have identified and/or classified individual and consumer motives (Blackwell, Miniard, & Engle, 2006; Maslow, 1970; McGuire, 1976; Murray, 1938; Rokeach, 1973). Maslow's work is among those most well accepted. Maslow identified five levels of human motives. In his hierarchy of needs, he suggested that when, and only when, lower-level needs were met individuals progressed on to satisfy higher-level needs. Then, when lower-level needs again became unmet, the individual was motivated to satisfy the lower-level needs before returning attention to higher-level needs. Maslow included need categories of (1) physiological, (2) safety, (3) belongingness and love, (4) esteem, and (5) self actualization. Consumer apparel consumption can easily be matched to each of these levels of needs.

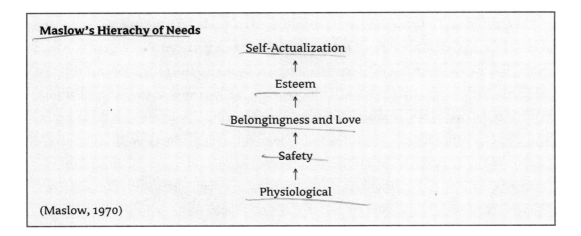

Maslow's Hierachy of Needs

Self-Actualization

↑

Esteem

↑

Belongingness and Love

↑

Safety

↑

Physiological

(Maslow, 1970)

APPAREL APPLICATIONS

1. Both manifest and latent motives are highly influential in apparel consumption.

2. Identification of key consumer motives for specific market segments is a powerful tool in creating apparel products that will satisfy consumer needs.

3. Apparel products can simultaneously satisfy multiple motives.

Information, Learning, and Memory

The sequence of consumer information processing in simplest terms involves acquiring or accepting stimuli, manipulating those inputs to obtain meaning, and then using that information to think about goods and services.

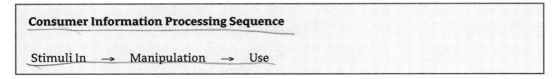

Consumer Information Processing Sequence

Stimuli In → Manipulation → Use

The acquisition of information-related stimuli occurs either by active or passive search. First, consumers scan their internal memory for information. Then, if needed, they engage in external search. How much external search occurs is influenced by the relative costs and benefits of that search. Higher levels of search result when the consumer seeks greater comfort and opportunity to increase the chance of maximizing satisfaction and when the consumer enjoys the shopping or searching experience and gains a positive feeling from obtaining product knowledge. Market conditions, buying strategies, and individual characteristics also influence the amount of external search. Market conditions are characterized by how many alternatives exist and how different from each other the alternatives are. Buying strategies such as prior decisions to buy specific brands or nationally advertised brands, or buying the cheapest brand tend to curtail external search. Individual factors include the consumer's product involvement, experience, open mindedness, and perception of risk.

Passive search involves the information consumers acquire during the normal process of everyday living. Without intending to gather information, consumers are bombarded by thousands of stimuli in rapid succession throughout the day. The attention of the consumer is allocated to these stimuli both voluntarily and involuntarily. In some cases a consumer may make a conscious effort to focus on an incoming stimulus such as a message on a billboard seen while traveling in a vehicle. In other cases, attention is involuntary, yet still the stimulus is received and available for further processing. While the human brain has marvelous capability, there are limitations to the number of stimuli that can be received and processed. Generally, attention is allocated extremely rapidly, yet only a limited number of stimuli can be attended to at one time. Some stimuli require more attention than others. For example, routine processes such as walking or viewing an ad seen previously may require very little attention while new stimuli require greater attention, even focus.

FIGURE 2.13 Shopping in a mall is a form of external search.

FIGURE 2.14 Without intending to, consumers obtain information through exposure to billboards.

Marketers have learned to capitalize on an understanding of attention variables and find that the following techniques are useful in gaining consumers' attention: motion, isolation, size, color, intensity, location, surprise, distinctiveness, human attraction, entertainment, connecting with consumers' needs, asking consumers for permission to send them stimuli, and paying consumers to pay attention (Blackwell, Miniard, & Engel, 2006). Humor is also an effective tactic. Consumers then allocate their attention-based on factors such as individual attention span; adaptation, including negation of effect for prolonged exposure; perceptual vigilance or watching for specific information; and perceptual defense or screening potentially threatening stimuli.

As stimuli are first introduced into the information processing system, consumers begin an encoding process whereby the original sensations, received as electrical impulses, are assigned mental symbols. Much of this occurs automatically. Initially, the features and organization of the stimuli are organized and then synthesized or combined with other information already held by the consumer. This synthesis stage is influenced by multiple factors, including the features and context of the stimulus and the consumer's experience, personality, motivation, attitudes, and adaptation level. Consumers learn to both discriminate between stimuli and to level stimuli into categories with similar stimuli. For the marketer, this discrimination and leveling is extremely important. For example, whether a product-related stimulus is "leveled" into a category with favorably perceived products is very different than if it is seen as similar to poorly regarded stimuli.

LEARNING

Learning occurs when stimuli are given attention, which results in a relatively permanent change in behavior. Such change can be either observable, such as purchase of an apparel product, or unobservable, such as development of an opinion. Learned behaviors can be physical, affective, or symbolic. Problem solving, including thinking or manipulation of symbols and insight or gaining new understandings of relationships is learned behavior. Symbols such as language, slogans, and logos are tools for learning and play a major role. For example, children at very early ages have had sufficient exposure to product logos and learn to identify them easily, often long before formal language is mastered.

Examination of learning has led to several useful applications for apparel marketers. Some of these include discrimination, stimulus generalization, reinforcement, shaping, modeling, ecological design, rate of learning, extinction, and forgetting. **Discrimination,** as noted previously, is the ability for consumers to distinguish the differences between two stimuli or perhaps new products. **Stimulus generalization** is the use of one response for similar stimuli unless the products are differentiated in some way. Store and family branding rely on the concept of stimulus generalization hoping that the consumer will see no difference between the store and national brands or between one branded product and other products produced under the same brand.

FIGURE 2.15 Slogans provide a reference point for an apparel company to maintain a loyal consumer base.

Reinforcement involves providing a reward for specific behavior. A behavior modification perspective suggests that providing rewards can alter behavior. **Shaping** builds upon that concept by reinforcing sequential behaviors that gradually move the consumer toward a desired behavior, like brand loyalty. **Modeling** involves allowing the consumer to observe the behavior of others and the consequences of that behavior. **Ecological design** employs principles of learning by using physical surroundings to change behavior. Store design including store layout and traffic patterns, in-store music, and fragrances are example of the application of ecological design. Learning rate information suggests that while initial learning may occur rapidly with exposure, the rate declines over time. Repetition, reinforcement, and practice schedules influence both the rate and strength of learning.

FIGURE 2.16 Many credit card and retail companies use rewards programs in order to encourage brand loyalty.

Finally, extinction and forgetting are factors in learning. **Extinction** suggests that consumers will unlearn behaviors if they are not reinforced. A shopper formerly loyal to a favorite store may lose that loyalty after time if they have not had reason or occasion to shop there and be reinforced by positive experiences. Similarly, **forgetting** refers to the loss of learning due to non-use or interference from other learning. New information may replace older learning.

MEMORY

An understanding of memory is important for marketers of apparel goods. Learned material, perhaps encouraged by a carefully orchestrated advertising campaign, must be retrievable. Multiple theories exist of how memory occurs including single memory formats where all learned material resides in a single register but that the level at which consumers are capable of processing varies from shallow to deep. An activation model suggests that consumers have variable abilities to activate memory and retrieval. Current popular theory describes memory as occurring in three distinct storage registers: sensory, short-term, and long-term. Information is first received by sensory memory. It then moves to short-term memory which is much like a work space for information processing where new information is combined with older information. Finally, the information is transferred to long-term memory. Whether the information is coded in a meaningful manner is extremely important for later retrieval. Semantic concepts, scripts, and mental pictures aid in coding and storing information.

Tips for applying what is known about memory include some of the following ideas. Memory is dependent on cues received and relevant cues can be used to stimulate recall. Since a limited amount of information can be processed at one time, "chunking" can be used to allow more information to be processed and retained. For example, for most people it is easier to remember

> **Multiple Store Memory**
>
> Sensory Memory $\rightarrow$ Short-Term Memory $\rightarrow$ Long-Term Memory

a 10-digit telephone number as two sets of three digits and one set of four digits rather than as a string of 10 digits. The order in which information is presented influences the amount remembered. Information presented in the middle of a message is most likely to be forgotten. Messages that encourage immediate rehearsal stimulate retention by actively engaging the learner in the act of repeating the information. Repetition is a useful memory tool. Finally, advertising messages with unique aspects and messages that have personal meaning, are likely to be remembered best (Loudon & Bitta, 1988).

APPAREL APPLICATIONS

1. Apparel products and marketing efforts bombard consumers with multiple stimuli and compete with thousands of other stimuli for attention.

2. Understanding and applying the attributes of attention allocation can increase the performance of apparel design and marketing communications.

3. Effective apparel advertisements and visual merchandising endeavors can be enhanced by applying principles of learning and memory.

Key Terms

Attitude	Autonomic	Classics
Conspicuous consumption	Consumer behavior	Cultural myopia

Culture

Ego

Forgetting

Market maven

Modeling

One-sided message

Psychoanalytic theory

Self-concept

Social class

Stimulus-response theories

Syncratic

Discrimination

Extinction

Human behavior

Material components

Motive

Passive Search

Psychographics

Self-concept/product image congruence

Social theories

Subculture

Trait and factor theories

Ecological design

Fads

Id

Matriarchal

Non-material components

Patriarchal

Reinforcement

Shaping

Stimulus generalization

Superego

Two-sided message

Ideas for Discussion and Application

1. Identify specific items of clothing or accessories such as a hat, shirt, or manner of wearing items that indicates membership or affiliation with a gang or social group. Why do you think they have taken on such meaning? Discuss what allows that affiliation to be recognized. What influence does it have and what are the reactions of others to such symbols?

2. Think about current logos or branded products that are "in" within your social group. Why do you think they are "in"? Who made the choice?

3. Identify and discuss some of the material and non-material components of culture related to apparel that you currently find in retail stores and the local environment.

4. Identify current trends in apparel. How are they being shaped by culture? Are they also influencing culture?

5. Select a specific subculture and identify an apparel product targeted particularly to them. Is more than one subculture involved? How do you know?

6. Review current print or electronic advertisements for apparel goods. Which social class is being targeted? How do you know? What do you know about the media usage patterns of each social class?

7. Reflect on the last time you were influenced by members of your social or family group. How did that occur? Was it beneficial?

8. Consider how the use of social group influence benefits apparel marketers. What concrete evidence do you see of the application of social group influence to marketing?

9. Find examples of one-sided and two-sided advertising messages. Critique the effectiveness of each.

10. Visit a local mall or shopping area. Identify stores that cater primarily to shoppers in each of the stages of the innovation adoption cycle.

11. Consider your own household or family unit. Select a recent purchase and identify who assumed the roles of initiator, influencer, buyer, and users. Could one individual assume more than one role?

12. Have you been given as a gift an item of apparel you didn't like? How could the theory of self-concept/product image congruence have applied in that situation?

13. Think of the last impulse purchase you made. Did your process follow the attitude development sequence for high or low involvement purchases?

14. Make a collection of apparel product logos. Quiz your peers to see how many they can identify successfully.

15. Look for advertising messages that use the concepts of chunking, message order, repetition, uniqueness, and personal meaning. Do you think these techniques increase retention?

unit
>>two

the creative processes and design

>> **chapter three**

creative processes

O f all the steps involved in producing apparel, the creative process is perhaps the most exciting and complicated. This step involves developing concepts for a line of garments with ideas gleaned from historical, political, economical and cultural events, to name a few. Sources of inspiration often overlap. The objective of this chapter is to explain, in some detail, just what is involved in developing apparel designs. There are several steps that will be covered in this chapter. They are line development, researching fabric and findings, creating first drafts by various methods, and assembling slopers or test garments.

Developing Designs

Before we go into detail about the processes, it is important to note that there are two separate routes to developing designs. The first and most widely known is simply designers and design houses creating apparel for the ready-to-wear industry or through haute couture. These garments bear the designer's name or label and are easily recognized. The other route is where mass merchants such as Wal-Mart, The Limited, Talbot's, and other large-scale retailers have in-house product development departments where designers work for the company to create apparel suited for their target customers. Sometimes, these designers are well-known, such as Isaac Mizrahi for Target, or they might be newcomers to the industry. In large companies that sell apparel under their own in-house label, a product development team works with individual buyers to develop silhouettes, colors, fabrications, seasonality and timing of delivery.

The steps involved in the creative process will be examined in the following order:

1. Ideas for inspiration
    >> historical
    >> economical
    >> social
    >> cultural
    >> political
2. Developing a Theme
    >> focus of entire line or groups of garments
    >> influence of society
3. Developing the Garment
    >> source fabric
    >> formal sketches and first drafts
4. Making the Pattern
5. Constructing Production Samples
    >> Edit the line

What Inspires Design?

Designers choose the colors, silhouettes, and fabrics of their collections. What inspires a designer? The entire world. Designers attend art galleries, read and listen to the media, go to movies, travel, study history, and observe what people are wearing. All of these things provide inspiration.

Although there are many examples to support the premise that fashion is influenced by movie stars and famous personalities, we will examine two of these. Personalities and media events have great influence on fashion trends and supply tons of inspiration for designers. An example is First Lady Jackie Kennedy. She was considered an icon of fashion and because she was constantly being shown on television and in the newspapers, whatever she wore was quickly copied by the women of America. Her style was considered modern, yet classic. Because of her fame, designers who created garments for her were also thrown into the limelight. Retailers and designers scrambled to sell garments that copied her style.

More recent examples of celebrity influence on fashion are pop stars Russell Simmons with Kimora Lee-Simmons. Russell Simmons, a pioneer of hip-hop music, made baggy jeans, loose oversized shirts, and Adidas tennis shoes popular as he wore these in the earlier days of performing. He went on to develop a line of apparel called Phat Farm. Kimora Lee-Simmons, previously married to Russell Simmons, now offers a line of clothing for women called Baby Phat, which sells upbeat, trendy, colorful garments that cater to teens and college-age consumers.

FIGURE 3.1 Jackie Kennedy was a style trend-setter while First Lady and remains a classic fashion icon today.

The Arts

Cultural events can influence designers. These influences include theatre, film, television, art exhibits, and music. An example of art influencing fashion is that of Yves Saint Laurent's (YSL) designs that mirrored costumes from the movie, *Dr. Zhivago* in the late seventies. He also gave a nod to abstract artists such as Mondrian and Picasso in his lines. YSL became known for his Mondrian dress. He was influenced by the art of Matisse, Mondrian, Andy Warhol, and Tom Wesselman (Breward, 2003). Films are a unique way of introducing fashion forms to the public. Some films introduce unforgettable icons in the fashion timeline.

Designers are continually influenced by movies. For example, we see examples of Grecian- and Roman-inspired evening gowns on the catwalks and on the Red Carpet. Some examples of possible influential movies might be *Troy* or *300*. The influence of the movie and television industry on fashion can be seen in the costumes worn and trend being translated into runway garments by designers. There is also evidence that the specific clothing designed for the stars heavily influence what is found in ready-to-wear collections. An example might be *Sex and the City*, where the fashions and shoes worn by the stars of this show became a very popular trend. Clothing in movies like *The Devil Wears Prada* showcases designs by Prada, Marc Jacobs, and Chanel.

Technology

Technology is a source of inspiration for designers. During the late sixties, the space program was prominent in the media as well as the advent of science fiction movies which fueled the consumer for styling that mirrored futuristic textiles and silhouettes. New technology provided

FIGURE 3.2 YSL's Mondrian dress is an example of the influence of fine art on fashion.

FIGURE 3.3 New fibers as a result of technological advances, such as Halston's ultrasuede garments

fabrics for astronaut's space suits as well as textiles used inside the space ships. These events served as inspiration for designers such as Andre Courreges, who designed around this theme.

Advances in textile technology also inspire designers. A popular example of influence on design was the development of ultra-suede, a multi-component, non-woven fabric that is composed of polyester fibers embedded in a layer of polyurethane foam. The surface appears and feels like suede and the fabric can be dry-cleaned or machine washed. This fabric, in its introductory stage, was considered a status symbol and was very expensive. Many designers used this new textile. Halston is perhaps one of the most well-known for his ultra-suede garments. Other examples are the 1960s double- knit revolution where manufacturers were able to inexpensively produce varieties of polyester double-knit fabrics that were washable. The fabric was very popular and suitable for simple, straight silhouettes. Garments made in this fabric were seen in menswear, as well as women's apparel.

When asked how he created his clothes, Yves Saint Laurent replied: "I put my ideas down on paper, which are turned into samples and, if necessary, are revised by me." (Seeling, 2000).

History

Using history as a resource gives the designer countless ideas. From the ancient Egyptians to the Colonial Americans, designers will pull out isolated parts of the costumes worn during certain times such as the translucent, pleated garments worn by the Egyptians or the ornate sleeves that adorned Elizabethan gowns. At other times, many different silhouettes will be utilized and modernized by the designer to create a cohesive theme for a season's line.

Historical influences can be seen on the runway today, in Grecian-inspired gowns and garments that mimic the design lines of Madeleine Vionnet.

Economy

The world's economy can have a great influence on designers' lines. A surplus or deficit in natural fibers such as cotton, linen, or silk can affect the kind of fabrics available for use. Exchange rates can also determine the cost of materials which directly affects the selling price of the garment. The years during World War II (1942–1945) had great impact on women's clothing and the array that designers presented for purchase. Ensembles were more functional than beautiful with skirts cut closer to the body and shorter in length because of low availability of fabrics (Cassin-Scott, 1994).

Another economic force influencing designers has come about because of the global **sourcing** of production. Depending on the country in which production is taking place, certain designs might be restricted or limited based on fabric, findings, or the labor involved. This directly impacts what garments are produced for sale to consumers.

Society

Societal influences are broad and can be subtle. People usually dress alike in order to be affiliated with a certain group whether it is an income bracket, church organization, fraternity, or club. The designer's challenge is to be aware of the social norms and create garments that are adaptable to the rules of current styles. The rap music culture had great impact on fashions during the mid-1980s. Trends were short-lived and seemed to disappear as quickly as they came. An example can be seen in this picture of Run DMC, with striped training pants and tennis shoes.

FIGURE 3.4A Historical inspiration from Grecian dress by Max Mara

FIGURE 3.4B Historical inspiration from a Vionnet dress by Zac Posen

FIGURE 3.5 Run DMC's influence on fashion: the all-black Adidas track suit

Many elements of society serve as inspiration for designers. Some examples of societal influences are: The prevalence of casual dressing, especially in the workplace; women who are more independent in their thinking and are not so easily swayed by what the fashion designers offer; cult movements such as the hippie era. The Hippie movement was characterized by loose-fitting garments, open macramé vests, beads, sandals or bare feet, and a general disheveled look. This look sought to oppose high fashion garments as a show of resistance to society in general and to the norms and values of the 1960s of extravagance and wealth.

FIGURE 3.6 The Hippie look characterized by long hair, wild flowers, and beads

Culture

Designers must be sensitive to the shifts of interests of their target markets. It is essential to be aware of what is happening globally, locally, and within the arena of the designers' sphere of influence. Research, planning, and inspiration are key to pulling these elements together. In order to be on top of this influence, trends must be tracked closely by reviewing demographics and psychographics. These elements do not work in isolation but overlap each other. Let's look at an example of cultural elements.

Influences from exotic cultures have been a recurring theme in many designers' lines for years. Shapes, motifs, colors, and lines from many parts of the world are incorporated into couture lines. In Figure 3.7, we see two examples of how YSL showed collections inspired by different cultures. In Figure 3.7a, a Bombara dress is shown from his Africaine Collection of 1967. In Figure 3.7b, a Russian influence makes this garment colorful and rustic from his 1976/77 Winter Russian Collection (Seeling, 2000).

FIGURE 3.7A
YSL's Bombara
dress, Africaine
collection, 1967

FIGURE 3.7B
YSL's 1976–77
Winter Russian
collection

Politics

This element can sometimes have a far-reaching impact on a designer's clothing line. Current political events can affect everything from the length of hemlines to the colors of garments. Examples can be seen in mini skirts worn during the Vietnam War and camouflage prints.

It has been proposed that during years of American presidential elections, patriotism is more widely displayed in some designer's lines with the use of national colors—red, white, and blue. There is probably not enough evidence to support this, but political forces do influence designers with respect to trade laws and policies in this increasingly diverse global market. During years when the United States engages in war, olive drab green, military looks, and camouflage prints seem to be more prominent in designs.

It is important to note that designers use multiple and overlapping elements to conceive their clothing designs and ultimately determine the direction of fashion with surprising innovations that react to current events. Consumers react negatively or positively to the options that they are given. Both consumer and designer determine the course of fashion.

FIGURE 3.8 Political influences allow for the popularity of camouflage in mainstream fashion.

Developing a Theme

A theme is determined by the designer and gives cohesiveness to the line. Often, designers have multiple themes within one line. An example of this is a spring line with themes such as flowers, the color green, or trapeze silhouettes. Decisions for themes are guided by the designer's sources of inspiration. The styling of garments within a theme has some commonality, such as color, fabric, trims, or silhouettes.

As designers assemble pictures, clippings, sketches, and color fabric swatches, themes come together in this creative process. Here is an example from Marc Jacobs' spring/summer 2003 collection where he showed a line with a 1950s theme with feminine dresses and pencil straight skirts. In yet another of Jacobs' collections, fall/winter 2005, his collection displayed a theme of embellishments along with trapeze line coats.

At the development stage, the designer decides what body type he or she is designing for and how the garments will look on real people. Other factors that guide development include:

1. Season
2. Color
3. Fabric
4. Target Market
5. End Use

Season

Usually, designers will focus on spring or fall seasons. Still others include a resort line which comes out during the late winter time period. The season being designed for obviously affects the type of fabrications used, colors, textures, and silhouettes.

FIGURE 3.9A Marc Jacobs Spring 2003 collection

FIGURE 3.9B Marc Jacobs Fall 2005 collection

FIGURE 3.10 Yohji Yamamoto is known for his black designs.

FIGURE 3.11 Valentino's signature color may be red, but in 1968 he created an all-white collection.

Color

Many elements are considered when deciding on color. Sometimes, color will determine the theme and at other times, the theme will dictate the colors used in the line. Research has shown that color is the single most important factor that appeals to customers in the process of shopping. So, the colors used in a line may be critical to the success of the line.

An example of a statement being made with color can be seen in the collections of Yohji Yamamoto whose signature color of black triggered a revolution in the fashion world during the 1980s when bright colors for apparel were the norm.

Valentino is also known for his signature use of color. In 1968, he presented a "white" collection. This collection marked a high point in his career. Because of the attention given to him as a result of this collection, he was asked to design the wedding dress for Jackie Kennedy when she married Aristotle Onassis. Valentino is well known for his consistent use of red in his evening wear. It has become his trademark.

Color choices are influenced by culture, the arts, the environment, and certainly seasonality. Professionals in the fashion industry spend a great amount of time analyzing color cycles and predicting colors for upcoming seasons. Designers make use of this information by hiring firms like the Color Marketing Group, the Color Association of the United States, the Color Box, Colorplay, Huepoint, and others, who supply them with much-needed color forecasts.

Another color service, Pantone, Inc., has a system of colors (Textile Color System) of 1,700 colors that are coded with six-digit numbers. These color cards are provided to clients who include designers as well as major companies that have in-house product development departments such as Gap and Wal-Mart. The colors adapted for a specific season then become the standard by which all of the apparel for a specific group of merchandise is measured.

Fabric

According to Sue Jones, in her book entitled *Fashion Design*, "Fabric is to the fashion designer what paint is to the artist: the medium of creative expression. Some designers work directly with the fabric, others might draw out ideas on paper and then search for an appropriate material. Choosing suitable fabrics is the key to successful designing. It is not only a matter of what one likes visually but also weight and handle, price, availability, performance, quality and timing. The suitability of a fabric for a fashion design comes from a combination of yarn, construction, weight, texture, color, handling and pattern or print, as well as additional performance factors such as warmth, stain-resistance and ease of care. The designer must have a reasonable expectation as to how a fabric will behave; a fabric cannot be forced into a style or shape that is not compatible with characteristics, both practically and visually."

Sometimes, the fabric determines the design rather than the other way around. Fabrications that have sold well in the past are often repeated in designers' lines in newer, updated colors. An example would be using wool gabardine suiting, which is a basic fabric. The designer would simply change the colors used in the forward line. Another consideration for the right fabric is the level of skill needed to execute the garment. If the fabric is difficult to work with and requires a high level of skill, this also affects the production cost of the garment.

Beautiful fabric does not always look great once it is sewn into a garment. Complementary fabric must also be found to complete the designers' concept for the line. This affords the designer the opportunity to develop as many combinations of designs as possible around the desired theme. Once this step is complete, the designer is able to weed out the weaker designs and focus on those most likely to sell.

Target Market

Of course, the designer must always be mindful of the target market when developing a theme. For example, polyester gabardine (very popular in the late 60s) would not be the fabric of choice for a current consumer who buys moderate to higher priced apparel. Target markets are usually determined by age, income level, lifestyle, gender, and size. These areas certainly overlap in terms of who the consumer will be. The question to be answered is: Who am I designing for?

End Use

The end use of the line of garments is always the primary concern. Is it casual, workplace, professional, or evening wear? Sometimes, designers might start at this end of the process because of restrictions related to the intended price points, or a specific target market that dictates certain styling. An example might be a designer for Liz Claiborne, where garments are priced within a certain range. The designer has to adhere to these constraints in developing garments which might affect the type of fabric used, the trims, or the kinds of silhouettes. Each of these factors overlap and is not isolated in influencing the designers theme.

Sourcing

Sourcing refers to the process of selecting raw materials or components and also choosing contractors to produce the garments. In this context, we refer to sourcing as locating a purchase source. This has become increasingly challenging for designers as they are purchasing goods from all over the world. Another term often used is **outsourcing**, which refers to the process of selecting and using a company to produce garments created by a designer. This can be a complex step in the design process.

Globalization has become a fact of life in the textiles and apparel industry and designers have a more difficult time when confronting the broad array of sources and countries from which to choose for the whole production of their designs. Countries such as Japan, China, Taiwan, Korea, and India have experienced high growth in the textile industries in the last 10 years.

The questions facing designers are: Where will they locate the fabric, buttons, and findings to produce the line? Will it be domestic or imported? Is there enough fabric available? How much does it cost to do any special dyeing or texturizing? Key questions and issues surrounding sourcing will be explored further in a later chapter.

Sketches and First Drafts

The designer documents his or her ideas in sketches and first drafts. The media used can be as simple as pen and paper, photography, pages from magazines, and other sources that have the potential for developing the theme.

Some of the more traditional methods are:

>> keeping a sketchbook where ideas are drawn as they come

>> tear sheets—pictures from books, magazines, or newspapers

>> creating mood boards—a collection of images and ideas from research to formalize the theme concept

>> developing a storyboard—includes a mood board and final sketches with fabric swatches and even trim and findings that enable the viewer to understand the theme.

>> CAD (computer-aided design) drawings – helps designers speed the sketching process.

At this point in the process, the designer has fully developed the theme, feels comfortable with the design sketches, and has acquired the fabrics and materials to support the theme.

FIGURE 3.12 AutoCad sketches of garments

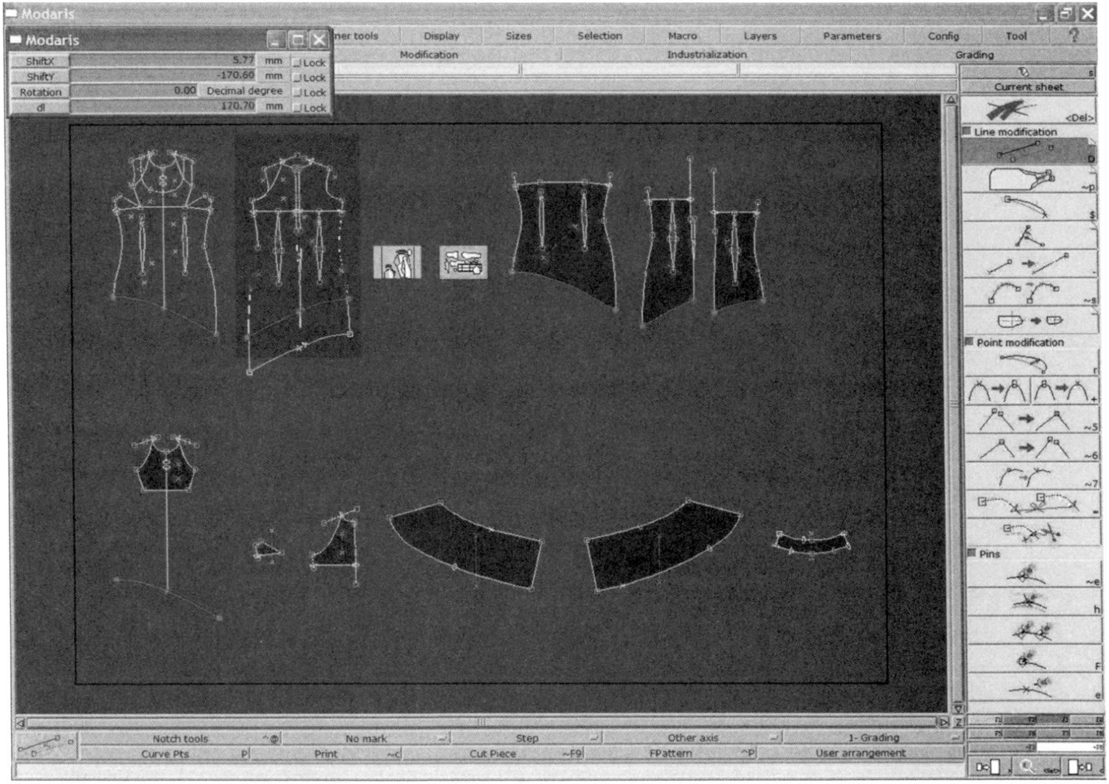

The next step is to start creating patterns and slopers for the garments. Patternmakers analyze the sketches and develop pattern pieces that are laid out on fabrics, cut, and sewn together to create a first garment. There are several methods to developing a pattern.

>> Drafting

>> Flat pattern design

>> Draping

Drafting is a method that creates a pattern by using the body measurements of a typical target customer. Computer-aided design (CAD) is now commonly used to speed this process.

Flat pattern design is a precision-based drawing that requires accurate measurements and proportions. This method is used for garments that follow the contours of the body without complicated lines. Flat patterns are developed from a set of basic pattern blocks as well as from CAD programs that are able to plot the measurements that are entered.

Draping is a method that involves fitting a **muslin** (toile) on a mannequin or on a real body. When the shape and fit are exactly what the designer envisions, the toile is removed and copied to pattern paper.

Muslin/Toile

After a pattern has been cut for the design, it has to be tested by making a garment in muslin, calico, or a fabric of similar weight and behavior to the final fabric. This is done in order to visualize any deficiencies in the design lines or fitting problems. The first fabric sample is called a toile (a French word for a lightweight cotton). In the U.S., the first garment is called a muslin (Jones, 2002). At this point, any needed alterations or adjustments in the design can be made easily because it is fitted on a mannequin or person. Only the designer and workroom staff actu-

FIGURE 3.13 Garment being draped on a mannequin and model

ally see this step. Critical decisions are made as the designer reviews each toile closely and compares each one to see if it fits with the theme of the entire group. It is at this stage that design lines are changed and some garments are actually eliminated. Usually the pattern cutter, sample maker, seamstress, and designer collaborate on the toile with the designer making the final decision.

When the pattern has been finalized, it is marked with seam allowances, darts, grain lines and any other marks that will facilitate the construction of the garment.

Construction of Production Samples

At this point, the designer reviews each garment and determines if it fits within the theme of the line. Several events can cause a garment to be deleted from the line, such as high cost of fabrics and findings which won't allow the garment to fit into the price structure of the line, bad design lines, or bad fit, design lines that don't work with the fabric, or simply a change of mind by the designer. This editing process takes place several times until the line is finalized and presented on the runway. The finished apparel lines are shown to the public in different venues determined by the target market and designer. Couture and ready-to-wear collections are usually shown twice a year for spring and fall seasons.

The Final Word

The design process can take anywhere from six to eight months, but not longer, because designers are expected to present a finished line each season. Each step has to be organized and move fairly quickly. The customer ultimately holds the key to the success of the line. Success is reached when a number of orders are actually put into production for sale to the customer. Companies may aspire to launch products that will become a mainstay in fashion society, or they may project short-term success with a trendy award-winner. Today's consumers, maneuvering through a saturated market, rely on much more than branding and name recognition in their selection of apparel. Designers are challenged to show an understanding of culture, economics, lifestyles, and global mobility in every step in their creative processes.

Key Terms

Drafting   Draping   Muslin   Outsourcing   Sourcing

Ideas for Discussion and Application

1. How have movies influenced fashion? Cite three films you believe influenced fashion and write about the ways in which this is evident to you.
2. How do you think war impacts fashion?
3. What is the primary difference between ready-to-wear and couture?
4. To what extent do the steps in the creative process overlap? Explain and support your explanation with examples.
5. What recent political events have had the most impact on today's current fashion trends?
6. State three changes in fashion that have occurred in your lifetime.
7. Cite two examples of ethnic influences in today's fashion trends.

Activities

1. Research a current designer's collection and write about what may have inspired the collection. Use at least three of the various concepts discussed in this chapter.
2. Design a garment using the lines and design elements found in the historical source. Use historical costume books, magazines, and Internet sources for inspiration. Write the catalog or advertising text that would sell this garment.

designers

OBJECTIVES

>> *Identify significant fashion designers and their contributions to the industry.*

>> *Recognize modern American icons and the trends they started.*

>> *Evaluate oriental inspirations and materials used for design.*

This chapter introduces the reader to a limited review of specific fashion designers who have become legends or icons in the fashion world. While all designers have contributed to the growth and development of the fashion industry, some were pioneers in terms of their contributions to design. The chapter is divided into sections for what we consider pioneers, classic designers, modern American icons, European innovators, and Far Eastern inspirations. The key contributions of these designers will be examined so that the student of apparel will have a deeper appreciation and understanding of major design elements that have served as a base for the current fashion industry and some of the trends that we continue to see today.

The Pioneers

We begin our study with who we consider to be the pioneers of fashion. These men and women were innovators and elevated the craft of creating garments to levels that set the standard for fashion for all time.

Charles Worth

Charles Frederick Worth is considered the founder of haute couture because he was the first to convince customers to wear what he told them to wear rather than catering to their tastes. Note the portrait of this great designer. He was so popular, that clients actually went to his home to have garments made for them. Originally from London, he created garments for Elisabeth of Austria and Napoleon III's wife, Eugenie. He signed his creations as works of art and presented a new collection every year. He is known for promoting sales and change in the fashion world.

Paul Poiret

Paul Poiret is sometimes referred to as the "first designer." Born in 1879, Poiret started his fashion career as an errand boy for an umbrella-maker. He stole silk remnants from his employer and used them to drape garments on a 15 inch wooden doll. He is considered the "fashion liberator" of women because his designs offered style to women. He became the first designer to create his own perfume. Poiret was actually a former apprentice of Charles Worth.

Inspired by the Art Nouveau movement and a possible "new" dress that would satisfy the suffragette movement, Poiret designed a simple, narrow robe with a long skirt that started just below the bust and fell to the floor in a straight line. This design immortalized him. The new dress was modest, young, supple, and moved with the wearer without confinement. Poiret continued to tinker with this silhouette by raising the bust higher and making the skirt tighter, which resulted in the hobble skirt in 1910. The hobble skirt was not popular for very long because it restricted the ability of the wearer to take normal steps. He became the first real designer of the twentieth century because of the mark he left on everything that he touched, from apparel to

FIGURE 4.1 (top left) Portrait of Charles Worth

FIGURE 4.2 (bottom left) A gown designed by Worth

FIGURE 4.3 (above) A model for Gimbel's in a Poiret creation

accessories. He died in 1944 in poverty, forgotten by society at that time, but definitely remembered in modern fashion history as the "first designer."

Elsa Schiaparelli

"Shocking" is the word that comes to mind when this designer is mentioned. She is remembered for her daring and eccentric designs. Culottes and pants were plentiful in her collections when these silhouettes were not commonly shown by couture designers. She is also well known for her use of bolero jackets. Elsa was born in 1890 in Rome to a well-off, cultured family. Her career in fashion began when she met Paul Poiret. Compared to other designers of that day, her designs were considered shocking. She developed a new color of pink, called hot pink. Today, that color is sometimes referred to as "shocking pink." Elsa considered herself to be as much an artist as designer. In addition to her new color she created a fragrance called Shocking. Her twenty-seven year career included her association with leading Surrealist artists of her day, which greatly influenced her designs.

Born in Italy, she moved to Paris, where she opened her fashion salon in 1927 and became enormously successful. Her creations were valued for their wit and an irreverence for tradition that was refreshing at the time. One of her most famous designs is an evening gown worn by the Duchess of Windsor with lobsters hand-painted on by Salvador Dali on a white background. Other gowns from her collection were made with fabrics inspired by Picasso's paintings.

Also known as Schiap, she was the first designer to use shoulder pads and created a man-tailored woman's suit in 1931 which showed that she was ahead of her time. The woman's power suit later became the professional uniform in the 1980s. It is believed that Schiaparelli's superb

FIGURE 4.4 Schiaparelli's famous "Lobster" dress

FIGURE 4.5 A flowing gown by Madeleine Vionnet

FIGURE 4.6 Balenciaga's Spanish-influenced design

workmanship in her garments was overshadowed by the attention given to the surface of her designs - colors, textures, etc. The Schiaparelli silhouette was cut close to the body, with a small waist and wide shoulders.

Madeleine Vionnet

Known as the mistress of the bias cut, Vionnet invented the bias cut and used elaborate draping in her designs. Even today, her designs remain unsurpassed. Born in 1876, she left school at the age of 12, despite her talent for mathematics. She later became a seamstress in Paris. At the age of 16, she traveled to England to become a laundry woman where she continued to perfect her designs. She worked like a sculptor to achieve her designs on the female body. It is speculated that Vionnet's love of mathematics inspired her designs that incorporated geometric shapes such as triangles and rectangles. Soft fabrics such as crepe, velvet, and satins were used in her garments. Vionnet is known for having tried to protect her designs from copies. Vionnet is not as well known today as Chanel but her designs are considered the "Rolls Royce" of couture.

Cristóbal Balenciaga

Cristóbal Balenciaga is considered the architect of couture. His designs were stark with clean lines that resemble sculpture. Somber colors were the norm, such as black sometimes mixed with browns. His garments were compared to works of art.

Born the son of a Basque tailor, he learned how to sew at an early age. Balenciaga's gowns are known for their dramatic detail with influences from flamenco. Many designers, such as Andre Courreges and Emanuel Ungaro learned their craft from him. Balenciaga left the house in 1968, not wanting to compete with mass production trends that had taken hold in the fashion industry. The house is now owned by Gucci.

The Classics

The classic designers are in a class by themselves. While it is not possible to cover all of the works of these great designers, a few of the most outstanding will be mentioned. These designers were successful because of their ability to create timeless garments that stand the test of time and consumer loyalty. Their designs are still being copied today with modern twists added to them.

Coco Chanel

Born Gabrielle Chanel in 1883 in France, Chanel was the second child of an unmarried couple. When she was 12 years old, she was forced to live in an orphanage when her father abandoned her after her mother's death. She experienced much unkindness during this time, which made her tough, and forced her to become an expert at survival. She also learned to sew during this time. Chanel is considered a designer in the modern sense, in that she was innovative and thoughtful about what women really wanted in apparel. She pioneered the use of jersey knit in garments. In 1926, she created a black dress constructed with crepe de chine fabric, which became known as the evening uniform. We know it now as the "little black dress." The foundation of Chanel's look was mobility for women. Chanel closed her salon in 1939 during the war.

At the age of 70 in 1954, she made a comeback to the fashion world and reopened her design house. What she showed in her first collection was not well received by the fashion world. They poked fun at her designs. Chanel showed them the future of design, and they thought it was the past. In her collection, she showed tailored suits with braiding, gilt buttons, chains, and sling-

FIGURE 4.7A AND B Coco Chanel and her classic black dress

back shoes with contrasting toe caps, and shoulder-chain purses. When Chanel died in 1971, her annual income was $160 million.

Valentino

Valentino Garavani is known as the 'Master of the Dress' by the fashion world. He is shown in Figure 4.8 along with some of his designs. He launched his design house in 1960, where he made extravagant couture gowns for the wealthy. His dresses are very romantic, feminine and are reminiscent of ancient Rome.

His signature color is red. However, one of the highlights of Valentino's career was a collection of all white gowns presented in 1968. One of his most famous clients was Jackie Onassis, who chose one of his gowns for her wedding to Aristotle Onassis.

FIGURE 4.8 Valentino and his ladies in gowns

Christian Dior

Dior is sometimes referred to as the "gentle dictator" in fashion circles. In 1949, he was perhaps the most well-known designer in the world. He was often criticized by Chanel for having created the "New Look." This silhouette took women straight back to the constraints of the past with waist cinchers. Dior was known as a brilliant marketer of his products. In his fashion shows, his models made theatrical appearances. He was the first designer to change the hemlines on the whole line from one collection to another from season to season.

FIGURE 4.9A Dior's look of the 1990s, by John Galliano

FIGURE 4.9B Dior in the 2000s, by John Galliano

FIGURE 4.10A Yves Saint Laurent

FIGURE 4.10B YSL's "smoking jacket"

Yves Saint Laurent (YSL)

Born in 1936, Yves Saint Laurent became Dior's successor in 1958, where his goal was to preserve haute couture and luxury in garments. Considered the 'genius of the century,' his collections were often influenced by old civilizations, artists and even students in college. His designs reflected the trends occurring in the streets and everyday life. He is given credit for designing "Le Smoking," a female version of the tuxedo. His consistent use of basic shapes with decorative devices and his generous use of color in his designs is what continues to make him popular and widely sought after.

Pierre Cardin

In 1951, Cardin showed his first collection. He is best known for the bubble dress—fabric gathered at the hemline, making it very puffy. Cardin was an astute businessman and made innovative decisions in selling his garments. Earlier, he had worked with Dior and Balenciaga, but did not duplicate their designs. By 1959, Dior was the first couturier to ever produce a ready-made collection. At that time, there was no such word in French for ready-to-wear. Because of this marketing strategy, he was expelled from the Chambre Syndicale but was later allowed to rejoin. He is regarded as fashion's scientist because he developed his own material, Cardine, which consisted of bonded fibers that were stiff enough to hold the geometric shapes incorporated in his designs.

FIGURE 4.11 A tailored women's suit by Pierre Cardin

Modern American Icons

American style most likely developed as a result of the United States' isolation from the fashions of Paris during World War II. The flow of trends and fashion information was interrupted and America had time to develop its own trend in apparel. American women were more active and more independent than their European counterparts, hence, the beginning of sportswear—comfortable, simple, and classic. Several Americans stepped up to the challenge of creating fashionable garments for this new customer. A few of them are discussed here.

Ralph Lauren

According to Seeling (2000), Lauren is known as the cowboy of American fashion because of his affinity for designing boots, jeans, and suede jackets with fringe. He is an excellent marketer, much like his counterpart, Calvin Klein. He is famous for his polo trademark. His garments appeal to the rich as well as the common consumer. His clothes are a status symbol of the twentieth century.

Calvin Klein

Klein was one in a group of designers who dressed women in feminine versions of menswear. He started his business in 1960. His collections included pant suits with gangster stripes, single-breasted blazers, dress-shirt collars and white linen three-piece suits. The hub of Klein's aesthetic is sexuality (Seeling, 2000). The cut of his garments appeal to customers and this is ensured by the marketing and promotions used by the company to entice clients. His advertising campaigns have played a part in the softening of the strict rules of society in terms of what is wearable and what is acceptable. His designs are not necessarily trendsetting but express timeless appeal.

FIGURE 4.12 Ralph Lauren's all-American, feminine look

FIGURE 4.13 Calvin Klein's simplistic yet elegant designs

Donna Karan

With the evolution of the power female executive of the eighties, there was a need for women to dress in clothing that displayed that power. Donna Karan met that need and had a global psychological impact on women's clothing with her designs. Karan trained in the house of Anne Klein where she worked with Louis del'Olio to keep the label going after Anne Klein's death. She presented her first collection in 1985, sensual, with jersey and wool crepes, black stockings, and distinct jewelry. These proved to be basic pieces for the working professional female.

European Innovators

During the era of the sixties, change was everywhere and the young generation demanded it. Fashion was varied, unconventional, and very radical compared to earlier times. This mindset spilled over into fashion and many designers achieved fame during this period of change and revolutionary ideas. A few designers of this time will be discussed.

Sonia Rykiel

Rykiel's career started out unintentionally as she searched for warm maternity clothing and began to knit her own garments. This necessity turned to profit when she began selling her garments in her husband's shop. Her knit garments consist of jumpers, jackets, skirts, wide pants, scarves, and capes. She is known as the Queen of Knitwear in fashion circles and has become internationally famous for her expertise in executing slim, elegant knit garments that are both flattering and comfortable to wear.

Karl Lagerfeld

Karl Lagerfeld took a decidedly different track in developing his career. Rather than opening his own design house, he chose to work freelance for noted designers. This strategy proved to be

FIGURE 4.14 Sonia Rykiel is known as the queen of knits.

FIGURE 4.15 Karl Lagerfeld revived the classic Chanel look for a new generation.

FIGURE 4.16 Emanuel Ungaro's evening gowns feature vibrant colors and patterns.

FIGURE 4.17 A flamboyant design by Christian Lacroix

successful for him and provided much fame. He first worked for Chloe, where he remained for 20 years. From there, he moved to Fendi, where he designed fur collections. His most successful stint has been that of reviving the style of Chanel. Lagerfeld has proven himself to be a master at bringing the spirit of Chanel into all of his collections. He has taken her elements of design and raised it to higher levels in his collections.

Emanuel Ungaro

Ungaro started his career with Balenciaga and spent six years there where he perfected the technique for strong cutting of garments. As a result of this training, his first garments were severe combinations of blazers and shorts. He later developed his own style and now has become known for mixing flowers and bright, vivid colors in his designs with softer, feminine silhouettes. Ungaro does not sketch his designs. He works directly on the body of a model, sometimes it is said for as much as 12 hours a day (Seeling, 2000).

Christian LaCroix

The eighties were a time of excess and the designs of LaCroix imbued that excessiveness in the lavish, luxurious fabrics, brilliant colors, and daring trims and silhouettes. LaCroix trained with Hermes and later took over the house of Jean Patou. His designs caused a stir because of their bright, bold colors, lavish accessories, and the puffed-up short skirt. Some of his designs were clearly not wearable but they were fun to look at. He opened his own house in 1987 with the financial backing of LVMH and has continued to be known as the "celebrated prince of fashion."

Oriental Inspirations

Along with Kenzo, who was the first Japanese designer to establish himself in Paris, many compatriots followed him as they expected to use Paris as a springboard for entering the international market. These designers are known for developing their design proportions based on the materials used rather than trying to shape the body.

Yohji Yamamoto

Yohji Yamamoto's first garments were perceived as dark, somber, and strange. These garments actually represented a revolution in fashion that offered an alternative to the body's exposure. Black was the only color used. Eventually, the fashion world embraced his collections. He is regarded as a master of cutting and allows the material to determine the shape of the garment.

Kenzo

Takada Kenzo, a Japanese designer, is renowned for bringing a sense of fun to his refined versions of hippie garments (Seeling, 2000). Kenzo was the first Japanese designer to open his design house in Paris. In his designs, he has incorporated elements from the kimono and combined it with elements from other cultures to produce garments that are fun, whimsical, and include lots of color.

Issey Miyake

Miyake is famous for recreating the Fortuny pleats in his garments of synthetic fibers and new colors. In his designs, art and craft merge and he believes that the fabric should dictate the shape of the garment rather than creating the garment to fit the shape of the body. He has researched many new fabrics and materials and has several factories working with him as he seeks to join technology and tradition. Miyake continually experiments with new materials to create unique garments. He developed a layered and wrapped look that became his hallmark. He also created wire constructions that were lacquered and used together with bamboo structures to mold

FIGURE 4.18 (above) Yohji Yamamoto's signature black

FIGURE 4.19 (top right) A layered look from Kenzo

FIGURE 4.20 (bottom right) Issey Miyake's geometric design

bodice shapes that resembled the armor of a samurai. His use of wrapping and tying techniques for fastenings on his garments is based on Japanese tradition (Milbank, 1985).

A Final Note

The reader has been provided with a brief overview of a very short list of key contributors to the exciting world of fashion. It is vital for students of apparel to be aware of couture designers and what they are known for. Couture designers have essentially raised the bar, so to speak, in apparel, because consumers have higher expectations of the apparel they wear, not only with respect to price, but color, fabrication, styling, and construction techniques. Being aware of the level of attention and detailing paid to couture increases the knowledge of the every day consumer.

Knowing what designers have presented in the past and what is currently being shown in the fashion world informs the consumer and gives them a comfort level about the apparel products being shown for sale by regular retailers. The garments sewn and made by past designers are also considered works of art because of the attention paid to every detail of the garment. Having an understanding of how the fashion industry has evolved gives clarity to professionals, students, and consumers and allows comparisons to be made between the apparel of yesteryear and garments of today. The question to be answered at the end of the day is: Does the apparel of today meet the standards of past decades in terms of quality in construction, design, and fabrication?

Ideas for Discussion and Application

1. What significant contributions did the following designers make to the development of fashion as we know it today?
   a. Coco Chanel

b. Charles Worth

c. Balenciaga

d. Poiret

2. Research two designers—one from early eighteenth century and one from the twentieth century. Compare their designs, techniques, and inspiration. How they similar? How are they different?

3. Search the Internet or local stores for a trendy garment and compare it to the fashion lines of any older nineteenth-century garment. What are the differences and similarities?

4. Select one designer and trace the evolution of their designs from their first collection to their current collection. How have they changed in silhouette, fit, color, styling, and textiles? What is unique about this designer's style?

5. Visit a local department store that carries couture garments. Document the names of the designer clothing that you find there. If possible, try on a few and evaluate the fit and construction of the garments. Examine the details and construction to decide if the price fits the quality of the garment.

6. If possible, visit a museum to view an historic costume collection. Check your local listings for exhibition information.

>>>unit
three

apparel factors

styles and trends

Apparel styles and the fashion trends created by acceptance of specific styles are essential components of apparel analysis. **Apparel fashion** is simply defined as apparel or accessories worn during a specific time period by a majority or large number of people. It refers to trends of dress at a given time. While variation is likely to be evident, an overall look is easily identifiable. Fashion adoption and fashion changes occur to the extent that people want something new or desire to wear apparel similar to that worn by others. **Style** generally refers more specifically to the lines, cut, colors, or other attributes that make garments distinct from one another.

As styles are accepted or rejected, fashion trends are formed. Fashion forecasters diligently study market conditions including street fashions, note the lifestyles of consumers, analyze sales statistics, survey publications and information services, and scan world events in an effort to predict fashion trends. Useful tools for forecasting include contract or in-house fashion and consulting services, professional publications; consumer research via secondary sources, surveys, focus groups, or interviews; scanning and shopping national and international cultures and markets; and analyses of market data and presentations. See chapter 13 for select examples.

Fashion trends often emerge as style ideas presented by more than one designer or manufacturer based on their independent analysis of the market. Common elements may signal a change

---

Processes and Tools for Forecasting Fashion

Fashion forecasters
- Study market conditions including street fashions
- Note lifestyle components of consumers
- Analyze sales statistics, survey publications and information services
- Scan world events in an effort to predict fashion trends.

Useful tools for forecasting include
- Utilizing contract or in-house fashion and consulting services
- Conducting consumer research via secondary sources, surveys, focus groups, or interviews
- Scanning and shopping national and international cultures and market
- Analyzing market data and presentations

---

in the times, and result in a fashion trend. With the explosion in communication venues, regional, national, and international trends now move at a heightened pace. Hence a trend may gain acceptance only to be discarded in a few months, may linger a year or two, or may be retained as a fashion classic.

The movement of fashion occurs on two levels simultaneously. One level is the rapid-paced forum created as designers, manufacturers, retailers, and the media seek to innovate and create demand. At the level of the consumer, individuals interpret fashion to meet their specific needs. Seasonality is an additional factor that affects fashion presentation, change, and acceptance. Climate, geographic location, and holidays present seasonal influences on consumer acceptance of products and styles. These can have both accelerating and retarding effects on fashion trends.

Elements Relating to Style

Style was defined earlier as the lines, cut, colors, or other attributes that make garments distinct from one another. Style also refers to the elements or parts that are combined to form garments. These include styles of sleeves, collars, necklines, skirts, pants, dresses, coats and jackets, etc. that form the building blocks of fashion trends. By varying proportions and combinations of these fundamental elements new fashions are created in an ever evolving sequence. Similarly, collars, necklines, and sleeves provide variation.

To further understand how these parts are combined to create desirable apparel products, it is useful to look to key elements and principles of basic design as applied to apparel. Understanding such key elements provides apparel marketers with a foundation for designing and predicting apparel trends.

Elements of Design

The attributes included here are elements of design: (1) line; (2) shape, form, and silhouette; (3) color; and (4) texture; and principles of design (1) balance; (2) proportion; (3) emphasis; (4) rhythm; and (5) harmony and unity. Discussion of each of the elements and principles of design will be organized by the categories' functions and values, types and characteristics, and design implications. They are the fundamental building blocks used to create design. Through variation and combination countless designs are possible.

Line

Line, defined as a continuous mark, functions to measure the distance between two points, indicate shape, provide movement, and determine direction (see Color Plate 2). It provides boundaries for shapes and breaks up visual and physical space. In apparel, line is created by the edges, openings, seams, darts, pleats, fabrics, details, and trims of the garment or accessory. Lines can fulfill diverse functions and can be of distinct types each with unique characteristics (see Table 5.1).

DESIGN IMPLICATIONS OF LINE

The use of lines can be manipulated to create illusions of height and width and to express visual meaning. Since vertical lines move the eyes up and down, the sensation recorded in the brain is likely to be length or height. This can be useful in adding visual inches to a figure or creating a long, lean look. In contrast, horizontal lines, since they lead the eyes across a garment, tend to increase apparent width and can be used to add emphasis or widen a specific area, such as the bust (see Color Plate 4).

Straight lines tend to suggest strength and stability and historically have yielded masculine images while curved lines suggest greater femininity. Dramatic effects can be achieved by

TABLE 5.1 Functions, Types, and Characteristics of Lines

Functions and Values of Lines
Provide paths for the eyes follow
Create direction, width, and length
Enclose space to create shape
Define the shape of the body
Create character by opposition, transition, or radiation
Create optical illusions of body size and shape (see Table 5.4)
Express visual meaning

Types and Characteristics of Lines
Straight
    Bold, solid, formal
Vertical
    Carry the eye up and down
    Appear strong, dignified, or formal
    Increase apparent height or length
    Decrease apparent width
Horizontal
    Carry the eye across the body
    Appear stable, restful, or calm
    Increase apparent width
    Decrease apparent height
Diagonal
    Create eye movement
    Appear active, excited, or restless
    Can both decrease and increase apparent height and width
Curved
    Relaxed, soft, or graceful
    Increase apparent size and shape
Restrained
    Flattened arc
Circular
    Complete or nearly complete circle

diagonal lines as they suggest movement and action. Creative application of lines as they occur in the component parts of garments and accessories yields tremendous variety in design possibilities (see Color Plates 5, 6, and 7).

Shape, Form, and Silhouette

Shape or **form** refers to the outer contour of an object or garment (see Color Plates 8 and 9). When a line is drawn around an area, the enclosed space becomes a shape or form. The outline of the shape or form is the **silhouette**. Shapes, forms, and silhouettes, also, have a variety of functions, types, and characteristics (see Table 5.2).

DESIGN IMPLICATIONS OF SHAPES, FORMS, AND SILHOUETTES

Silhouettes employ basic shapes including squares, rectangles, triangles, and circles. The shapes formed by these silhouettes can be manipulated to create visual illusions that emphasize attractive body shapes and camouflage less attractive attributes. Facial and body shapes should be considered in conjunction with garment shapes.

Wide, full clothing shapes increase apparent size while straight, tubular shapes increase apparent height and decrease apparent width. Lines within the silhouette, such as those created by seams, darts, openings, pleats, design lines, and fabric design further divide the garment into

---

Making an Impression with Shape

London Fashion Week, September 2007, saw shape break the tedium of days of shows when a Gareth Pugh model stunned the audience by entering the runway with a black box on her head! Tilted on the model's head like a textbook illustration of perspective, the silver-flecked black fabric box aroused the attention of the audience and set the mood for the display of Pugh's collection (Burns, 2007).

TABLE 5.2 Functions, Types, and Characteristics of Shapes, Forms, and Silhouettes

Functions and Value of Shapes, Forms, and Silhouettes
Size, shape, and position combine as design factors
Apparel design is composed of one or a combination of simple shapes
Silhouette is a strong trigger for garment first impressions
Silhouette areas emphasized change with time

Types and Characteristics of Shapes, Forms, and Silhouettes
Straight
Rectangle
Tubular and rectangular with straight lines and tubes circling the body
Cylindrical dress shapes, straight skirts, and straight pants
Usually height greater than width creating dominant vertical lines
Increases apparent height

Square
Rectangular shape with equal apparent height and width

Triangle
Triangular: narrow shoulders and wide hem
Inverted triangle or wedge: wide shoulders and narrow hem
Waist may be defined

Curved
Circle and related curves
Roundness to some degree
May conform closely to body curves

Combinations
Curved and angular shapes can be combined in endless ways
Diamond: Curved midsections with narrow shoulders and hem
Hourglass: Fitted waist with rounded curves on larger shoulders and hem
Bell: Straight lines combined with rounded curves toward the hem

smaller shapes. In addition, shapes can be used to create mood by manipulating how the eye perceives garment features.

Historically, three fundamental silhouettes have evolved and returned in cycles. The bell silhouette is formed from a narrow waist, widening at the hips, and expanding to greater fullness at the hem. The tubular silhouette maintains uniform width throughout the length of the garment. Shoulder, waist, hip, and hemline areas are similar in width and emphasis. The bustle silhouette, sometimes created by the addition of padding or extra fabric at the rear hip, begins with a narrow waist, gathers fullness at the buttocks, and then flows downward to the hemline. Fashion cycles bring ever evolving changes to and recreations of these fundamental silhouettes.

Color

Color is the sensation aroused when the eye is stimulated by light waves. In simple terms, color is seen when light is reflected off items into the eye. Variety in the wave lengths of the light creates color variety. Color provides strong visual impact on the perception of apparel (see Color Plates 11 and 13).

FUNCTIONS, TYPES, AND CHARACTERISTICS OF COLOR

Colors can combine to provide unlimited interest. Each color has a characteristic hue, value, and intensity. **Hue** refers to the name of the color, such as red, yellow, or blue. **Value** refers to the lightness or darkness of the color. Values are made by adding white or black to a hue to form a **shade** (darker) or tint (lighter) of the hue.

Intensity refers to the brightness or dullness of a hue. The intensity of a hue can be decreased by adding its complementary hue to it. A complementary hue is the hue that is located exactly opposite on a color wheel. Color wheels are commonly used to show relationships among colors (Pegler, 2006).

In many cases, the terms *hue* and *color* are used as synonyms. Hue is actually, more narrowly, one aspect of color. A color wheel shows hues and the ways they can be used together. Primary hues are the building blocks of color. All other hues can be made by mixing these hues: red, yellow, and blue. Secondary hues are created by mixing equal amounts of two primary hues. The secondary hues are orange, green, and violet.

Intermediate (tertiary) hues are created when equal amounts of adjacent primary and secondary colors are combined. The primary hue is usually stated first when the color is named: blue-violet, blue-green, yellow-green, yellow-orange, red-orange, red-violet, blue-violet, blue-green, yellow-green, yellow-orange, and red-orange. While, black, gray, and beige are considered neutral colors.

Hues are classified as warm or cool. Warm hues (red, orange, and yellow) reflect more light and appear to advance and stimulate, while cool hues (green, blue, and violet) absorb more light and have a calming effect.

Color schemes are the ways colors are used together.

Monochromatic schemes use tints, shades, and intensities of a single hue (see Color Plates 14 and 15). **Analogous schemes** use adjacent colors from the color wheel such as green and blue or red, orange, and yellow (see Color Plates 16 through 18).

Complementary schemes use colors that are opposite on the color wheel. There is great contrast in these colors, such as violet and yellow or red and green (see Color Plates 20 and 21). **Split complementary schemes** combine three colors. One color is combined with the two colors on the sides of its complement. Red combined with blue-green and yellow-green is an example.

Triad schemes combine three colors that are equal distance from each other on the color wheel. The primary colors of red, yellow, and blue create a triad scheme. Accented neutral schemes combine white, black, gray, or beige with a bright color accent. In general, color is seen in relation to nearby colors providing both coordination and contrast.

As a component of society, color has developed both symbolic and psychological meanings. As a result, color symbolism plays an important part in communication via apparel. Sports teams gain recognition with fans through the adoption of a team color; black may be worn during mourning; or a baby's gender may be indicated by clothing which is either pink or pastel blue. Symbolism and psychological meanings, however, vary with culture and subculture. While white may be the preferred color for wedding dresses in the U.S, red may be the preference in another location.

DESIGN IMPLICATIONS OF COLOR

Color offers tremendous opportunity for diverse design applications. Personal color, including skin, eyes, and hair, influences which colors look best on individuals since colors are not seen in isolation, but in comparison. Color can be used to enhance, minimize, and create visual illusions that influence perception (see Color Plate 22). For example:

Warm colors advance, increasing apparent size.

Cool colors recede, decreasing apparent size.

Intense colors advance, increasing attention and apparent size.

Dull colors recede, decreasing apparent size.

Light colors advance, increasing apparent size.

Dark colors recede, decreasing apparent size.

APPAREL APPLICATIONS

1. Because color is seen in comparison to nearby colors, personal coloring—such as hair, eyes, and personal coloring influences which colors look best. Based on the cast of their skin tone,

most individuals look best in either blue-based or yellow-based colors. These are colors with either cool or warm undertones.

2. Multiple authors have devised guides for selecting apparel and cosmetics that are best for individuals' personal coloring (Beauty by Jeanique, 2007; Color Me Beautiful, 2007; Jackson, 1980; Nicholson & Lewis-Crum, 1986; Nix-Rice, 1996; Style Makeovers, 2007; Wallace, 1983). Each recommends specific colors based on elements of personal coloring such as hair, eyes, or skin.

3. Effective use of color in apparel selection can substantially enhance the visual appearance of the body.

Texture

Texture refers to the surface quality of an apparel or accessory item. It includes not only the visual aspect or look, but also the feel and hang or drape of the fabric (see Color Plate 25).

FUNCTIONS, TYPES, AND CHARACTERISTICS OF TEXTURE

Texture is a sensory attribute which provides both visual and tactile interest. In addition to influencing perception, it affects the way fabric can be manipulated, used, or draped. While visual texture refers to the qualities inferred from only visual input, tactile texture refers to the qualities experienced by touch.

Texture can be either structural or printed. Structural texture is created when the fabric or garment is manufactured. Printed texture is printed onto garments or surfaces after construction. In many cases, especially from a distance, it is difficult to tell which method was used. Structural texture is usually created by one of four primary methods.

Fibers, yarns, fabrication methods, and finishes can create texture. Fibers create texture through the inherent or engineered characteristics of the raw materials. For example, wool, because of the scale-like structure of its surface provides a rough texture. Polyester, by contrast, can be extruded as a long continuous monofilament that yields a smooth texture. Yarns create texture through the length of fibers or production methods. Short staple length fibers create fuzzy yarns that produce soft or textured surfaces. Yarns made with bumps, nubs, or uneven twists, in turn, create textured fabrics. Fabrication methods, also, create texture through the way yarns or fibers are formed into fabric. Fabrics using a satin weave where yarns float across other yarns before being entwined allow light to be reflected from the long surface yarns, creating a shiny fabric. Pile weaves, through the introduction of more than two sets of yarns, break up the reflection of light and create increased visual and tactile texture such as in the case of velvet or pile carpet. Finishes given to fabric can, also, change or impart texture. Slick waterproofing creates a smooth surface while the addition of glue and flocking creates added texture.

DESIGN IMPLICATIONS OF TEXTURE

Texture influences not only visual elements but also the drape of fabrics and the way they will lay on the body. Some fabrics cling to the curves of the body while others are less likely to mould. Illusions can be created by the use of texture. Bulky, stiff, and rough textures give the illusion of increased size. This feature can be used to provide emphasis and attention where desired. In general, textures should be selected in relation to the overall size of the garment or figure. Proportion, incorporating contrast and similarity, are important design considerations.

Printing processes can also be used to impart diverse textural qualities before and after garment construction. Printing techniques can produce overall design or emphasis elements and greatly influence the look and feel of a garment.

Principles of Design

Five foundational principles guide the development and analysis of good apparel design. While the elements of design discussed above provide the component parts for good design, the principles of design focus on effective interrelationships of those design elements. The principles of design include balance; proportion and scale; emphasis; rhythm; and harmony, unity and variety.

Balance

Balance is the perception that the elements in a design are equal in visual weight. Lines, shapes, colors, textures, and patterns are designed and combined so that their weight, both actual and visual, is evenly distributed.

FUNCTION, TYPES, AND CHARACTERISTICS OF BALANCE

Balance creates a feeling of visual harmony, stability, or comfort. The eye is the measure of balance. Balance is created by both structural and added components and is required for both vertical and horizontal aspects of design.

There are three types of vertical balance.

Symmetrical or formal: The elements on either side of an imaginary center line are identical.

Asymmetrical or informal: Elements on either side of the imaginary center line are different but have equal visual weight (see Color Plates 26 and 27).

Radial: The major elements radiate from a central point.

Horizontal balance on the human figure is almost always asymmetrical because of the body's anatomy.

DESIGN IMPLICATIONS OF BALANCE

Harmony is created when a design is well balanced. Formal balance suggests a quiet, dignified mood. Informal balance creates a dynamic, active mood. In asymmetrical balance, not only the size and number of shapes, but also their distances from the center line, colors, and textures are influential. For example a rough, boldly colored accent flower placed at a distance from the garment midpoint may have greater visual weight in counterbalancing other elements than a smooth pastel flower placed near a center seam would have. In general, apparel designs where the center of interest is above the center line are usually more pleasing (see Color Plate 28).

Proportion and Scale

Proportion refers to the relation of the size of the parts of a garment or outfit to the whole and to each other. It includes how the lines and shapes divide the garment into parts and how one part or space compares to the garment and the body. **Scale,** a related and sometimes interchangeable term, refers more narrowly to how the size of one shape compares to another.

FUNCTIONS, CHARACTERISTICS, AND DESIGN IMPLICATIONS OF PROPORTION AND SCALE

Proportion enhances harmony. It can be used to flatter or enhance a figure. Usually, a garment is more pleasing and interesting if it is divided into unequal parts. Designs composed of equal space divisions may be monotonous. Variation adds interest. Proportion is often based on an ideal, yet ideal proportions differ with time and culture. Historically, the Golden Mean has been applied as an ideal proportion. For apparel, this uses a proportion of 3:5:8: ⅜ of the total human figure is above the waist and ⅝ of the total figure is below the waist.

Out of scale situations occur when one shape overpowers another. Ideally, proportions that flatter the natural figure are more likely to be pleasing and remain in style longer. Applications of color, prints, and textures must be scaled to the intended use. Details such as buttons, pockets, cuffs, collars, and yokes should be scaled to the size of the total garment and the wearer. As with the other elements and principles of design, proportion and scale can be used to create visual illusions.

Emphasis

Emphasis is the creation of a focal point or center of interest. It is visually the most important element or area. The eye is drawn to that point and is retained there for a bit of time. Emphasis supplies a resting place in a design and saves the eyes from over stimulation (see Color Plate 29).

FUNCTIONS, CHARACTERISTICS, AND DESIGN IMPLICATIONS OF EMPHASIS

Emphasis provides a center point for the design and usually requires that only one area or feature is the most visually important. A single design element must dominate. All other elements become subordinate. Subordinate areas complement the dominant one since more than one dominant element creates confusion.

Repetition and contrast are effective ways to create emphasis. A center of interest can be created by highlighting one large item or several smaller items.

Patterns and motifs can be used as either dominant or subordinate elements.

Four types of patterns can be incorporated: Realistic or naturalistic patterns duplicate natural or man-made objects; stylized patterns apply artistic variation to natural forms; geometric patterns incorporate the strict use of lines and geometric shapes; and abstract patterns flow from artistic imagination and do not represent anything natural or man-made.

Dominant elements can be used to call attention to or accentuate positive personal attributes. Emphasis can be used to create visual illusions, minimizing or showcasing specific traits. Shape, texture, detail, color, size, position, contrast, and repetition are additional tools to create emphasis. Advancing and receding visual effects can be used to create emphasis.

Rhythm

Rhythm in apparel and in ensembles leads the eye from one part of the design to another in a smooth and organized manner. It creates a fluid path of motion for the eyes by allowing them to begin with a dominant feature and progress easily from that dominant point to subordinate areas.

FUNCTIONS, CHARACTERISTICS, AND DESIGN IMPLICATIONS OF RHYTHM

Rhythm provides a pathway for the eyes and serves to unify the design by creating smooth visual movement from area to area. By providing transitions between garment areas, rhythm can be used to enhance pleasing personal characteristics. Rhythmic movement can be created in four primary ways: **repetition, progression, continuous line,** or **radiation**.

Repetition repeats lines, shapes, colors, or textures. Repetition can be either uniform, repeating like units, or alternating, repeating two or more design elements in an alternating manner. A knife-pleated skirt or a shirtdress with brass buttons marching down a center placket are examples of uniform repetition.

Progression or gradation uses a gradual increase or decrease of a single design element such as color or shape. A scarf with a motif of gradually larger circles illustrates gradation. Continuous line uses either real or suggested lines to lead the eyes. Curved lines, perhaps depicting the stems of abstract flowers could be used to move the eyes to desired locations within a garment. Radiation employs visual movement outward from a central point. Sunburst and star motifs employ this tactic. Subtle application of these techniques is usually most pleasing. Harmony is created by effective use of rhythm.

By providing a path for the eye, rhythm can lead the eye toward positive personal features or away from negative features. Curved continuous lines suggest a feminine quality. Culture-based values for the curves of the female figure may be the underlying root. Ruffles, in other cases, may suggest a light or gay mood. Frilly necklines on social or party attire return often to popularity. Gradation and radiation create dynamic or active moods. Dynamic radiating forms in fabric print or garment construction, often in vivid or contrasting colors, create drama. Rigid continuous lines imply stateliness or grandeur. Formal wear, including single color tuxedos for men, and long, lean flowing evening gowns for women are examples.

Harmony, Unity, and Variety

Harmony occurs when all design elements—including apparel and accessories—work together to create a pleasing visual effect. It implies that not only within the garment the parts relate well to the whole but also that the garment or ensemble is appropriate for the wearer and the occasion. Harmony has the two essential elements of unity and variety. Unity infers a sense of completeness. A unified outfit is one that appears well integrated and provides a complete look. Unity is often created by the repetition of one or more similar elements or qualities. However, variety is useful and is achieved by introducing an unusual or interesting point of contrast. Variety combats visual boredom.

Harmony provides a comfortable visual image. Elements within an outfit with harmony appear to "fit"—they fit within the garment as well as to the person and the social environment. Unity reflects a design that is complete and tied together while variety offers diversion from designs that may not include sufficient visual interest. By departing from a predictable template, variety creates visual interest that provides a spark of excitement. Harmony is created through unity and variety together.

Since harmony is the outcome of the effective use of the elements and principles of good design garments and ensembles that have harmony will be more accepted by consumers. This is because unity is the result of careful coordination, variety is the spark that provides visual interest, and garments without variety may appear boring.

More broadly, all of the elements and principles of design work together to create apparel products that appeal to customers. Savvy designers and consumers learn to use these tools to create fashion that fulfills their needs including enhancing their native features and attributes (see Table 5.3).

Personal Apparel Selection

Although the elements and principles of design provide the foundations for the creation of apparel, discussion of apparel style is incomplete without consideration of the personal attributes and applications of consumers. Personal attributes, wardrobe planning, and a mention of shopping are important.

TABLE 5.3 Advancing and Receding Design Elements

Visually Advancing	Visually Receding
Colors	
Bright	Dull
Light	Dark
Contrasting	Blended
Warm	Cool
Lines	
Solid	Broken
Wide	Thin
Straight	Curved
Vertical	Horizontal
Shapes	
Straight	Curved
Textures	
Rough	Smooth
Heavy	Light
Coarse	Fine
Opaque	Sheer
Crisp	Soft
Patterns	
Large Scale	Small Scale
Geometric	Natural

(Rasband, 2001, p. 32)

Physical Considerations: Body Types

Figure is the term used to refer to the shape of a woman's body. **Physique** is the term for the shape of a man's body. Since natural figure or physique is the underlying form on which fashions are draped and displayed, consideration of body form is useful. Body shape is important to how apparel looks. Even more important to the overall look of apparel on an individual is the proportion of body parts to the whole and to each other. While there is no universal ideal body size and shape, societies, based on cultural norms and values, tend to create preferred proportions and attributes. Individuals and the designers who create for them can, then, use the elements and principles of design just described to aid individuals to accentuate positive physical attributes and minimize physical liabilities.

Strategies for Attracting and Avoiding Attention to Specific Areas

Attract Attention

The goal is to attract and hold the eye.

Add an accent or applied decoration

Employ bright or light colors

Use warm hues

Use textured, clingy, or shiny fabrics

Select large or busy prints

Avoid Attention

The goal is to not attract the eye and to move it on to other assets.

Avoid accents or applied decoration

Employ dull and dark colors

Use cool hues

Use flat, soft, or dull fabrics

Select plain fabrics without pattern

Individuals can carefully analyze their physical body with the aid of books on the topic, computer programs, and consultants. A full range from simple analysis in the mirror to sophisticated analytical methods of tools are available. Understanding one's personal figure or physique is instrumental in maximizing opportunities to select and use apparel effectively.

TABLE 5.4 Strategies for Increasing and Decreasing Apparent Width and Height at Specific Locations

Increasing Apparent Height and Decreasing Apparent Width	Decreasing Apparent Height and Increasing Apparent Width
Select	*Select*
Sold colors	Contrasting color separates
Same color top and bottom	Pattern mixtures
Monochromatic scheme head to toe, including hose and shoes	Layers
Long ties	Textured fabrics
V-necks	Cuffed pants
Vertical stripes	Contrasting or patterned hosiery
Long diagonal lines	Double breasted jackets
Design elements that move the eye vertically	Horizontal stripes
	Gathers or ruffles
	Design elements that move the eye horizontally
Avoid	
Busy patterns	*Avoid*
Textured fabrics	Slim silhouettes
Short pants	Narrow ties and lapels
Cuffed pants	Monochromatic color schemes
Wide lapels	Vertical stripes
Vests	
Gathers or ruffles	
Many accessories	

Once personal physical assets and liabilities are known, it is then possible to apply the elements and principles of design to highlight the assets and camouflage the liabilities. This process of using design to create optimal visual effects is primarily based on two fundamental concepts. These are (1) attracting and avoiding attention and (2) increasing and decreasing apparent width and height. These concepts can be applied to the total silhouette as well as to areas within that silhouette. For example, attracting attention and increasing or decreasing apparent height or width can be used equally well to accentuate or diminish shoulders, hips, waists, thighs, legs, etc. The key is to consider what impact the design element will have on the movement of the eyes.

Physical Considerations: Personal Coloring

Hair, skin, and eye color are important factors in individual clothing selection. In most cases, the natural colors of an individual's hair, skin, and eyes are found in the same palette. Apparel colors can be selected to further enhance that natural relationship (see Color Plate 30). While many systems have been produced to analyze personal coloring and to aid in the selection of appropriate coloring to show off the natural beauty of the individual, the simplest system will serve to illustrate the concept. Since eyes, hair, and skin naturally coordinate with each other, it is possible to select colors based on one of those attributes. Skin, for example, may be seen as having either cool or warm undertones. Cool skin tones include taupe, olive, charcoal brown, pale pink, and cool beige. When viewing such skin a blue undertone is visible. Hence cool colors and those with blue undertones are most likely to be flattering. Warm skin tones include warm brown, terra cotta, golden beige, and ivory. When viewing warm-toned skin a yellow undertone is visible. Thus, warm colors and those with yellow undertones are most likely to be flattering. While this is a simple method for determining personal color type, it illustrates the concept that personal coloring can be used to optimally make apparel selections.

Wardrobe Planning

Wardrobe planning enables individuals to make optimal apparel selections. Prior to developing a personalized plan, it is important to consider several key factors. These include (1) lifestyle, (2) personality, (3) physical attributes, (4) climate, and (5) social standards. Lifestyle is created by the way individuals spend their time. This is influenced by employment, associates, interests, travel, income, family structure, and sport and leisure activities.

Personality can creatively be expressed through clothing choices. Physical attributes, as described previously in this chapter, can be highlighted or camouflaged by clothing.

Climate plays a vital part in clothing selection with varying temperatures creating diverse clothing needs. Seasonal and geographic variances must be accommodated.

Social standards refer to the norms created by groups of people. These influence what is considered appropriate in overall dress and in dress for specific occasions.

In general, successful wardrobe planning can have multiple benefits. Looking and feeling one's best, increasing wardrobe flexibility, saving money, and increasing personal enjoyment from clothes are some of these benefits. By considering the lifestyle, personality, physical attributes, climate, and social standards, individuals are better prepared to look their best in each situation. Planning carefully allows the wearer to invest energy in decisions prior to "walking out the door" and then be freed from worry about clothing or appearance, ready to focus on the activity at hand. Wardrobe flexibility is increased when a wardrobe plan includes garments that can be combined in different ways to create multiple outfits. The parts work harmoniously together.

Money is saved by creating a wise spending plan and limiting costly clothing selection errors. Most importantly, wardrobe planning limits clothing related frustrations and allows the wearer to make the choices that are best for them. Knowing that the look is well planned and executed increases positive self-confidence and general clothing enjoyment.

WARDROBE INVENTORY AND EVALUATION

It's really not enough to just create an inventory of a current wardrobe. It is vital to evaluate the status of individual garments and accessories. A simplified system for inventory and evaluation includes sorting items into one of three categories: items that are loved and worn often, items that are worn occasionally, and items that are never worn. Deciding why each item falls into a specific category is important. For example, looking for commonalities in the well loved category can provide useful clues for future purchases. Items that are never worn can tell the story of purchases to avoid. Careful consideration of the second category, occasionally worn items, can also provide useful clues. Perhaps a minor change or alteration in style or fit would make the item more useful. Perhaps only a repair is needed.

A useful next step is to discard, recycle, or give away those items which are judged to be not useful. These may primarily come from the third category, items that are never worn. Unused items take up valuable storage space. Exceptions to the "discard if not used" rule might be specialty items where the use has not been recent but is anticipated.

Creating an actual list or inventory of remaining items is next. One basic system uses a grid that includes spaces for recording personal activities and then clothing items and accessories identified as either basic or supporting/extending to match those activities. More detailed inventories include attributes such as color, fiber, fabric, source, cost, age, season, details, and more. Many commercial wardrobe inventory tools are commercially available to assist with this process.

The final step in this sequence is analysis of the inventory. Once individual garments and accessories have been assessed, it is time to evaluate how the items work together within the context of the lifestyle and needs of the wearer. Using a grid format during the inventory process facilitates observing inadequacies or shortcomings in the total wardrobe. Notations of these, along with an understanding of a few fundamental wardrobe planning guides, then facilitates decision making regarding future wardrobe purchases. Specific apparel purchases can be planned, recorded, and incorporated into a wise shopping strategy.

Oprah's Guests Share Tips

On the show "Oprah Cleans Out Her Closet" guests Jessie Garza and Joe Lupo from Visual Therapy shared tips for avoiding "closet bulge." Here are the tips:

>> Create "yes," "no," and "maybe" piles
>> Ask for each piece of clothing: "Do I love this?" "Is it flattering?" and "Is it the image I want to portray?" If any answers are no, it belongs in the "no" pile.
>> From the three piles take one of three actions: Keep the "yes" pile; get rid of the "no" pile: and from the "maybe" piles, create an archive. This archive can include items with sentimental value. The archive can be stored in an attic or basement, but not in the closet (Oprah, 2007).

WARDROBE PLANNING GUIDES

Many guides exist to help consumers individually build effective wardrobes. Most are built on the concept that a few carefully selected garment pieces can be combined to create multiple outfits. For example, Fenner (2004) suggested that one dress, two jackets, three bottoms, and four tops can create 40 independent outfits for a woman. For a man, one sport coat, two pairs of trousers, three suits, and six tops provide similar flexibility.

Johnson and Foster (1990) recommended breaking the wardrobe into smaller units and creating wardrobe wheels, which are groups of clothes that are related in color and can be worn together. A central garment is placed at the hub of the wheel with other compatible garments placed as spokes of the wheel. Additional garments and concentric wheels create increasing numbers of outfit possibilities.

Rasband (1996) proposed the use of clusters of garments. Each cluster works with existing wardrobe items but extends the options in a new, yet unrelated, direction. She suggested starting with a pattern to inspire the color scheme and then to plan for five to eight top and bottom pieces, selecting pieces that are simple in style lines and shape, selecting pieces that will work with at least two other pieces, choosing pieces such that no two are alike, selecting accessories to complement, and gradually expanding the clusters to meet all wardrobe needs.

CLOSET ORGANIZATION

While closet organization may not at first appear to be an element of style, effective closet organization and maintenance can provide several useful functions that extend the style attributes of fashions. An orderly closet can increase the total enjoyment of being able to manage apparel and personal style. By arranging items within a well planned closet, money can be saved. Items that are hung or folded properly will retain their shape better, style elements will be maintained, and wear-life extended. When closet contents are neatly contained within the confines of the closet, they don't spill out into the rest of the room taking up useable living space. A well arranged closet can aid in visualizing which items and style elements go well together and, thus, not only extend wardrobe possibilities, but also speed up and simplify daily clothing choices.

Items within a well organized closet should be (a) visible, (b) accessible, and (c) grouped. Visibility of items increases the likelihood that they will be seen and worn rather than forgotten. This increases the options for multiple combinations and extends the potential of the total wardrobe. Accessibility means that items are within easy reach. Frequently used pieces may occupy eye-level positions while less often used, or special occasion items, are on upper or lower shelves. However, all should be easily accessible. Finally, grouping apparel items by categories or clusters by use or occasion can assist in viewing coordination options and making selections.

While few closets seem to have adequate space regardless of their dimensions, a few tools can prove useful. Double-hung rods can double the amount of hanging space and seriously reduce wasted space. Shelves placed above the rods provide extra storage space and serve to protect the garments below from dust. Shelves, bins, baskets, and hooks placed on the inside walls of the closet can be useful. Doors that open outward rather than sliding across can be fitted with a mirror, bins, or hooks. Outward swinging doors also increase visibility into the closet. Adequate lighting and a light-reflecting paint coat further increase visibility. Numerous closet fittings are available commercially for either do-it-yourself or custom closet configurations.

APPAREL CARE AND FIT

Proper care and fit of apparel items enhances and extends their life.

CARE

After investment of time and money in the selection of apparel goods, it is important to care for and protect that investment. Caring properly for these items saves money by extending the life of the garment or accessory and delaying the need for replacement. In addition, items continue to look their best and provide optimal style and service when they are well maintained. Care while dressing decreases the chances of soiling or damaging garments. Opening all fasteners before putting items on reduces the opportunities for tears; removing jewelry reduces snags; and care with hair products, makeup, and deodorants reduces soil.

Once worn, dirty or damaged items should be readily cleaned or repaired and then replaced in the closet ready to use. If possible, allowing clothes to air briefly before returning them to the closet is beneficial. Clothes need to "breathe" a bit. This is one good reason for discarding unwanted items to allow those that remain more space. Padded hangers provide a bit of width, which aids with this need. Additionally, they support the garment better than narrow wire hangers.

Some items fare better when stored folded. Sweaters and other knits, for example are more likely to retain their shape when folded. Out-of-season storage is a good idea. Clothing that will not be worn for a few months should be cleaned and stored carefully. Cleaning prior to storage is important as stains tend to set with time and many stains, especially food, attract insects. Seasonal storage in a separate location is also beneficial because it frees space for items currently being worn.

FIT

Fit is an important aspect of apparel selection. Garments that fit well are both comfortable and have a flattering appearance. Just as other attributes of apparel such as silhouette, color, and style change with fashion, so does fashion influence and change what is considered to be a good fit. Close-fitting garments give way to baggy ones as fashion trends shift. However, some general fit guidelines are appropriate regardless of the current trend.

Grain is one of the first indicators of good or poor fit. Grain refers to the lengthwise and crosswise yarns in a woven fabric. They create a grid for the garment and the body underneath. Generally, the lengthwise yarns run perpendicular to the floor and the crosswise yarns run parallel to the floor. Exceptions to this rule would occur when a garment is cut on the bias to accomplish a specific look or drape. When the grain does, indeed, run perpendicular and parallel a garment is said to be "on grain." This is an indicator of good fit. Conversely, when the grain does not run perpendicular to the floor, for example, when it is being pulled in some direction by a body part, the fit is not right or needs inspection.

Wrinkles are a second indicator of fit. Wrinkles indicate tension on the fabric. This suggests that there is either an excess or a shortage of fabric covering a particular area. In many cases following the line of a wrinkle can serve as an arrow leading to or away from an ill-fitting area. Ease is also an indicator of fit. There are two types of ease, wearing ease and design ease. Wearing ease is the extra fabric needed to allow the body to move within a garment. **Design ease** is the extra fabric needed to create a visual effect. When ease—especially wearing ease—is insufficient, the garment is too tight.

Shopping

Understanding of apparel styles, the art elements and principles of design, personal apparel selection criteria, and wardrobe planning underlies the actual purchase of apparel products. Effective selection and shopping practices are founded upon these concepts and enable appropriate choice of styles and application of trends. In addition, specific shopping strategies and skills can be applied to optimize the apparel selection process.

Shopping Strategies

Prepare
  Create a wardrobe procurement plan (described earlier in the chapter)
    List individual items by style, color, anticipated cost
    Prioritize needs
    Consider finances
      Plan ahead to spread out expenditures
      Delay some purchases
      Allocate most resources to multiple wear items
        Frequently worn items
        Multiple season items
Seek Information: Reduces errors, increases efficiency
  Scan publications and media
  Evaluate useful information in advertisements
  Find and evaluate prices and sources
Decide where to shop
  Evaluate the attributes of various retailers/vendors
    Department stores
    Specialty stores
    Discount stores
    Secondhand stores
    Direct mail
    Internet
  Evaluate vendors
    Location/access
    Merchandise carried
    Price vs. quality
    Image and clientele
    Services

Shop
  Shop with a plan. Know what is needed.
  Control impulse buying
  Evaluate shopping alone or with an objective friend
  Determine time to shop
    Seasonal: Early best selection, later reduced prices
    Daily: Evaluate store traffic
  Practice good grooming
    Dress comfortably, attractively
    Wear comfortable shoes
    Wear items for which coordinates are needed
    Wear clothes that are easy to put on and off
  Carry color/fabric swatches if possible
  Utilize sales associates/Develop sales resistance
  Try on apparel items
    Wear appropriate undergarments and accessories
    Check fit
    Move in garments: sit, bend, stretch, etc.
    Evaluate quality of components and construction
    Purchase the highest quality allowed by financial constraints
    Check color in natural lighting
    Arrange for alterations if needed
  Recheck item against wardrobe plan
Make purchase or continue search
Evaluate purchase
  Return home
  Rethink the selection in relation to the total wardrobe plan
  Check garment versatility/use in the context of personal wardrobe needs
Enjoy the purchase or return it

Personal Wardrobe Consultant

Lauren Rothman's title at Saks Fifth Avenue is personal wardrobe consultant. She might also be called a personal shopper, stylist, or fashion consultant. Her job is to be a fashion guide for consumers at Saks. Typically, she sees two to four clients a day. For each, she communicates with them on a regular basis and prepares for their visits to the store by walking the retail floor, pulling any clothes or accessories that they might want to know about, and keeping a diary of their preferences, needs, and wants. Prior to each appointment, Lauren assembles total looks for her clients. This includes not only clothing, but also shoes, handbags, lingerie, cosmetics, and anything else to create a head-to-toe look (Silverstein, 2007).

Key Terms

Analogous schemes	Apparel fashion	Asymmetrical balance
Balance	Color	Color schemes
Complementary schemes	Continuous line	Design ease
Emphasis	Figure	Grain
Harmony	Hue	Intensity
Line	Monochromatic schemes	Physique
Progression or gradation	Proportion	Radial balance
Radiation	Repetition	Rhythm
Scale	Shade	Shape or form
Silhouette	Split complementary schemes	Style
Symmetrical balance	Texture	Value

Ideas for Discussion and Application

1. Research and discuss the interplay between the two simultaneous influences in the movement of fashion: (1) designers, manufacturers, retailers and the media seeking to create demand, and (2) individual consumers seeking to interpret fashion to meet personal and family needs.

2. Consider necklines and collar types. Look at your face and shoulders in the mirror. Which collar and neckline styles do you think will be most flattering?

3. Analyze your personal figure or physique. A digital photo taken in a leotard can provide an objective image. Classify your figure type. Then identify the elements of line, shape, and silhouette that will make the most of your positive attributes.

4. Peruse both men's and women's fashion magazines. Find examples of each of the following: symmetrical and asymmetrical balance; proportion and scale; emphasis; rhythm, including repetition, progression, continuous line, and radiation; and harmony, unity, and variety.

5. Using the simplified system for wardrobe inventory and analysis in this chapter, sort your wardrobe items into each of the three categories: loved and worn items, occasionally worn items, and never worn items. Make appropriate decisions to retain or discard items.

6. Take a look at your closet. What improvements from this chapter could you make to its organization?

line

is created by edges,
openings, seams,

vertical

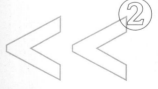

Carmen Marc Valvo
2008

**darts, pleats,
fabrics, and trims**

lines

carry the eye
up and down

Etro
2008

horizontal lines

carry the eye across the body

4

diagonal lines

create eye movement

5

Herve Leger
2008

(opposite)
Kishimoto 2008 (left)
and Louis Vuitton 2008 (right)

curved lines

6

yield a relaxed, soft, and often graceful air to garments

7

Dior 2007

silhou >>> 8

rectangles +
squares +
triangles >>> 9

Balenciaga
2008

ette

is the
outline of
a garment
shape or
form

can provide
the basic
silhouette
of garments

Alexander McQueen
2007

color

is the sensation
around when the
eye is stimulated
by light waves >> 11 >>

Alexander McQueen
2002

color

can be used as subject

Valentino's red dresses
1963 – 2008

matter, concentration, or designer trademark¹³

mono- ⑮
chromatic

⑭

color schemes use a single hue

Michael Kors
2007

(opposite)
Nina Ricci
2007

Alexander McQueen
2008

16 17 analogous

color schemes use colors
that are adjacent on
the color wheel

Jonathan Saunders
2007

Pucci
2008

analogous

color schemes can stretch across an entire collection

comple-
mentary

color schemes
use colors that
are opposite on
the color wheel

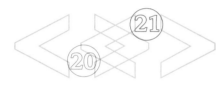

Dior
2005

(opposite) Louis Vuitton
2008 (left) and Proenza
Schouler 2008 (right)

etrical

27

design balances
differences on
either side of
an imaginary
center line with
equal visual
weight

Versace
2008

the **28**
center of
interest
is visually the most
important element

emphasis
can be used to create
visual illusions
29

(opposite)
Ralph Lauren
2007

Balenciaga
2007

personal coloring

30 is important in apparel selections; hair, makeup,

Chanel
2006

and jewelry should interplay with style choices

chapter six

fabrics and findings

Any student who sets out to understand the fashion world must understand fabrics, their origins, and how they are made. **Fabric** can be defined as the textile material from which most ready-to-wear garments are made. Fabric is probably the single most important factor in determining the quality of a garment. With this in mind, the chapter will give the student an overview of fibers, yarns, fabrics, and findings.

Fibers

Let's begin by looking at the most basic unit of fabrics: **Fibers**. In order to gain an understanding of fibers, it is necessary to examine the properties of fibers because these properties contribute to the characteristics of the fabric in which they are used. Knowledge of a fiber's properties will help in predicting the performance of the fabric in finished products. Let's consider some of these properties.

Fiber Performance Properties

>> Abrasion is the ability of a fiber to withstand the rubbing or abrasion it gets in normal use.

>> Absorbency is the percentage of moisture that a dry fiber will absorb from the air under normal temperature and moisture conditions. Fibers that absorb moisture easily are called hydrophilic fibers, while fibers that resist absorbing moisture are referred to as hydrophobic fibers.

>> Cover is the ability of a fiber to expand and to occupy more space for protection or covering.

>> Chemical effects describe how fibers react when they are in contact with various chemicals.

>> Elasticity is a fiber's ability to increase in length when stretched or pulled under tension and then return to its original state.

>> Flammability is its tendency to burn or ignite.

>> Flexibility is its ability to bend easily and repeatedly without breaking.

>> Hand is how a fiber feels to the touch.

>> Luster is the light reflected from its surface.

>> Pilling is the balling up of fibers on the surface of fabrics.

>> Resiliency is its ability to return to its original shape after bending, twisting, or a combination of these.

>> Specific gravity is a measure of the weight of the fiber.

>> Static electricity is its ability to transfer electrical charges.

>> Strength is the ability to resist stress.

>> Thermoplasticity is the ability of fibers to withstand heat exposure. A thermoplastic fiber softens and might even melt when heat is applied.

>> Wicking is the ability of a fiber to transfer moisture along its surface.

FIGURE 6.1 Cross-section of a fiber under the microscope

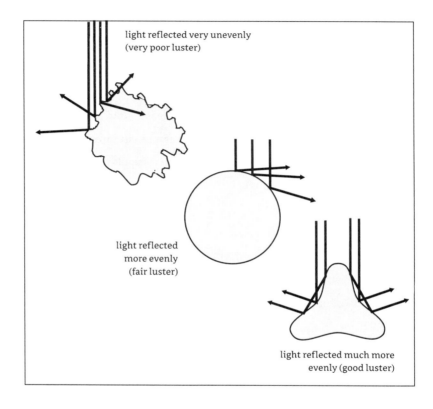

Sources of Fibers

There are basically two sources for fibers: natural and man-made. Natural fibers are found in nature and man-made fibers are manufactured through the use of science and technology. Many of the man-made fibers were developed out of necessity to try to copy or improve on natural fibers or to meet the needs and desires of consumers. Fibers are classified according to their length and can be either staple or filament.

Staple fibers are short fibers that can be measured in inches or centimeters. All natural fibers, except silk, are staple. Manufactured fibers can be cut into shorter lengths but are produced as filament. **Filament fibers** are long, continuous strands that are measured in yards or meters. Silk naturally occurs as filament.

Natural Fibers

As stated earlier, natural fibers occur in nature from three sources: animal, plant, or protein. Natural fibers have unique properties that provide comfort, durability, and beauty to apparel. Evidence of use of natural fibers such as linen and cotton dates back thousands of years.

COTTON

Cotton is the most widely used fiber in the world and has been in use for more than 5,000 years. It is a seed fiber and is composed mostly of cellulose (plant fiber). The fibers of cotton are short and grow in a boll or seed pod of the cotton plant. Cotton is typically cultivated in warm climates. The fiber used for fabric is grown on the seeds that form the flowers of the cotton plant. Both the seed and the fiber are encapsulated in a boll, which opens at maturity to reveal the cotton fiber. Many different species of cotton are produced all over the world.

FIGURE 6.2 Cotton is a seed fiber composed mostly of cellulose. It grows encapsulated in a boll until maturity.

Cotton is soft and breathes, providing the wearer with coolness in hot months and warmth in colder months. It is highly absorbent, dries quickly, inexpensive, washable, and extremely durable. High moisture content makes it static-free and it also takes dyes, printing, and other surface treatments easily. It is commonly used in children's apparel and can be treated to be flame retardant, UV protective, wrinkle and water resistant.

FLAX

We know this natural fiber as linen. It comes from the stem or stalk of the flax plant. This fiber is harvested by pulling the entire plant from the ground. The fiber lengths are between 2 and 36 inches long. Linen is the oldest fiber known and has been found with relics from the Stone Age. France, Belgium, and the Netherlands have the ideal soil and climate for growing flax, but it is cultivated in Germany, Austria, and Finland. At least 20 varieties of flax are grown in Western Europe.

Flax is a fast-growing plant, reaching maturity in just 100 days. It is valued for the fibers of its stalk and its seed. The fibers used to create linen textiles are found within the stalk, centered within a wood core and surrounded by bast.

HISTORY OF LINEN

Linen's earliest use can be traced back to Egypt in 8000 BC. By 6000 BC, the Phoenicians were purchasing linen fabric and exporting it for sale in England and Brittany. The Romans embraced

FIGURE 6.3 The natural fibers used to create linen come from the stalk of the flax plant.

FIGURE 6.4 Sheep being shorn for their wool.

this fiber wholeheartedly, cultivating it throughout the Empire and using the fabric for clothing and bedding. By the Middle Ages, linen had spread across the continent and was gaining ground in Northern and Central Europe. The seventeenth century saw the establishment of the first linen factories in France, with mostly Flemish weavers and lacemakers. The Wars of Religion brought the fiber to the British Isles as these Huguenot workers were exiled to England and Ireland. Their skill made Irish linen famous for its quality throughout the world. This reputation still holds to this day.

The modern age of linen arrived in the nineteenth century, when French scientist Phillipe de Girard, in 1810, designed a way to spin flax mechanically. This invention spurred the setup of textile mills throughout Europe and introduced new spinning and **weaving** techniques that increased production and expanded the variety of finished products. Today, the innovation continues as new harvesting, manufacturing, and finishing techniques are continually developed, making this ancient fiber a state of the art fabric embraced by the twenty-first century (*Butterick Home Catalog*, Summer 2002).

WOOL

Wool is the fiber from the fleece of sheep or lamb. It is a protein fiber, since hair is protein. About 40 different breeds of sheep produce about 200 types of wool fibers. Wool fibers have many positive properties such as good resiliency, good drape, no static, warmth, and slow moisture absorbency. However, it is vulnerable to moths, pilling, and can be expensive.

Australia and New Zealand lead the world in wool production, with China, South Africa, and Argentina running close behind. The process of transforming the fiber to fabric is basically the same everywhere. Shearers cut close to the skin to preserve the length of the fiber, removing the fleece from the animal's body with electric hand clippers. It is a quick process and takes about five minutes.

Wool has been used as clothing for humans since the Stone Age. Wool textiles were considered one of the riches of Babylon. It was so valued as a commodity that people distinguished sheep for food from sheep for fleece. The warm wool clothing spun and woven in ancient Babylonia was instrumental in spreading civilization beyond the temperate climates of Mesopotamia. Between 3000 BC and 1000 BC, the Persians, Greeks, and Romans distributed sheep throughout Europe, expanding the wool trade into what is now Spain, North Africa, and the British Isles. By 50 BC, the Romans had established a wool plant in what is now Winchester, England.

Wool was England's main export during the Middle Ages and contributed to its growing foreign commerce. The voyages of Columbus and Cortez were partially financed by the thriving

Did You Know?
Dyed-in-the-wool
Early yarn makers would dye wool before spinning it into yarn to make the fibers retain their color longer. In sixteenth century England, that practice moved writers to draw a comparison between dyeing of wool and the way children could, if taught early, be influenced in ways that would stick with them throughout their lives. In the nineteenth-century United States, the wool-dyeing practice gave an idea to eloquent Federalist and orator, Daniel Webster, who used the term to refer to a certain type of Democrat whose attitudes were as unyielding as the dye in unspun wool. Of course, Democrats were soon using the term against their opponents, too, but over time the partisanship of the expression faded and it is now a general term for anyone or anything that seems unlikely or unwilling to change.

> **Did You Know?**
> In the seventeenth century, spinning was the duty of the eldest unmarried daughter. This is where the term, "spinster" comes from.

wool trade in Spain. These explorers took sheep to the New World on their journeys. By 1665, the sheep that had been brought to the Colonies had grown to 100,000. King George III made wool trading a punishable offense in the colonies. Despite this law, the wool trade flourished. The invention of the spinning wheel, combing machines, and water powered looms helped bring the Industrial Revolution and caused rapid expansion to the wool industry. These inventions created an insatiable demand for wool because of the increase in speed of production (*Butterick Home Catalog*, Summer 2002).

SILK

Silk is a natural protein fiber and is produced by the larvae of a moth. It is universally accepted as a luxury fiber. Silk has many unique properties not possessed by other fibers:

>> dry hand

>> natural luster

>> good moisture absorption

>> high strength

>> good draping qualities and flexibility.

Silk is produced by a process known as sericulture, which begins when the silk moth lays eggs on specially prepared paper. When the eggs hatch, the larvae are fed fresh, young mulberry leaves. The commercial production of silk is dominated by the Mulberry Silk Moth, *Bombyx Mori*. This literally means the cocoon is fed on mulberry. After about 35 days and four moltings, the silkworms are approximately 10,000 times heavier than when hatched and ready to begin spinning a cocoon, or a chrysalis case. The silkworm produces silk in two glands and forces the liquid silk through openings in its head in order to form a thick, smooth wall around itself. These two strands are coated with a water-soluble protective gum called sericin. When the silk comes into contact with the air, it becomes solid. Japan is the major producer and exporter of silk while a few other countries like China and Italy also have sericulture industries.

A BRIEF HISTORY OF SILK

Silk production started in China about 5,000 years ago where the *bombyx mori* silk moth existed. Its food is the white mulberry which existed in abundance. The most common story about how silk production was started was told by Confucius. He said that the Empress Xi Ling-Shi, the Lady of the Silkworms, accidentally dropped a silk cocoon into a cup of hot tea around 2640 BC. When she retrieved the cocoon, out came a silken thread. She liked the delicate beauty of what she retrieved and decided to encourage the development of silk into a textile. One can surmise that the Chinese were wearing silk garments while the Europeans were still in the Stone Age.

Silks from China were sold in Japan and Asia, where the Romans first saw this beautiful fabric in the third century BC. It is said that Julius Caesar favored it and wore it, as did his officials. China maintained a monopoly of this industry for 2,500 years until the secret of sericulture was smuggled out of China by Persian monks, who also carried silkworm eggs with them. From there, it traveled to Persia, Japan, Korea, India, Greece and much later, to Spain and Italy. By the fifteenth century, the French had imported the techniques from Italy. Lyons became an important

FIGURE 6.5 Silkworms are the larva of *Bombyx mori*, a domesticated silk moth. Silkworms secrete liquid silk which solidifies when it comes into contact with the air.

center for silk production and a succession of French kings encouraged the industry. By 1942, silk's single largest market was women's hosiery, which was replaced by nylons. Other man-made fibers have been developed in an attempt to replicate a fabric with the qualities of silk, but none have been able to replace the true beauty and versatility of real silk. This resilient fiber remains unparalleled.

Man-Made Fibers

According to the American Fiber Manufacturers Association, by 1992, the manufactured or man-made fiber industry was a $12 billion per year industry and employed thousands of workers around the world. The industry continues to grow as researchers seek to modernize and make production more efficient as well as designing innovative textile products, not only for apparel, but for industrial uses as well. The scope of this industry is wide, with fibers being used in many areas such as the medical field, space shuttle, fire resistant apparel, tea bags, and disposable diapers, to name a few. Approximately 25 percent of all manufactured fibers are used for industrial products, 45 percent are used for home furnishings, and the remaining 30 percent are used in apparel. See FiberSource.com for the latest in-depth industry information.

Man-made fibers are composed of materials found in nature, such as wood pulp, petroleum, natural gas, and air. These elements are not in their natural state and require different kinds of chemical reactions to reach a fibrous state. There are two types of man-made fibers: cellulosic and non-cellulosic. **Cellulosic fibers** are made from natural plant cellulose (same as cotton) and require minimum chemical steps. Two common cellulosic fibers are rayon and acetate. **Non-cellulosic fibers** are made from molecules of carbon, hydrogen, nitrogen, and oxygen. These elements are found in natural gas, air, and water which have been chemically synthesized. Some common non-cellulosic fibers include acrylic, nylon, polyester, and spandex.

Let's consider some of these man-made fibers. While the overview will not be extensive, the focus of this section will be on the most commonly used man-made fibers specifically found in apparel.

Cellulosic Fibers

RAYON

Rayon is 100 percent cellulose and has the same chemical composition and molecular structure as the natural cellulose found in cotton or flax, except that the rayon chains are shorter and are not as crystalline (Kadolph, et al 1993). The wood pulp is chemically converted into a soluble compound which then goes through the spinning process. Rayon was the first man-made fiber produced. The process was discovered in 1891 and is still in use today. The credit for the invention is given to Count Hilaire Chardonnet, who dissolved the pulp from mulberry trees in an attempt to duplicate silk. By the late 1800s, he had established an industry for "artificial silk" in France. Many advances have been made in the process since the first American rayon plant opened in 1910.

The name rayon was given to this invention because there was much consumer confusion when it was dubbed "artificial silk." The name rayon comes from "ray" because of its sheen, and "on" to suggest its similarity to cotton. Rayon lost its market share in the late 1970s because of new fabrics such as nylon and polyester. Recently, the fiber has rebounded and is now considered a luxury fiber. There are several types of rayon fibers, named according to the cellulose conversion process. The most common are viscose rayon and cuprammonium. (*Vogue Patterns*, November/December 1992.)

One of rayon's most outstanding characteristics is its drapeability. It is highly absorbent as well as easy to dye. It is widely used as blends with other fibers and serves to enhance wool and

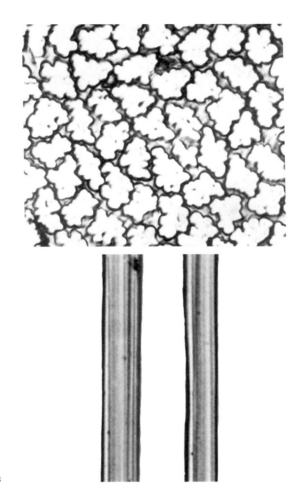

FIGURE 6.7 Rayon fibers

silk in fabrics. Its major drawbacks are its relative lack of strength and dimensional stability. It loses strength when wet, shrinks during laundering, and wrinkles easily.

The newest product of rayon is called Tencel. It was developed in 2000 and is widely used in sportswear and is often dyed to resemble denim textiles.

ACETATE

This fiber originated in Europe in 1869 but was not commercially used until after World War I. Acetate fibers were used on the wings of aircraft during the war. Acetate, like rayon, was called "artificial silk" until 1924 when the Federal Trade Commission assigned it the name cellulose acetate. This fiber was first produced in the United States in 1924 by the Celanese Corporation. Acetate has a combination of properties that make it a valuable textile fiber. It is relatively inexpensive and has good draping qualities. It is widely used in satins, brocades, and taffetas because of its luster, body and beauty. Other important uses of acetate are lining fabrics, robes and loungewear, and formalwear. (*Vogue Patterns*, November/December 1992.)

LYOCELL

Lyocell is 100 percent natural in origin and is produced from the cellulose of wood pulp in a process that is environmentally friendly. It is shrink and wrinkle resistant and has the absorbency of a natural fiber. Lyocell is also washable and dries quickly. Often combined with other fibers such as cotton, wool, or polyester, its properties help to produce a variety of fabrics from crepes to corduroy. It is commonly used in dresses, suits, sportswear, upholstery fabrics, and home furnishings. It is often produced in both woven or knitted fabrics and has a soft peach-skin surface. Tencel is a common brand name for lyocell.

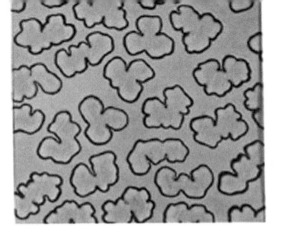

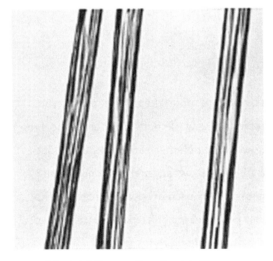

FIGURE 6.8A AND B Cross-section of acetate fiber

FIGURE 6.9 A garment made from Tencel

Non-Cellulosic Fibers

NYLON

Nylon was the first synthetic fiber and the first fiber conceived in the United States. In 1928, the DuPont Company decided to establish a fundamental research program in order to diversify the company. By 1939, DuPont was making a polyamide fiber known as nylon 6,6 and introduced it to the public in the form of women's hosiery, which was an instant success. The name nylon was chosen for the fiber. The name has no special meaning other than it sounds like cotton and rayon.

Nylon has a combination of properties unlike any fiber in use in the 1940s. It was stronger, more resistant to abrasion, had excellent elasticity, and could be heat set. Because it was light-weight, had high strength, and was resistant to chemicals, it was suitable for ropes, cords, sails, parachutes, and other industrial products.

POLYESTER

Polyester was produced in the United States in 1951 by DuPont under the trade name Dacron. Sometimes this fiber is referred to in the textile industry as the workhorse fiber because it is the most widely used synthetic fiber. Polyester is produced by the polymerization of the product formed when an alcohol and organic acid react. This fiber resists wrinkling, has good dimensional stability, and washes and dries easily. Polyester is widely used in apparel because of its easy care characteristics. Some other common uses for polyester are knitted fabrics, and fiberfill for pillows, comforters, bedspreads, and other quilted household fabrics.

ACRYLIC

Acrylic was first produced in Germany in 1893. Later, in 1944, DuPont developed the fiber in the United States and started commercial production in 1950. Acrylic fibers have wool-like

Brawny Knit Twill — Here's a masculine doubleknit outfit of 100% texturized "non-glitter" Dacron® polyester that's snag-resistant and easy-to-care-for. The jeans (about $17) and the shirt-jac (about $28.50) possess striking contrast stitching and find an ideal complement in the Lee "El Greco" knit shirt (about $16) which features Mediterranean scenes. The Lee Company, 640 Fifth Ave., New York, N.Y. (212) 765-4215.

Lee® A company of VF corporation

FIGURE 6.10 Men's leisure suit made of polyester

HAS IT.™

LYCRA®

FIGURE 6.11 (top left) Acrylic sweaters

FIGURE 6.12 (above) Spandex swimsuits

FIGURE 6.13 (bottom left) Micromattique

characteristics in terms of how they feel and look. However, these fibers resist moths and mildew, which makes acrylic a good choice for garments made for colder climates, such as jackets, coats, sweaters, and other heavy knitwear. Craft **yarn**s are another use for acrylic yarns because of the variety offered in colors, textures, and weight of yarns.

SPANDEX

Spandex is an exceptionally strong fiber and can stretch up to 400 percent without breaking. Many apparel manufacturers now include a small percentage of spandex to the fabrics used for sportswear. This fiber enhances the drape and helps the garment mold to the wearer's shape. Spandex has a high luster and a soft hand and is often found in swimwear. The brand name for spandex is Lycra, which is still owned by DuPont.

MICROFIBERS

The textile industry is constantly looking for ways to improve products. A recent trend has been the development of microfibers. This is a very tight fabric made from polyester or nylon yarns. These yarns are approximately 100 times smaller than a human hair and have properties that lend themselves to many uses in fabric production. Microfibers have excellent moisture retention, wrinkle resistance, and a smooth, soft hand. They are commonly combined with other fibers, though many garments made for easy travel are made with 100 percent microfiber.

A new group of manufactured fibers have taken the spotlight as technology continues to tinker with chemicals and naturally occurring elements. These are called smart textiles with the intent of adjusting to the specific physical needs of the wearer such as body temperature or moisture. Other innovations in smart textiles are fibers that offer impact protection for the wearer and protection against skin-tear wounds and trauma. Many of the developments in smart textiles have implications for safety, space travel, and high-performance end uses.

Yarns

A yarn is a strand of natural or man-made fibers or filaments that are twisted or grouped together for weaving or knitting in constructing fabric. The characteristics of yarns are determined by the fibers used, the texture, performance qualities, and the end use of the fabric. Yarns are divided into two classifications according to their use: weaving yarns or knitting yarns. Staple fibers or filament fibers may be used for producing yarns. Staple fibers are spun or twisted into yarns. Yarns that have two or more single yarns twisted together are called ply yarns. Because of their nature, filament fibers don't require as much twist to become yarns. Technology has afforded us the ability to create novelty yarns and bulk yarns which are used in sweaters, dresses, and outer garments.

Twist in yarns brings the fibers closer together, making them more compact, which produces a harder yarn with lower luster but increased strength. The characteristics of finished fabrics are determined by the amount of and direction of twist in the yarns that were used for production. Yarns can also be categorized by fiber content, method of spinning, and raw materials used.

Methods of Fabrication

Weaving and knitting are the most common methods of making fabric. Weaving is the process of interlacing two sets of yarns at right angles. This can be accomplished by hand or by machinery. Knitting can be described as the process of using one set of yarns to form loops which are caught into other loops, eventually forming rows that are attached to each other.

Weaving

Weaving is the most common method for making fabric. Woven fabrics have been found as far back as the Egyptian tombs. In ancient times, fabric was woven on a loom by hand. These looms were small, and large quantities of fabric could not be produced quickly. Today, the textile industry uses high speed, high performance computerized looms that can produce hundreds of yards of fabric in a short time. Hand looms are still used in producing some fabrics.

Weaving is completed by interlacing lengthwise and crosswise yarns. The yarns that run the length of the fabric are called warp yarns. These yarns are usually stronger and have less stretch. Yarns that run crosswise are called woof, weft, or filling yarns. These yarns have more stretch and are weaker than the warp yarns.

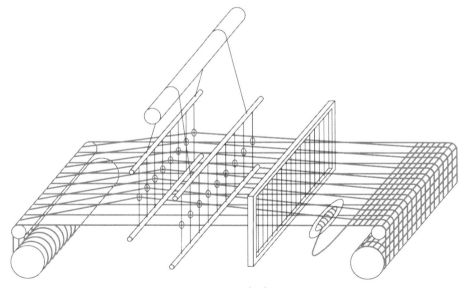

FIGURE 6.14 A weaving loom

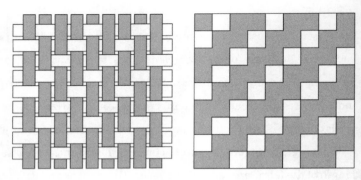

FIGURE 6.16 Twill weave

FIGURE 6.15 Plain weave

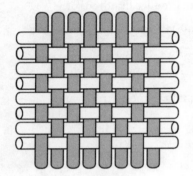

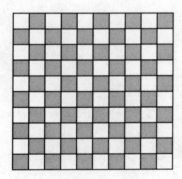

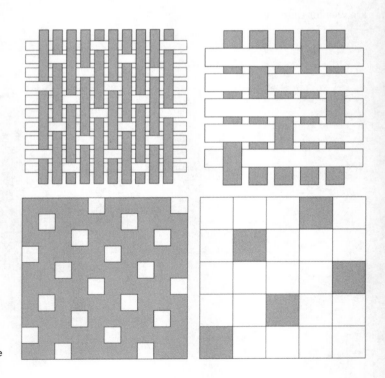

FIGURE 6.17 Satin weave

Basic Weaves

The three basic weaving methods used in producing fabric are the plain weave, twill weave, and satin weave. Almost all other fabrics are some variation of these three basic weaves.

PLAIN WEAVE

This is the simplest of the three weaving methods. The filling yarns pass over and under the warp yarns. The yarns alternate in each row to form an even, balanced weave. Most plain weave fabrics have no wrong or right side unless they are printed or finished differently. Some examples of plain weave fabrics are broadcloth, taffeta, and percale. Plain weave fabrics are used in all forms of apparel and home furnishings.

There are variations of the plain weave, known as ribbed weave and basket weave. A ribbed weave fabric has pronounced rows, or ribs, on the surface in the filling direction. Examples are poplin and faille. A basket weave variation has two or more yarns grouped side by side in each direction and are woven as one yarn. Hopsacking is an example of this plain weave variation.

TWILL WEAVE

A twill weave can be recognized by the parallel diagonal ridges visible on the fabric surface. The filling yarns pass over and under one or more warp yarns, forming this pattern. Each successive row shifts to the right or to the left to give this diagonal line effect. Twill weaves are usually heavier with more firmness and are used in fabrics that require durability such as denim, chino, and gabardine. The diagonal ridges are called wales and may run from the upper left to lower right (called left-hand twill), or from upper right to lower left (called right-hand twill), or in both directions (called herringbone).

SATIN WEAVE

Satin weave fabrics have yarns that float on the surface to give it luster or shine. Either the warp yarns or filling yarns pass over four to eight yarns at a time. This weave produces fabrics that are smooth, lustrous, and rich-looking. It is commonly used for **linings** and evening wear, but is found in basically every kind of outer garment. One drawback of this particular weave is that it snags easily.

Selvage

Along each edge of woven fabric, the **selvage,** or self-edge, can be found. It is formed by the filling yarn when it turns to go back across the fabric in the other direction. This edge is usually stiffer, firmer, and more tightly woven than the face of the fabric. The selvage does not ravel and it is usually between ¼ and ½ inch wide. It is found on both edges of the fabric. The selvage ensures that the fabric will not tear during the finishing and printing processes. The warp yarns are always parallel to the selvage.

Fabric is woven in various widths, depending on its end use, the type of yarns used, and the type of loom used to do the weaving. Fabrics for apparel are woven in widths from 35 inches wide up to more than 60 inches wide. Some looms are capable of weaving widths up to 72 inches. Commonly found in fabric stores, fabrics will be 36 inches wide, 44–45 inches wide, and 60 inches wide. Put-up is the term used to indicate how fabric is packaged when it is sold.

A bolt of fabric refers to the fabric rolled or folded onto a cardboard or metal form. Fabric sold to manufacturers and retailers is placed on a roll put-up where it is wound around a cardboard tube. If the fabric is folded, it is wrapped around a rectangular cardboard with fiber content and other label information on the end of the bolt. This method is commonly found in fabrics of 45-inch and 60-inch widths. In more expensive fabrics, the fabric is not folded, but wrapped around long, tubular cardboard put-ups. This method prevents wrinkling and distortion of the fabric. Labeling information is usually placed at the end of the tube. Other fabrics, such as velvet, velveteen, and other pile fabrics are put-up on metal frames so that the surface does not come into contact with any other part of the fabric (which would crush or distort the pile).

Grain

The direction in which the yarns run is referred to as the **grain**. Lengthwise grain runs in the same direction as the selvage. This is usually the strongest and sturdiest direction of the fabric. Most garments are cut with the lengthwise grain running vertically, up and down the length of the garment. This direction has more strength, durability, and less stretch. Garments cut on this

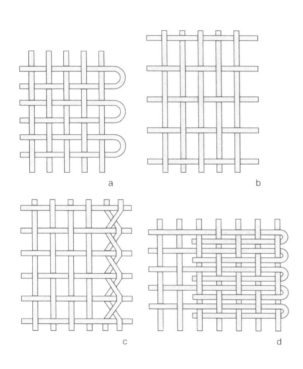

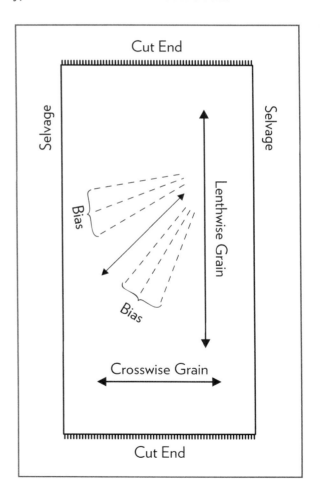

FIGURE 6.18 (top) Edge of fabric showing selvage

FIGURE 6.19 (right) Grain direction

FIGURE 6.20 A knitting machine

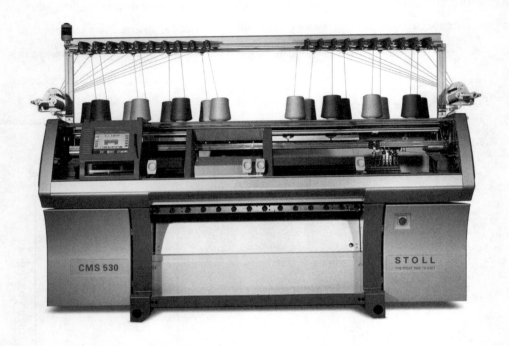

direction tend to hang more evenly on the body. Crosswise grain runs across the fabric from selvage to selvage. It is the same direction as the filling yarns and has a slight amount of stretch. **Bias grain** runs diagonally across the fabric. Garments cut on the bias have more stretch but could easily cause distortion in the way the completed garment hangs. True bias is created by folding the fabric at a 45-degree angle so that the crosswise grain is parallel to the selvage. True bias has the most stretch. Many couture evening gowns are cut and constructed on the bias. Designer Madeleine Vionnet is famous for having perfected this technique.

Knits

Knitting is the second most widely used process of producing fabric. Knitted fabrics have invaded the apparel market because consumers now demand comfortable, easy-care apparel. Knitted goods have also grown because of their distinctive properties such as resistance to wrinkling, blending of natural and manufactured fibers, and their ease in production. The lead time for production of knit fabrics is much less than that of woven fabrics.

Knitting is done by hand or knitting machines that duplicate hand stitches or patterns. In the textile industry, some machines produce knit fabric while others knit the entire item, such as socks and hosiery. Knit fabrics also have a crosswise and lengthwise direction. The lengthwise rows of stitches are called wales and the crosswise stitches are called courses. Knit fabrics are versatile and can be made from a variety of fibers.

There are two kinds of knits: Weft knits and warp knits. Weft, or filling knits, are made with only one yarn. Hand-knitting is an example of a weft knit. Most weft knits have two-way stretch in both directions but are prone to run because of their construction. Warp knits are made with several yarns. The fabric is flat and is constructed by looping the multiple warp yarns so that they interlock. So each yarn is made up of two yarns. This method makes the fabric run-resistant.

Most historians agree that knitting began in Scotland in the fifteenth century. The first stocking firms appeared in Nottinghamshire, England, in 1589 (Wingate, 1984). In 1758, a rib-knit machine was invented by Jebediah Strutt, but circular machinery-producing tubular knit fabrics were not produced until the middle of the nineteenth century. The circular knitting machines used in today's textile industry are highly developed and efficient.

Dyeing, Printing, and Finishes

Dyeing

Dyeing is the process of imparting color to fibers, yarns, and fabrics. Dyestuffs (color substances) that are used to produce color are either natural or synthetic. Prior to 1856, only natural dyes were known. Sources of dyes were insects, shellfish, plants, flowers, and minerals. The nature of the fabric to be dyed influences the type of dyeing process used. The first synthetically produced dyestuff was discovered by William Henry Perkin in 1856 when he discovered the colored substance known as mauve as he experimented with aniline, a coal tar based substance. Some common dyeing processes are:

>> Solution dyeing—man-made fibers are dyed in the solution before the filament is formed

>> Fiber dye or stock dye—fibers are dyed before the yarns are spun or woven into fabric

>> Yarn dye—yarns are dyed before they are woven into fabric. Examples are gingham checks, plaids, and stripes.

>> Piece dye—the cloth is dyed after fabrication

>> Cross dye—fabric of two or more fibers are placed in a dye bath containing two or more kinds of dye. The result is that each fiber type will be dyed by the dye for which it has an affinity.

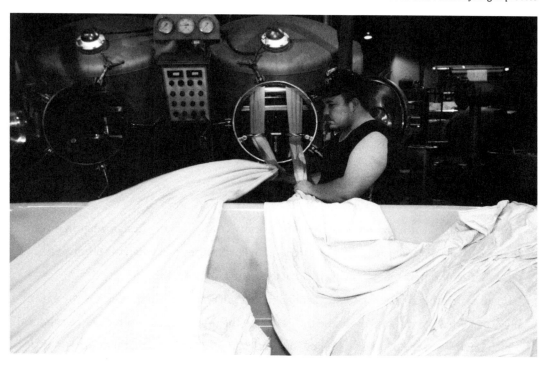

FIGURE 6.21 Fabric dyeing in process

>> Solid dye—fabric from one fiber is dyed one color

>> Union dye—mixes dyes for fabrics made from two or more fibers so that the fibers will dye the same color.

Printing

Variation of fabric design lends itself to artistic expression and inventiveness. The process of printing involves using the same color substances used for dyeing. These substances are thickened with resins to prevent color from bleeding through the design outlines on the fabric. There are a few major methods used for printing fabrics:

>> Direct or roller printing involves separating the individual colors in a design where a roller is used for each color that is part of the design. Actual printing occurs when the fabric passes over a series of rollers that revolve in a vat of dye (Wingate, 1984).

>> Discharge printing is used when there are no more than two colors in the design. The entire piece of cloth is dyed a solid color and the design on the roller is then covered with a chemical which removes the color when it is applied to the fabric. The result is that the background is left colored and the design is white (Wingate, 1984).

>> Screen printing is completed by placing a fine mesh screen fabric, usually made of nylon, polyester, or metal on top of the fabric to be printed. Colored paste is forced through the openings by pulling a squeegee back and forth across the fabric.

Technology has certainly contributed to the advancement of methods of dyeing and finishing fabrics in the textiles industry. There are two categories for fabric design that we will consider in this section: structural design and applied decoration.

FIGURE 6.22 Printed fabric

Structural designs are achieved during the construction of the fabric by combining yarns, introducing novelty yarns or fibers, weave variations, varying knitting designs, or combining colored yarns to create special effects.

Other decorative designs are applied to the surface of the fabric by printing, embossing, adding a relief design element, or using chemical reactions. We will focus on the printing application. Printing is achieved by applying color or chemicals to the surface of the fabric after it has been woven. Several major methods of printing are discussed earlier but there are many other methods for imparting designs to fabric.

Prints on fabrics are very mutable from season to season and from year to year. Depending on trends, prints can swing from florals to geometrics to plaids and back again. Some seasons, prints are scarcely seen on the runways, however, florals tend to be the most popular when prints are shown in collections.

Current technology allows print designs to be prepared on the computer, which utilizes inkjet technology to print onto the face of the fabric. This method is used for short yardages and some accessories, such as scarves.

Finishes

Finishing is the final step in the fabrication process and includes all of the processes that follow the weaving or knitting of the fabric before it is cut for garment production. There are two groups of finishes: aesthetic finishes and functional finishes.

Aesthetic finishes include procedures to achieve a specific characteristic on the fabric. Some of them are calendering, bleaching, napping, sizing, and lustering. Functional finishes have the end use in mind and contribute to the wearability of the garment. Some explanations of both groups of finishes are discussed below.

>> Anti-static finishes serve to reduce the dryness in garments, thus reducing the static electricity, which is caused by the dryness. This finish is applied with chemicals that absorb moisture from the atmosphere onto the surface of the fabric.

>> Anti-microbial finishes are often found in garments that are in direct contact with the skin, such as diapers, underwear, and bed linens. This finish is also commonly referred to as anti-bacterial. The chemicals used for this finish prevent or reduce odor-causing germs as well as eliminating fungi (mold and mildew) that are common threats to cellulosic fibers. These fungi produce stains, odors, and weaken the fabric.

>> Flame-resistant finishes were initiated by the Flammable Fabric Act Amendment in 1967 to prohibit the use of fabrics that burn rapidly and might be dangerous in apparel. This finish is applied in various methods depending the fiber content and the end use.

>> Bleaching is a finish accomplished by using bleach to clean and whiten greige goods. This process is often used for cotton and linen whose natural fibers are off-white. The goal is to uniformly remove impurities in the fabric and to achieve a high, even, degree of whiteness on the fabric surface. This also allows the bleached fabric to uniformly accept dyes. Bleaching is also an aesthetic finish and is used abundantly in producing variations in denim jeans.

>> Mercerization is a process that uses an alkali (caustic soda) on a fabric in order to increase luster, softness, give greater strength, and improve the fabric's affinity for dyes and other finishes. This process is most commonly applied to cotton, linen, and some rayon fabrics.

Now, let's look at some aesthetic finishes.

>> Calendaring is a mechanical finish performed by a series of rollers through which the fabric passes. There are several types which produce different effects on the fabric.

FIGURE 6.23 Glazed fabric finish

>> Luster finishes produce a change in the way light is reflected off a fabric. Some examples of this process are: glazed fabrics, such as chintz and polished cotton, cire, and moiré.

>> Sizing is another form of starching, where fabrics are immersed in a mixture of waxes, oils, glycerine, and softeners. This process adds stiffness, weight, and body to the fabric.

>> Napping is a process that produces a raised group of fibers on the surface of the fabric. This is done by machines that brush up the fiber ends. This process results in fabrics with a soft hand and the surface fibers tend to lay in one direction.

>> Each of these finishes accomplishes specific tasks and contributes to comfort, durability, and consumer satisfaction.

Findings

Findings can be defined as all other materials in a garment besides the fabric that is essential in making the garment. Examples are **interfacing**s, **interlinings**, zippers, trim, buttons, thread, and labels. The quality of findings is just as critical as the fabric quality used to make the outer garment. The performance of findings can influence a consumer's decision to buy, return, or discard a garment. Findings must meet the same performance requirements as the fabric. The American Society for Testing and Materials (ASTM) has developed standardized test methods and performance specifications for a selection of findings which include zippers, elastic, buttons, snap fasteners, and thread (Brown, 2001).

Thread

Thread is used to hold fabric sections together by way of seams. Fabric sections are joined to create apparel or home furnishings. It is vital that thread be strong and possess the ability to hold fabric sections together and at the same time, be aesthetically pleasing.

Threads are usually selected according to the fiber and weight of the fabric in which they are being used. General guidelines suggest using natural fiber threads for natural fiber fabrics and synthetic fiber thread for synthetic fabrics. The main types of thread used in garment production are spun thread and corespun thread. There are several kinds of threads on the market for constructing garments:

>> Cotton-wrapped polyester is an all-purpose thread designed for hand and machine sewing on all fabrics, both natural and synthetic, woven and knit. This kind of thread is called corespun because of its construction. The synthetic core of polyester makes the thread fine and stronger.

>> Spun thread is basically made up of staple fibers spun into single yarns. Anywhere from two to six yarns are twisted together to make a thread. Spun threads are strong, have elasticity, and are abrasion resistant.

>> Topstitching and buttonhole twist thread is used in topstitching, decorative stitches, and in making machine or hand-stitched buttonholes.

>> Long-fiber polyester thread is smooth, even, and suitable for stitching by hand or machine.

>> One hundred percent mercerized cotton thread is used for natural woven fabrics. It is not strong enough for use in constructing knit garments.

Trims and Tapes

Trims and tapes are also chosen for compatibility with the garment in which they will be used.

>> Single-fold and double-fold bias tapes are available in solid colors and are used for casings, trim, and facings in garments.

>> Lace seam binding is used to finish seams and as a decorative touch in garment hems.

FIGURE 6.24 Various threads

FIGURE 6.25 Trims and tapes

FIGURE 6.26 Frog closings and buttons

>> Seam tape is used to stabilize seams, finish hems, or reinforce corners. This tape is usually 100 percent rayon or polyester.

>> Twill tape is similar to seam tape, but is narrower and is used to stabilize interior seams of garments.

>> Rickrack is a decorative trim and comes in ¼ inch, ½ inch, and ⅝ inch widths.

>> Braid is used for accents, scroll motifs, drawstrings, ties, or button loops and is available in loop, soutache, and middy styles.

>> Elastic comes in various widths and is used in casings to shape waistbands, wrists, and necklines. Elastics are found in woven or knit versions and should be compatible with the garment in which they are used.

>> Corded piping is an accent trim that is inserted in seams for definition or accents. Sometimes, contrasting colors are used for emphasis in garment collars, pockets, or necklines.

>> Additional forms of trim are lace edging, appliqués, beading, feathers, and studs.

Labels

Labels on garments must be permanently attached and must be legible during the life of the garment. Manufacturers commonly use a woven label with printed information that is sewn into the neck of the garment. It has also become a common practice to print the required label information directly onto the back neckline of the garment, especially in T-shirts. More details regarding specific labeling requirements will be covered in chapter 8.

Buttons and Closures

Buttons come in every conceivable shape, size, and color. All buttons have two holes, four holes, or shanks in order to facilitate attachment to the garment. Buttons with two or four holes are

FIGURE 6.27 Interfacing

usually flatter in shape while buttons with shanks underneath the button can be thicker with more dimension. Other closures used in garments are toggles, frogs, snaps, Velcro tape, and hooks-and-eyes.

Another primary closure is zippers whose teeth are made from metal or plastic. The teeth of the zipper are attached to a woven tape which is usually made from polyester or nylon. Polyester all-purpose zippers are commonly used in fabrics of all weights for skirts, pants, dresses, and blouses. Metal all-purpose zippers are more heavyweight and are used in coats, outerwear, and sportswear.

Interfacings and Underlying Fabrics

Linings, interfacings, underlinings, and interlinings all add shape and support to garments. These fabrics must meet the same performance and aesthetic requirements of the outer fabrics used in apparel. Linings are an extra layer of fabric used to prevent stretching and to finish off the inside of the garment. **Underlinings** and interlinings serve the same purpose, but their use is determined by the shape of the garment and how much support is required. Underlining is the method of using one fabric as a backing for another fabric. The two fabrics are treated as one piece in the construction process. Typical lining fabrics are lightweight, plain weave, and smooth texture.

Interfacings are extra layers of fabric (woven, knit, or non-woven) placed between the garment and the facing to add shape or body to the garment. Common placement for interfacings are necklines, collars, sleeve cuffs, pockets, and garment openings where buttonholes and buttons are part of the design. Interfacings come in a wide assortment of weights, from lightweight to very heavy. They are usually available only in black, white, or beige colors and are also offered as fusible or sew-in. Fusible materials have a chemical adhesive that is activated when heat is applied, usually by ironing, and secures the interfacing to the fabric without sewing. There are advantages and disadvantages for both kinds. Woven interfacings are stronger, do not stretch, but must be cut on grain and are more costly than their non-woven counterparts.

Key Terms

Bias Grain	Cellulosic fibers	Dyeing	Fabric	Fibers
Filament fibers	Findings	Grain	Interfacing	Interlining
Lining	Non-cellulosic fibers	Selvage	Staple fibers	Thread
Underlining	Weaving	Yarn		

Ideas for Discussion and Application

1. What is the difference between a cellulosic and non-cellulosic fiber?
2. Why is it important to understand textiles when evaluating apparel quality?
3. What is the difference between a staple fiber and a filament fiber?
4. Name and explain the three basic methods of weaving.
5. How is weaving different from knitting?
6. What is the single most important factor in determining garment quality?
7. Define *fiber*, *yarn*, and *fabric*. How are they related?
8. Select two garments from your closet to note the fiber content and discuss the fiber properties that contribute to the functionality and aesthetics of these garments.
9. Why do you think silk has remained a status fiber?

Activities

1. Visit a fabric store and explore the layout. Take notice of how the fabric is merchandised and segmented.

2. Go to a textiles, fabrics, and trim store and notice how fabrics and findings are merchandised and segmented.

3. Trace the source of a natural or man-made fabric back to its roots. Research its principle elements, the chemical or mechanical processes it undergoes, and the geographic route it travels, to finally become part of the clothing you wear. Write a report on sourcing that includes the relationship between companies and their global vendors.

chapter seven

the manufacturing process

The apparel production cycle involves several inter-related steps. As with the creative processes used by designers, the manufacturing process is both creative and technical and requires a high level of proficiency and knowledge to execute the steps for making successful garments.

The steps are as follows:

1. Evaluation of previous season's line and current trend analysis
2. Design
3. Sourcing, including costing
4. Pre-production
5. Production
6. Distribution
7. Promotion and sales.

In order to effectively accomplish these steps, lead time calendars or time/action calendars are used so that delivery and production deadlines are met. Now let's discuss each step.

Evaluation

Evaluation is guided by a development plan based on last season's sales, market research, trends, customer returns, and comparison of products. The development plan provides the general direction for the upcoming season in terms of color and style. During this stage, designers not only research fabric and color trends, they also look at the past season's sales and how many units each garment sold. The goals of the company also are taken into account. This is a critical stage and determines what the next season's line of apparel will look like.

At this point, the company decision-makers and the team of designers consider each piece in the line carefully, measuring it against past sales history, current trends, and considering what stage of development each garment or silhouette actually belongs to. For example, if they review a blouse with puffed sleeves and determine that the puffed sleeves are no longer trendy and experienced slow sales for the past season, this garment will most likely be pulled from the line and some new trendy detail might be exchanged on the blouse for the now no-longer-trendy puffed sleeves. The goal is not to make garments that are in the declining stage of the fashion cycle.

Let's examine the fashion cycle and why it is involved in the evaluation stage of production. There are several stages of design related to apparel:

Introductory phase—worn by trendsetters and innovators—usually sold at higher prices. Often, only the wealthy can afford these purchases. An example would be Jimmie Choo shoes when they were first introduced to mainstream consumers by way of television programming

FIGURE 7.1 A variation of the production cycle.

APPAREL PRODUCTION CYCLE (3 TO 6 MONTHS)

The processes noted in each cycle are occurring simultaneously for different products and different seasons. (Steps may vary slightly from firm to firm and will depend on whether the company is a traditional manufacturer or a manufacturing retailer.)

1 DESIGN　　　　　2-3 Weeks
Line Development and Preliminary Approval
Fabric Research and Development
Findings Research and Development
Artwork for Prints, Embroideries, and Screen Prints
Develop New Wet-Process Finishes
First Patterns
Prototype Garments

2 SOURCING　　　　2-3 Weeks
Precosting
Production Costing
Fabric Specifications
Findings Specifications
Determine Production Capacity Requirements
Consider Garment Placement Options
Begin Cost Negotiation
Obtain Color Lab Dips
Prototype Prints, Embroideries, and Screen Prints

3 PREPRODUCTION　　2-6 Weeks
Fabric Testing and Approval
Findings Testing and Approval
Wet-Process Finish Testing and Approval
Garment Specifications
Color/Shade Approval of Production Fabric
Care Label Approval
Preproduction Garments
Customs Preclassification
Production Patterns
Grading
Finalize Sourcing Decisions and Sign Purchase Agreements
Marker Making
Other Label Approval
Line Finalization

4 PRODUCTION　　　　1-2 Weeks
Production Fabric and Findings Arrive
Inspect and Test
Spreading
Cutting
Sub-Contract Pre-Assembly Sundry Operations (e.g., Embroidery)
Sample Garments Sewn
Production Garments Sewn
Wet Processing
Sub-Contract Post-Assembly Sundry Operations (e.g., Screen Prints)
Pressing
Finishing
Final Audit

5 DISTRIBUTION　　1-3 Weeks domestic, 3-5 weeks imports
Shipping
Customs Clearance
DC Audit and Inspection
Distribution to Retailers

6 PROMOTION AND SALES　　3-6 Weeks
Display at Retail
Advertising
Initial Sales
Reorders
POS Information Gathered

7 EVALUATION　　　2-4 Weeks
Previous Season's Sales Analysis
Analysis of Customer Returns
Competitor Comparison Studies
Market Research
Trend Identification
Development Plan for Upcoming Season

with the weekly sitcom, *Sex and the City*. They became a status symbol because of who was wearing them: Sarah Jessica Parker, Helen Mirren, Naomi Watts, Victoria Beckham, Jennifer Garner, Jennifer Lopez—and the list goes on—who make regular appearances in their Jimmie Choos at high-visibility awards ceremonies such as the Golden Globes and the Oscars. Regardless of unabashedly exorbitant retail prices, innovative styling and top-notch workmanship enabled the name brand to take on momentum. Strategic partnerships have led to the spawn of more than 60 stores worldwide. To be sure, women all over the U.S. are coveting Jimmie Choo shoes, regardless of cost.

Peak phase—widely accepted and worn by mass market. Garments are normally available in many fabrics and style variations. These items often go "on sale" and are promoted regularly by retailers. Gap, and its winning deck of cards that includes Banana Republic and Old Navy, has mastered the art of peak phase retailing while maintaining a loyal client base that spans a broad variety of demographic groups.

Declining phase—still being worn but purchased by fewer consumers at lower prices. At this phase, the item is on its way out. An example might possibly be Levi jeans before they developed a strategy to recapture lost market share with the standard five-pocket jean.

Fad—short life. An example is bell bottom pants in the 1990s. The rapidly changing nature of fads brings to light the tight interaction of shoes, pants, and accessories—when a pant hemline suddenly changes, as fads do, boots and shoes follow suit. This creates a wave of retail opportunities that piggy back on one another. If you've ever been swayed by the phrase, "That's so last year," to swap your bellbottoms for boot-cut jeans and your boot-cut jeans for pencil-straight skinny jeans, you've experienced a fad. The lesson is to hang on to those gorgeous platform shoes you only wore once; they may come back into fashion.

Classic—takes decades to move through the cycle. An example is the white oxford shirt. Trend forecasting is a vital skill during the evaluation stage. Many companies use outside sources to provide information to them regarding current trends in color and fabrications, as well as predicted silhouettes for forthcoming seasons. These sources might include the Tobe Report and Block Note. While the reports are general in scope, they provide insight to the companies because they represent an analysis of what has been found in the marketplace and predictions about what are likely to be popular colors and silhouettes.

There are also companies that provide only color predictions. Examples are the International Color Authority, The Color Box, and Concepts in Color. Two companies, Pantone and Standard Color of Textile Dictionaire International de la Couleur (SCOTDIC), also have developed color systems. They are a resource for many designers and retailers because they keep records in the form of dyed fabric. Many companies use one of these systems to set the color standard for apparel that is being developed in house. Trade publications are a research resource for getting information on developing, as well as declining, apparel trends. Fashion magazines are also important resources.

Evaluation sets the foundation for the remainder of the process.

Trade Publications	**Magazines**
Women's Wear Daily	*Accessories Magazine*
Daily News Record	*Vogue*
Earnshaw's	*InStyle*
Children's Business	*Elle*
Sportswear International	*Marie Claire*
Footwear News Magazine	*Seventeen*

Design

Design involves line development, preliminary line approval, fabric and findings research and development, first patterns, creating slopers and muslins, and finally, constructing prototype garments.

One of the first steps is to create a color story. This is developed by the designers who get inspiration from various sources as discussed in Chapter 3. Designers group garments together based on color, theme, fabric, or silhouette. At this point, designers decide the colors in which the garment will be offered. This is contingent on fabric availability, current trends, and sales projections. Often, not every garment in every color is purchased by the retailer. Many different techniques are used to illustrate designs. Some designs are developed using the draping technique, sewing a muslin and transferring it to a flat pattern, or by using sophisticated CAD programs which eliminate sketching. These techniques are discussed in detail in Chapter 3.

A comprehensive package of designs is called a line or a collection. Most ready-to-wear and couture designers create several lines per year—spring/summer, fall/winter, and resort. Not every designer is great at sketching or constructing garments. Advances in technology have made it possible to overcome these limitations. Designing is experimental, with the goal of combining the right silhouette with the right fabric and trim to create a beautiful, functional garment. Once the line has come together and the designer or manufacturer is certain about what the next season's line will look like, another department takes over and starts the sourcing phase of production.

FIGURE 7.2 Design color boards

Sourcing

Sourcing refers to the process of selecting raw materials or components and also refers to the process of contracting or choosing contractors to perform the production work. Sourcing is also the first step in calculating the cost of making your product. Sourcing materials, fabrics, and trim can be done at the wholesale level from mills, distributors, and jobbers. Usually mills and distributors require larger quantities to be ordered while jobbers sell smaller quantities but sometimes at higher prices. With jobbers, there is no assurance that they will have the same product in the future.

There are many options available for sourcing manufacturers today, such as using domestic production totally, cutting the fabric in the U.S. and sending it to another country for assembly, or simply using foreign production for the entire garment. According to an article in the *Houston Chronicle* on September 4, 2007, U.S. manufacturing has undergone many changes since the number of industry workers peaked at 19 million in 1979. The number of American workers has now dropped to 14 million. Many states whose industries were heavily manufacturing have lost thousands of jobs because of outsourcing of apparel and textile products to other countries. Some reasons that companies are outsourcing to other countries are that labor and the cost of materials are cheaper. Many domestic manufacturers have begun to source their production on a global scale, seeking out facilities that will provide the lowest cost for production and maintain quality standards.

Countries such as China, Vietnam, Indonesia, just to name a few, are competing for production and materials on a global scale while developed countries are downsizing and/or relocating textile and apparel capacities to smaller, underdeveloped countries.

There are several factors involved in these decisions. The costs involved must factor in labor, how the fabric will get shipped to the contractor, shipping finished goods, tariffs, and quotas. Another factor is timing or lead time, which is the length of time from design concept to transit of finished product to the retailer. Depending on the country in which production is taking place, this could be a critical issue in terms of getting product to the retailer on time. Production capacity, another factor, plays a major part in the decision of who will produce the goods. A company may not be equipped to handle large orders because of lack of up-to-date technology, manpower, or even physical restraints. A final consideration is quality of the product. Even though underdeveloped countries are in the business of producing apparel, many of them don't have the expertise on specialized manufacturing skills such as patternmaking, cutting, stitching, and finishing techniques that meet the standards for garments to be sold in the United States. Quality management is an issue that will only be resolved with intense training of the workers in these countries.

According to Kunz and Garner (2007), "In both the textile and the apparel markets, Asian countries claim 9 of the top 15 positions in terms of the size of their textile and apparel markets." It is suggested by Kunz and Garner that China and Asia are likely to remain the world's largest producers and exporters of textiles and apparel in the near future.

Costing

Costing is the process of estimating and then determining the total cost of producing a garment. Normally, after the sourcing process is complete, the manufacturer will calculate how much it costs to make one garment. This calculation includes cost of materials, labor, transportation, and general expenses. Once the cost for making one garment has been calculated, this figure is usually doubled in the apparel industry which gives the manufacturer or retailer an idea of what the final retail price will be. If this number does not fit with the general pricing strategy, whether too high or too low, then more sourcing is done until the right fabric, trim, and so forth is found.

Production costing is detailed and is based on a sample or sketch of a garment with written specifications. See example of a cost sheet below. Accurate calculations are necessary and can be done manually or by computer. According to Kunz and Garner (2007), "cost estimates must include not only the costs of materials and labor, but also, in the case of imported products, the inclusion of agent or broker fees, quota and/or tariffs, insurance, transportation, receiving, and quality assessment costs."

Cost Sheets

Cost sheets contain all the information necessary to calculate the cost of each specific garment being considered for production. The following information should be included on the cost sheet.

>> style name
>> style number
>> fabric costs
>> trim costs
>> cutting costs
>> assembly costs
>> packaging costs

>> other costs

>> first cost

>> wholesale cost

>> suggested retail cost

There are five main elements of the garment that should be included: fabric, findings and trim, labor, overhead, and other expenses such as labels.

Let's discuss each of these:

Fabric can make up 60 percent to 70 percent of the total cost of the garment. All fabrics used in the garments are included in the cost such as linings and interfacings. The amount of yardage needed for outer fabrics must be calculated separately from the accessory or inner fabrics, which are linings, interlinings, and interfacings. Most of the inner fabrics are likely to be stocked in-house by the manufacturer and will cost less.

Findings are defined as all materials other than fabric, such as thread, trims, closures, buttons, labels, shoulder pads, and elastic.

Labor costs involve **spreading**, cutting, sewing, pressing, finishing, and any wet-processing. These fees also include sample-making, **grading**, patternmaking, **marker making**, and pre-packing. Some of this work can be done in-house and is usually calculated by the production person who knows the capacity of the facility and what tasks need to be out-sourced.

Overhead expenses are part of operating the business beyond the direct costs of producing garments. These include, but are not limited to, such expenses as utilities, machinery, buildings, technology, and payroll.

Other expenses can include packaging, labels, and costs for processing finishes on the garments.

When all of these expenses are added up, the total cost of production might force the manufacturer into a wholesale or retail price higher than the desired figure. At this point, adjustments are made on controllable factors, such as fabric, findings, cheaper trims or eliminating trims, color choices offered, and sizes offered.

Pre-Production

At this point in the production process, many tasks are being undertaken simultaneously. Because this can get very complicated, many companies have personnel designated to track the progress of each task and some have incorporated technical systems to assist them. Some of the most important steps in pre-production are described below.

Color approval is a necessary step, especially for manufacturers that are filling orders for sale to retailers. Many retailers specify the exact colors and shades desired in each garment. Colors that are approved by using computers must be duplicated in the actual fabric. In order to maintain consistency of color, lab dips, strikeoffs, or shade bands are produced for comparison. A lab dip is a sample of the dyed fabric. A strikeoff is a print fabric sample. A shade band is a long, narrow swatch of fabric that is cut from different dye lots, with variations of the shade. Many retailers who develop their own apparel lines with an in-house product development division are very stringent about their color requirements of manufacturers. Oftentimes, this process must be repeated several times before it is approved and can sometimes delay the production process until the manufacturer meets the color requirements to fill the order.

Fabric testing and approval—Once the fabric has been approved for use in garments, testing is conducted for specific qualities that will enhance the overall quality and functionality of the garment. Examples are testing for flammability, moisture retention, luster, etc. During this period of lab testing, fabric performance is expected to be consistent and is closely watched for variances.

Findings testing and approval is similar to testing and approving fabric. In this step, closures and other findings are tested and approved for color match, durability, and overall appearance. This stage also includes testing and approving garment labels, which must meet the industry requirements.

Garment specifications with diagrams and instructions are written and must be exact at this stage so that production can be completed. During this step, production patterns are made. These are hard patterns which will be used in the cutting step.

Cut order planning is a step that translates the customer's orders into cutting orders. This step examines the width and availability of the fabrics required to make the garments. Some considerations in this step are the quantity of garments expected to be produced, the width of the fabric and how that affects the layout, and number of sizes and colors to be produced. Normally, two to five garments are made in each size for pre-production. If the garments are to be imported, they must be classified by U.S. Customs, which will determine any tariff rate or duty assessed to the garments. Considerations for classification are the percent weight of each fiber in the completed garment, the fabric construction (knit or woven), the gender of the intended wearer, and the description of the item.

When the United States, Canada, and Mexico formed the North American Free Trade Agreement (NAFTA) in 1994, they had problems documenting the types and quantities of products being traded. This became even more of a problem since Canada and Mexico both use the metric system of measurement. The three countries developed the North American

Classification System (NAICS) in 1997 in order to standardize the indentification of textiles and apparel products that are consistent with the rest of the world market (Kunz & Garner, 2007).

Under the North American Industry Classification System, all ready-to-wear apparel is classified into specific categories with designated assigned code numbers. These codes were developed to track trade between the United States, Canada, and Mexico under NAFTA of 1997.

NAICS (North American Industry Classification System)

Code	Classification
315	Apparel Manufacturing
3151	Apparel Knitting Mills
31511	Hosiery and Sock Mills
315111	Sheer Hosiery Mills
315119	Other Hosiery and Sock Mills
31519	Other Apparel Knitting Mills
315191	Outerwear Knitting Mills
315192	Underwear and Nightwear Knitting Mills
3152	Cut and Sew Apparel Manufacturing
31521	Cut and Sew Apparel Contractors
315211	Men's and Boys' Cut and Sew Apparel Contractors
315212	Women's and Girls' Cut and Sew Apparel Manufacturing
31522	Men's and Boys' Cut and Sew Apparel Manufacturing
315221	Men's and Boys' Cut and Sew Underwear and Nightwear Manufacturing
315222	Men's and Boys' Cut and Sew Suit, Coat and Overcoat Manufacturing
315223	Men's and Boys' Cut and Sew Shirt (except Work Shirt) Manufacturing
315224	Men's and Boys' Cut and Sew Trouser, Slack and Jean Manufacturing
315225	Men's and Boys' Cut and Sew Work Clothing Manufacturing
315228	Men's and Boys' Cut and Sew Other Outerwear Manufacturing
31523	Women's and Girls' Cut and Sew Apparel Manufacturing
315231	Women's and Girls' Cut and Sew Lingerie, Loungewear and Nightwear Manufacturing
315232	Women's and Girls' Cut and Sew Blouse and Shirt Manufacturing
315233	Women's and Girls' Cut and Sew Dress Manufacturing
315234	Women's and Girls' Cut and Sew Suit, Coat, Tailored Jacket and Skirt Manufacturing
315238	Women's and Girls' Cut and Sew Other Outerwear Manufacturing
31529	Other Cut and Sew Apparel Manufacturing
315291	Infants' Cut and Sew Apparel Manufacturing
315292	Fur and Leather Apparel Manufacturing
315299	All Other Cut and Sew Apparel Manufacturing
3159	Apparel Accessories and Other Apparel Manufacturing
31599	Apparel Accessories and Other Apparel Manufacturing
315991	Hat, Cap and Millinery Manufacturing
315992	Glove and Mitten Manufacturing
315993	Men's and Boys' Neckware Manufacturing
315999	Other Apparel Accessories and Other Apparel Manufacturing

FIGURE 7.3
NAICS codes

Marker making is a very important step in the manufacturing process. A marker is a diagram that shows the precise arrangement, or layout, of pattern pieces for a specific garment and the number of sizes to be cut from a single spread of fabric. The goal is to achieve an efficient layout with minimal waste of fabric without distorting the directionality of grain of the garment design.

Spreading is the process of superimposing lengths of fabric on a cutting table in order to prepare for the cutting step. This can be accomplished manually or by machinery. The number of layers of fabric or plies can range from 1 to 300 depending on the size of the order, the texture of the fabric to be cut, the cutting method, and the capacity of the spreader. A lay, or lay up, has about 24 to 32 plies. Directional fabrics, such as naps or one-way designs must be cut from one direction. This step saves time and reduces production costs.

FIGURE 7.4 Markers

FIGURE 7.5 Spreading

Grading is the process of increasing and decreasing pattern dimensions to reflect the various sizes produced. This step uses a computer-aided manufacturing system such as CAM. It can also be done manually but would be time-consuming. Manual grading requires skill and is a painstaking process taking many hours to complete while the CAM system quickly and accurately grades patterns to the desired sizes in a much shorter time (Brown, 2001).

FIGURE 7.6 An example of a graded bodice pattern.

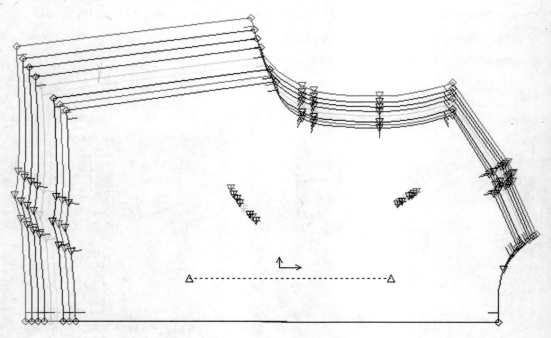

Production

The production process goes more smoothly when all the preparatory steps are completed according to the standards and deadlines. Production involves the cutting task, assembling sample garments, and the final assembly of garments, including applying decorative details and any necessary garment finishes.

Cutting the fabric can be a pre-production step or it can be done in the production phase, depending on decisions made by management. Because cutting involves several hundred pieces at one time, it is critical that accuracy is monitored. If only one piece is inaccurate, it can affect the fit, shape, and final appearance of hundreds of garments and create a loss for the company. Most companies use computerized machines to complete this task, but some employ people whose job it is to cut the fabric using manually operated machinery.

Making sample garments is done by assembling one or two garments for the designer and/or retailer to review. This is another strategic move to keep costs down and insure accuracy. Any errors or mistakes can be caught and corrected at this point. Sometimes, garments are deleted from the line if the final product does not resemble the original design concept.

Assembly of garments is commonly referred to as sewing. We will discuss two methods in which garments are assembled. The method of assembly is contingent upon the kind of garment, the price, and the level of sewing skill needed to execute the design.

>> Section work is a system where each operator on the assembly line works on only one part of the garment. An example is sleeves. Several sleeves would be bundled together and given to one operator. After the sleeves are assembled, they are passed onto another operator for the next task required. This system is also referred to as bundling.

FIGURE 7.7 Garments being sewn

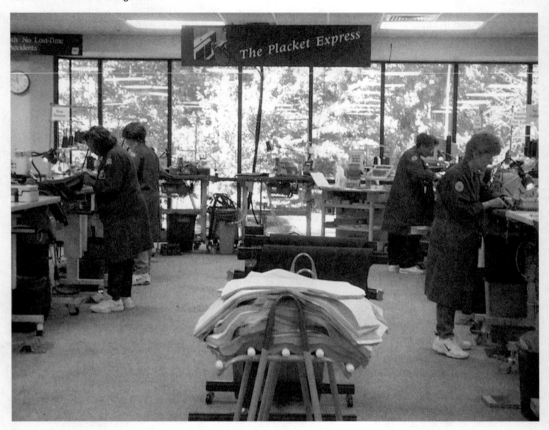

>> Complete garment construction is the assembly of the entire garment by one person, except for finishing details that might need other machinery for completion.

After the assembly is completed, the next step is to apply any finishes to the garment based on the design specifications. One common finish method is called wet-processing, where the garment has a rinse or wash applied to it, such as jeans. Other finishes at this stage are bleaching, frosting, acid washing, adding a color, dyeing, or overdyeing.

The final step in the production process is finishing the garment by adding buttons, labels, snaps, and more. Advances in technology have provided sewing machines that can be programmed to sew specific stitches and only need monitoring by an operator. Stitches and seam types required for assembling apparel in the United States were defined and classified by the American Society for Testing and Materials (ASTM) in 1997. This is known as ASTM D6193-97 Standard Practice for Seams and Stitches. This document identifies four seam classes and two stitching classes. Each class includes many seam types.

Distribution

At this point, the garments are made and have been inspected by quality control staff and are now ready to be delivered to the retailer. The orders are filled and packed according to the guidelines set forth in the purchase orders placed by the retailer. The critical factor is making sure that goods are delivered on time, as specified by the company that placed the order.

There are many ways to deliver goods to their destination—air freight, boat, and ground. The method of delivery varies based on the amount of the shipment, the destination, and the preference of the retailer. Some larger retailers specify their preferred delivery method when orders are placed. Any variance from this must be approved by the retailer, or the manufacturer could incur additional shipping costs. Some companies request drop shipments where goods are delivered directly to a brick-and-mortar store. This occurs in cases where companies have hundreds of locations and are not able to handle product adequately in a distribution center. The other method involves shipping all of the merchandise to a central distribution center, or DC (sometimes, several distribution centers).

Promotion and Sales

This is the final step in the production process. By this time, the garments have made it to the selling floor. In order to sell the goods, retailers must inform consumers about the product as well as persuade them to buy. Several methods are used to accomplish this:

>> Advertising—direct mail, posters, video display, brochures, newspapers, magazines, TV, movies, radio

>> Sales promotion—visual displays, trial offers, contests, special events, fashion shows, gifts with purchase

>> Publicity—press releases

>> Personal selling—using salespeople, showing goods during Market Week, trade shows, and more.

It is obvious that the manufacturing process is a continuous cycle, and no sooner than it is completed, it starts all over.

FIGURE 7.8 A fashion distribution center

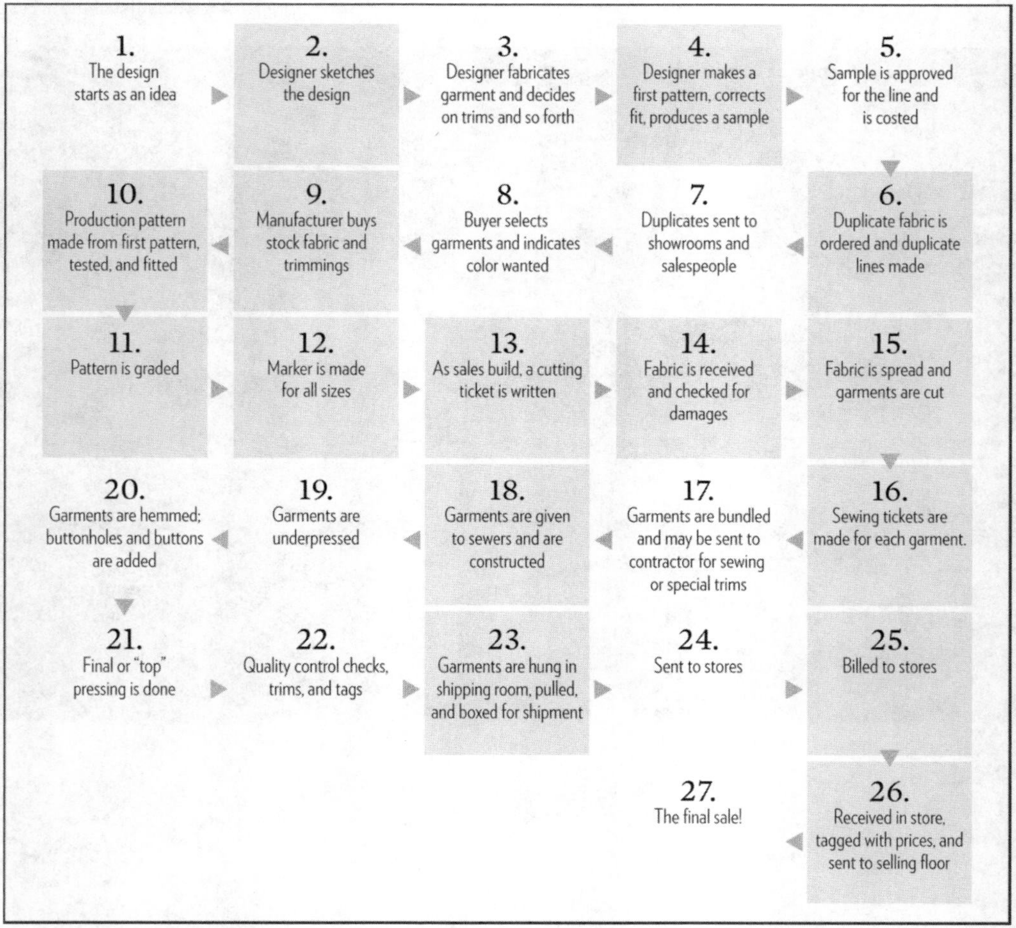

1. The design starts as an idea

2. Designer sketches the design

3. Designer fabricates garment and decides on trims and so forth

4. Designer makes a first pattern, corrects fit, produces a sample

5. Sample is approved for the line and is costed

10. Production pattern made from first pattern, tested, and fitted

9. Manufacturer buys stock fabric and trimmings

8. Buyer selects garments and indicates color wanted

7. Duplicates sent to showrooms and salespeople

6. Duplicate fabric is ordered and duplicate lines made

11. Pattern is graded

12. Marker is made for all sizes

13. As sales build, a cutting ticket is written

14. Fabric is received and checked for damages

15. Fabric is spread and garments are cut

20. Garments are hemmed; buttonholes and buttons are added

19. Garments are underpressed

18. Garments are given to sewers and are constructed

17. Garments are bundled and may be sent to contractor for sewing or special trims

16. Sewing tickets are made for each garment.

21. Final or "top" pressing is done

22. Quality control checks, trims, and tags

23. Garments are hung in shipping room, pulled, and boxed for shipment

24. Sent to stores

25. Billed to stores

27. The final sale!

26. Received in store, tagged with prices, and sent to selling floor

FIGURE 7.9 Major steps in the manufacturing process

Key Terms

Classic	Costing	Declining phase	Fad	Grading
Introductory phase	Marker making	Peak phase	Spreading	

Ideas for Discussion and Application

1. List each step in the manufacturing process and explain what occurs in each step.
2. Why are decisions about color critical to the design step?
3. What two factors are involved in considering sourcing of production of garments?
4. Why is a costing sheet necessary for apparel manufacturers?
5. What element makes up 60 to 70 percent of the total cost of a garment? Explain why.
6. Why is it important for colors to be approved during the pre-production process?
7. How does the marker making step affect the quality of the finished garment?

Activities

1. Select a garment that fits into each stage of the fashion life cycle. Explain why it qualifies for this stage.
2. Research current fashion trends by reading various sources such as WWD, DNR, Vogue, etc. and determine what you feel is a trend in the introductory phase of the fashion life cycle. Based on the criteria for each stage, try to predict how long it will take to move to the peak phase. Qualify your answers.
3. Research a product development department of a major corporation such as Target or Wal-Mart to learn how in-house labels are designed and produced.

chapter eight

industry standards and quality attributes

OBJECTIVES

>> Identify the sizing systems used in the apparel industry.

>> Understand the categories of sizes for consumers.

>> Understand the labeling regulations for apparel.

>> Describe attributes associated with determining quality of apparel.

>> Explain pricing lines in the apparel industry.

In order to make a correct assessment of the quality of apparel, the student must understand what the apparel industry requires in terms of labeling, sizing standards, and specific quality attributes.

Sizing

Sizing can be defined as the classification of the dimension of garments. In order to meet consumers needs, it is necessary to group apparel together in some logical system that consumers can easily identify and relate to their own physical apparel needs. Sizing makes purchases easier and faster. Sizes are grouped together based on gender, age, and/or body type.

There are two types of sizing being used in the industry.

>> Numbered sizing

This method uses two numbers for men's and one number for women's clothing. Men's clothing sizes are based on specific body measurements: waist, inseam, chest, and arm length. Women's clothing sizes are stated in numbers that correlate to a set of body measurements such as bust, waist, and hip. Each manufacturer determines how they will size their garments. There is very little consistency in the industry in terms of women's sizing.

>> Lettered sizing

Letters are used to designate sizes such as S/M/L/XL. This sizing method is common with low priced merchandise because it eliminates the need for precise measurements and lowers production costs and inventory requirements.

Major Sizing Systems

The three major sizing systems being used internationally are:

>> U.S. sizes

>> British sizes

>> European and Continental sizes

Issues in Sizing for Women's Apparel

What does a number size really mean? It's just a number, but it has so much power over the female consumer! It is understood that sizing of garments is the classification of dimensions and that sizes are grouped together based on gender, age, and/or body type to meet the needs of consumers. Size labels merely suggest to the consumer that the garment is suitable for their body dimensions. Sizes of garments vary widely, especially in women's garments (see Table 8.1).

TABLE 8.1 Size Conversions

Women's Suits, Dresses, and Coats

American	British	European
2	6	36
4	8	38
6	10	40
8	12	42
10	14	44
12	16	46
14	18	48

Men's Suits and Overcoats

American	British	European
36	36	46
38	38	48
40	40	51
42	42	54
44	44	56
46	46	59

Women's Shoes

American	British	European
6	4½	37½
6½	5	38
7	5½	39
7½	6	39½
8	6½	40
8½	7	40½

Men's Shoes

American	British	European
7½	7	40½
8	7½	41
8½	8	42
9½	9	43
10½	10	44½
11½	11	46

The first voluntary sizing standards for the apparel industry were published in the United States for men, women, and children in 1942 after a study was conducted by the National Bureau of Standards (now known as the National Institute of Standards and Technology).

These data were revised slightly in the 1970s to reflect height and weight changes in the population of America at that time. These revisions were withdrawn in 1983 and they have not been revised since that time. After 1983, sizing issues in the apparel industry have been turned over to American Society for Testing and Materials (ASTM) for review and updating.

Sizing in women's garments is problematic for many reasons. The lack of standardization creates dissatisfied customers, increases the likelihood of multiple markdowns on garments, and results in lower profits for retailers and manufacturers. Currently, each designer, retailer, or manufacturer has its own sizing system to match body dimensions to correlate to a specific number. For example, Coldwater Creek specifies that a size 12 has dimensions of 37.5 inches for bust, 29.5 inches for waist, and 40 inches for the hips. Some couture designers and better ready-to-wear companies use what is called **"vanity sizing,"** where the garments are cut larger to appeal to the vanity of consumers who like to think of themselves as smaller. Thus, a customer who tries on a size 8 dress and normally wears a size 10 or 12 is more likely to purchase the garment because of the smaller size designation (see Table 8.2).

A survey was conducted in 2003 by SizeUSA where more than 10,000 people were measured across the United States. They found that there was significant difference in the measurements of the average female compared to 60 years ago. In the 1940s, the average female wore a size 8. Currently, in America, the average female is size 14. Along with standardizing sizing for women, the apparel industry must now give some attention to the new dimensions of consumers in America.

TABLE 8.2 Comparison of Sizes				
Company	Size 6	Size 8	Size 10	Size 12
Isaac Mizrahi	38–27.5–39	39–28.5–40	40–29.5–41	41.5–31–42.5
J. Crew	34.5–26.5–37	35.5–27.5–38	36.5–28.5–39	38–30–40.5
Victoria's Secret	34.5–26–36.5	35.5–27–37.5	36.5–28–38.5	38–29.5–40
Spiegel	34.5–25.5–36.5	35.5–26.5–37.5	36.5–27.5–38.5	38–29–40

Categories of Sizes

Women

Women's Clothing includes dresses, blouses, pants, skirts, jackets, coats, and sportswear. The basic categories for women are:

>> Juniors

>> Misses

>> Petites

>> Plus-size

>> Plus-size Petite

>> Tall

Junior sizes are designed for shorter, slender, more youthful bodies that are still developing. These sizes are 1, 3, 5, 7, 9, 11, 13, 15, and 17. Sometimes, garments can be found in double ticket sizes such as 5/6 or 7/8 which means these items can fit as junior garments or missy garments. Sometimes the term missy is used interchangeably with misses. They both refer to the same body proportions.

Misses sizes are meant for adult females with average proportions, usually with a height of 5'7". These sizes start at size 0 and move up to size 20.

FIGURE 8.1 Women's fashion silhouettes

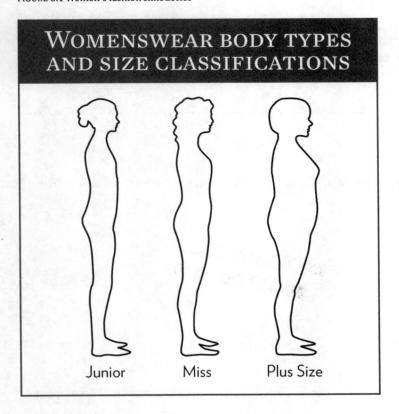

Petite sizes are designed for the shorter adult woman who is less than 5'4" in height. Garments usually have shorter sleeves, bodice length, and hemlines.

Plus-size garments are made for adult females who are average height of 5'7" but have larger body measurements. These sizes range from 14W to 30W. Plus-size Petite garments are made to the same specifications of plus-size garments but with shorter measurements that are very similar to the petite customer. Sizes range from 12WP to 24WP.

Tall sizes are made for the adult woman who is taller than 5'7". Garment measurements are slightly increased in leg length, hem length, sleeve length, and bodice length.

Menswear

This apparel is made for the adult male. Garments include pants, shirts, jackets, coats, and suits. Jacket and coat sizes are based on chest circumference and height. Sizes start at 38 chest and go up. Pant sizes are based on waist and inseam measurements. Waist sizes start at 32 and go up by 1-inch increments. Inseam measurements usually start at 28 inches and go up to 34 inches. For Big and Tall men's sizes, these measurements are higher. In order to differentiate in body build of men, sizes are coupled with descriptive terms: short, regular, long, slim, and portly or stout.

Men's shirts are sized based on neck circumference and sleeve lengths. An example is 15/34 which means the neck circumference is 15 inches and the sleeve length measurement is 34 inches. The sleeve length is measured by placing the tape measure in the center of the back and measuring the length from that point across the bent elbow to the wrist. Some inexpensive lines of men's dress shirts will combine the sizes to read 15/32-33 which prevents the retailer from having to stock a high quantity of inventory.

FIGURE 8.2 Menswear styles of collars, pockets, and vents

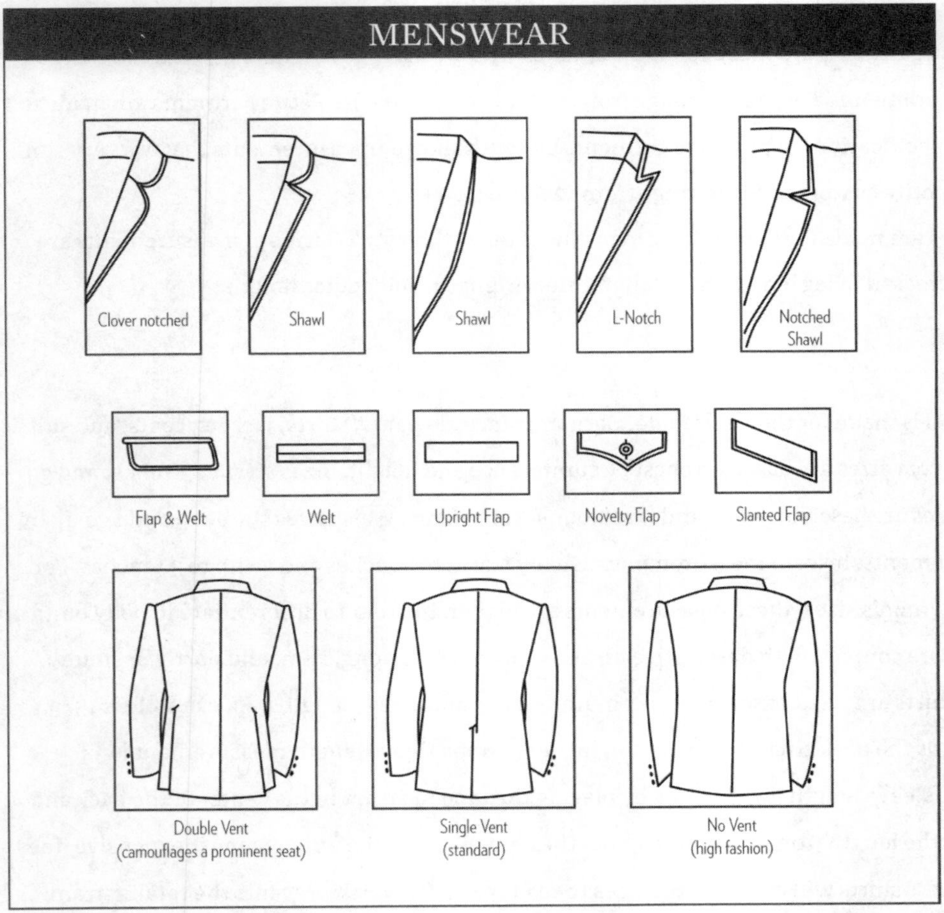

MENSWEAR

Clover notched

Shawl

Shawl

L-Notch

Notched Shawl

Flap & Welt

Welt

Upright Flap

Novelty Flap

Slanted Flap

Double Vent
(camouflages a prominent seat)

Single Vent
(standard)

No Vent
(high fashion)

Children's Clothing

Garment sizes for children are based on age and height and weight charts. Sizes are:

>> Infants—sizes are 0–3 months, 12–24 months

>> Toddlers—sizes are 2T to 4T

>> Children aged 3–6 years old are divided by gender.

>> Girls—4, 5, 6, 6X

>> Boys—4, 5, 6, 7

>> Pre-teen, Teens, and Young Juniors

   Girls—7, 8, 10, 12, 14 for girls ages 7 to 11 years

>> Prep, Student, and Teen

   Boys—8, 10, 12, 14, 16, 18, 20 for boys ages 7 to 17 years

Regulations on Apparel Labeling

There are major laws that affect apparel and textiles sold or manufactured in the United States. These laws are intended to regulate and standardize information for consumers on content, consistency, quality, and performance.

FIGURE 8.3 Examples of garment labels

Textile Fiber Products Identification Act

The Textile Fiber Products Identification Act was passed in 1960 in an effort to provide uniformity to the labeling of garments. This act stipulated specific requirements for garment labels. This is commonly referred to as the TFPIA and specifically requires information relating to the fiber content of textile products. This information must be contained on the labels conspicuously and be securely attached to the item for sale. This act refers to apparel and household textiles such as bedding, draperies, and more.

Regulations for apparel labels are administered by the Federal Trade Commission (FTC). The writing on the label may be woven into the label or printed on. The label can be attached in a variety of ways such as sewn, glued, and in some cases, manufacturers print the label onto the fabric of the garment. This is an increasing trend in garments that are washable, such as T-shirts. The labels must be permanently affixed to the garment with no risk of the label falling off.

The following items must appear on the labels:

>> Generic name of the fiber present in the fabric. Trade names of fibers can also be included but are not required. Foreign names of fibers are also permitted.

>> Percentage of fiber content by weight, listed vertically and in descending order by predominance. Any fiber that is less than five percent can be designated as "other fiber" unless it has a specific functional significance in the fiber, such as spandex for elasticity. If there are two or more fibers with less than five percent and have no functional significance, they must also be listed as other fibers.

>> Country of origin disclosure is required. This means that the country where the textile or apparel product is manufactured must be disclosed. For products made in the United States,

FIGURE 8.4 Label with trims identified

the manufacturer is responsible for insuring that this information is accurate. There are three categories of production in which apparel might fit:

- ≫ If the product is made entirely in the United States, using domestically manufactured materials, the label should read "Made in the U.S.A."
- ≫ If the product is made in the United States but composed of imported materials, the label must disclose this information. An example would be "Made in the U.S.A of imported fabric." It is not necessary to name the foreign country.
- ≫ If the product is partially made in the United States and partially made in another country, the label should show the manufacturing process performed in relevant countries. For example, "Assembled in Mexico of U.S. components."

As these rules relate to apparel, if the garments are sewn and assembled into finished apparel in one country from parts cut in another country, the country of origin is considered the country where the garments are sewn and assembled. In the case of knitted apparel, the country that produces the knit parts is considered the country of origin.

The Federal Trade Commission assigns the manufacturer's registered identification number known as the RN (registered number) or the manufacturer's name. What is commonly found is the RN rather than the manufacturer's name in the label. In some instances, a CA number is also shown on the label. This number refers to the Canadian manufacturer's number assigned to a specific manufacturer. In Canada, labels must contain a CA number, a 5-digit number to identify the textile products dealer.

When garments are composed of two or more components such as a lining, outer shell, or trim, the fiber content of each of these must also be identified separately. The manufacturer must list fiber content in the garment trim such as lace, ribbons, and so forth, and ornamentation such as embroidery.

The Wool Products Labeling Act of 1939 has been amended many times since its passage and is enforced by the Federal Trade Commission. It provides for mandatory fiber content labeling by percentages of all fibers present in products containing wool, reprocessed wool, or reused wool fibers in any amount. Its purpose is also to prevent false or misleading labels on woolen products.

Wool is defined as the fiber from the fleece of sheep or lamb or hair of the Angora or Cashmere goat. These fibers have never been manufactured or used and are called **new wool** or virgin wool.

Reprocessed wool, or recycled wool, is the resulting fiber when wool has been woven, or felted into a wool product, and has not been used by the consumer, and is now being converted back to a fibrous state.

Reused wool is the resulting fiber when wool or reprocessed wool has been spun, woven, knit, or felted into a wool product and has been used by the consumer and is now being converted back to a fibrous state.

FIGURE 8.5 Wool product labels

Flammable Fabrics Act

The Flammable Fabrics Act was passed in 1953 and has been amended several times. This act prohibits marketing of materials that are so highly flammable as to be dangerous when worn by the consumer. The purpose was to classify fibers according to how fast they burn under controlled testing conditions. All wearing apparel, regardless of material, falls under this umbrella. The Consumer Product Safety Commission administers this regulation and establishes the standards that garments must meet in testing for safety. The Flammable Fabrics Act requires a formal certification, known as a guarantee, which states that a fabric has met the minimum requirements under the corresponding Federal code for safety. While all garments are regulated, special attention is given to infants and children's sleepwear where safety issues are of greater concern.

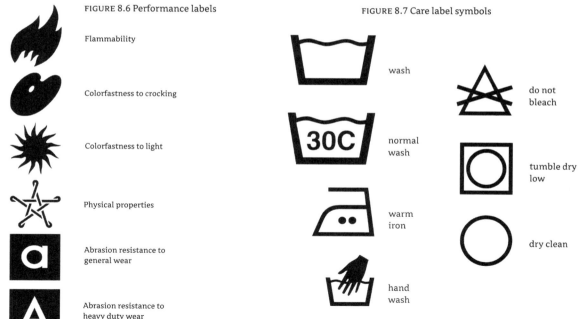

FIGURE 8.6 Performance labels

Flammability

Colorfastness to crocking

Colorfastness to light

Physical properties

Abrasion resistance to general wear

Abrasion resistance to heavy duty wear

FIGURE 8.7 Care label symbols

wash

30C — normal wash

warm iron

hand wash

do not bleach

tumble dry low

dry clean

Care Labeling of Apparel

Generally referred to as the Care Labeling Rule, this regulation, in effect since 1972, requires that care labels be affixed to most textile products (especially apparel) that are used to cover or protect the body. It also includes home textile products and applies to domestic and imported goods. The law is administered by the Federal Trade Commission and is intended to protect the consumer by educating them on how to safely clean and maintain the products that they purchase. It is the manufacturer's responsibility to provide the care label. There are steep fines for noncompliance.

The instructions must contain regular care guidelines for the ordinary use of the product. It is required that it be attached to the garment so that it does not come off unless removed by the consumer. The instructions must be clear and remain legible during the life of the garment. This rule provides that only one care method be provided in the garment. In order to meet the expanding global consumer base, universal symbols are now being consistently used in the care labels of garments. These symbols were developed in 1996 by the American Society for Testing and Materials (ASTM) and while they are not recognized internationally, their standard use makes it easier for consumers to understand without using various languages. There are five basic symbols (see Figure 8.7):

>> Wash
>> Bleach
>> Dry
>> Iron
>> Dry Clean

Many retailers and manufacturers include other information on the labels of garments that they sell in an effort to brand their product and promote customer loyalty. This information is entirely voluntary and is not consistent throughout the apparel industry.

Some of this voluntary information is:

>> Trademark—a name, word, or symbol used to identify and distinguish a company's products from another.

>> Brand—can also be called a name brand or national brand such as Evan-Picone or Levi.

>> Private Label—this is the retailer's private name for the line of clothing.

>> Licensing—some companies will license their names or trademarks to be used on other products. This may be denoted by a logo, trademark, or name such as Disney on children's apparel. A royalty fee is paid to the company for the use of the license.

>> Sizing—while not governed by law, manufacturers almost always indicate garment size on labels. Sometimes, the size is included on the fiber content label. Other companies attach separate labels in the side seams of the garment.

Quality Attributes

A very broad definition of **quality of apparel** is whether or not the garment meets the expectations of the consumer. Quality can be very subjective and is different for each consumer/product combination. To some people, quality is richness or refinement. To others, quality means high price, certain labels or brands, durability, or beauty. Each consumer has general and specific requirements in terms of what he/she perceives a quality garment to be. This section will examine some features associated with determining the quality of apparel:

>> physical features of apparel

>> performance features of apparel

>> price

>> perceived quality model

Physical Features

Physical features encompass the design and style of the garment. An example would be a dress with a full, gathered skirt, long sleeves, and V-neckline. The design is not subject to change in regard to this specific description.

The materials used in the garment are another factor. Consider the fabric, notions, trim and other components as part of the materials. Another physical feature is the construction technique used in the garment. Finally, the finish of the garment is also part of its physical features.

All of the items discussed above are part of the tangible form of the garment and contribute to its intrinsic attributes. Intrinsic in this context means features are not subject to change or alteration. Intrinsic qualities are created during the design process and production.

Performance Features

Performance features relate to how the garment benefits the consumer based on its function. Many properties, such as, how it feels on the wearer, thermal comfort, fit, and durability are considered by the consumer. The consumer considers if the garment performs the way it is expected to perform for the specific function for which it was purchased.

Unlike intrinsic qualities, which emerge during the production process and are not subject to alteration or change, extrinsic qualities originate outside the garment and are not inherent parts of the garment. Examples are price, brand name, visual merchandising, or advertising campaigns.

FIGURE 8.8 Example of a trademark

FIGURE 8.9 Customers shopping for apparel

Pricing

The price assigned to garments is another indicator of quality. Thus, pricing is considered an extrinsic quality because it can be altered or changed by the retailer without changing the garment. Besides the color of a garment, most consumers pay close attention to the price of the garment. Price plays a major role in the decision to purchase and also serves as a quality indicator in the mind of the consumer. If a garment has a high price, it is assumed that it is better quality than if the price is lower. Most consumers believe that there is a positive relationship between price and quality (Brown, 2001).

Ready-to-wear is grouped according to price. These groupings are called price lines and represent merchandise at various price levels, from most expensive to least expensive. The most common groups of prices in the ready-to-wear apparel industry are better, bridge, moderate, and budget pricing. Brand names are usually found in these price lines that are referred to as *prêt-a-porter* (a French term). Designer clothing is sold as haute couture by their own firms and design houses. Many high fashion designers are now also making clothing lines that appeal to the mass market and are selling these lines in department and specialty stores.

>> Better represents the highest price line carried in the store. The consumer associates this level of high pricing with high quality garments. This area is usually separated in the store.

>> Bridge merchandise falls in between better and moderate price lines. Its goal is to trade down and possibly trade up for consumers shopping for apparel. This bridge line can also be located between better merchandise and designer merchandise.

>> Moderate price lines are average prices; neither too high nor too low. These price points are associated with average quality of garments, as well.

>> Budget prices are the lowest prices. Consumers associate low quality with these price points but are still willing to make these purchases because the financial investment is low. Some companies refer to budget prices as value-pricing or every day low prices to entice the customer.

Perceived Quality Model

Perceived quality is the combination of intrinsic and extrinsic qualities. Research has been conducted on how consumers make decisions about purchases and how they reach these decisions based on perceptions and expectations for quality. Aesthetic and functional standards are formed in the mind of the consumer once it has been decided to initiate making a purchase. These processes are probably subconscious and are influenced by the information that the consumer has about the product. The Perceived Quality Model was proposed by I. Ajzen and J. Fishbein (Ajzen, et al, 1980) and sought to explain how consumers evaluate the quality of a garment.

This model attempts to quantify the process of evaluating perceived quality in a garment and takes place at the point of sale, while the garments are in use, or when the garment is being discarded. The model shows that no two purchases are alike and demonstrates that every consumer evaluates garments differently. Table 8.3 shows a comparison of two consumers, A and B, evaluating the same T-shirt using the perceived quality model.

The following steps are recommended to evaluate a garment using this model:

1. Select the features of the garment that you are evaluating that would make you conclude that it is high quality.
2. Assign a weight to each one of the selected features in terms of importance in determining quality.

FIGURE 8.10 Perceived quality model

$$Q = \sum_{f=1}^{n} w_f\, r_f$$

Overall quality score = Sum of (weight of each feature x rating of each feature)

Q = overall quality score; a number ranging from 0 to 100 representing a consumer's evaluation of a garment's quality, with 100 as maximum quality and 0 as absence of quality

Σ = sum

n = number of features used in the evaluation; varies depending on consumer and garment

f = feature used in evaluation a garment's quality; the features used depend on the consumer and the garment

w = weight; a percentage ranging from 0 to 100 representing the contribution or importance of the feature to the overall quality evaluation, wtih the weights of all features totaling 100%

r = rating; a number ranging from 0 to 100 representing how well the garment performs on that feature, with 100 asmaximum performance and 0 as absence of performance

TABLE 8.3 Comparison of Two Consumers' Evaluations of a T-Shirt using the Perceived Quality Model

Consumer A's Perceived Quality Evaluation:

Feature	Weight (Importance)		Rating		Contribution to Quality
Brand name	10%	X	70	=	7
Color	10%	X	60	=	6
Comfort	5%	X	20	=	1
Country of origin	2.5%	X	70	=	3.5
Durability	2.5%	X	10	=	.25
Ease of care	2.5%	X	10	=	.25
Fabric	5%	X	40	=	2
Fit	10%	X	60	=	6
General appearance	20%	X	60	=	12
Shrinkage	5%	X	60	=	3
Style/fashion	15%	X	80	=	12
Price	10%	X	50	=	5
Total	100%	X		=	58
					Overall Quality Score

Consumer B's Perceived Quality Evaluation:

Feature	Weight (Importance)		Rating		Contribution to Quality
Color	30%	X	70	=	35
Fit	10%	X	90	=	9
General appearance	15%	X	60	=	9
Style/fashion	25%	X	80	=	20
Price	20%	X	80	=	16
Total	100%	X		=	75
					Overall Quality Score

3. Rate the garment by observing how well it meets each feature.

4. Multiply the weight of each feature by the rating assigned to it.

5. Add the contribution of all features to get the overall quality score for the garment. There are no right or wrong answers. This calculation allows the consumer to quantify their expectations of quality and determine if garments score above or below average. For example, in the table, a score of 70 is average. If Consumer A has a T-shirt with a score of 58, then the score is unacceptable and the garment is not accepted as good quality. Consumer B has a T-shirt with an overall score of 75 (which is higher than the average) and is accepted as good quality.

Key Terms

New wool	Quality of apparel	Reprocessed wool
Reused wool	Sizing	Vanity sizing

Ideas for Discussion and Application

1. Why is lettered sizing more common in low cost apparel?

2. Why do you think the apparel industry has been reluctant to standardize sizing in garments for women?

3. What impact, if any, did the TFPIA have on consumer purchasing decisions?

4. What is the difference between a CA number and an RN number? Are they both required to be shown?

5. Why was the Flammable Fabrics Act passed?

6. List the five basic care instructions and illustrate the symbols for each one.

7. Explain the difference between physical features and performance features of a garment.

chapter nine

shoes and handbags

OBJECTIVES

>> *Identify the different components of shoes and how they are constructed.*

>> *Compare shoe designs of the past to modern trends.*

>> *Understand how handbags developed through time.*

It is believed that most women in the United States own an average of 30 pairs of shoes. **Shoes** are often used to reflect the wearer's status and economic position. The higher the price of her accessories, the more one is perceived as being wealthy or fashionable. Shoes reflect social history and record special times in our lives.

As shoes and handbags have developed during the twentieth century, the impulse to buy these items has nothing to do with need, but more to do with being in step with the latest fashion trends. Practicality and comfort issues have become secondary considerations for shoe and handbag consumers. This chapter provides a brief overview of how the shoe and the handbag developed and discusses the construction process of shoes and their classifications by silhouette.

History of the Shoe

Early shoes were developed from necessity as man sought protection for the feet through the use of leaves, grass, or bark tied under and around the foot with vines. This makeshift shoe evolved into the sandal in warmer climates. Animal skins were also utilized, especially in cold climates for protection and keeping the feet warm.

FIGURE 9.1A AND B Ancient sandals

FIGURE 9.2 Elaborate Elizabethan shoes

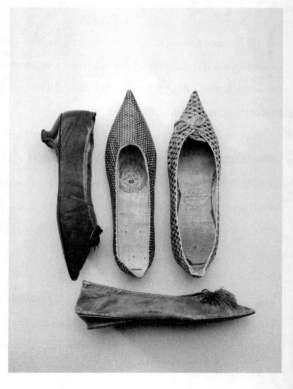

Shoes continued to develop during the Roman Empire as the Romans produced a variety of footwear. The military sandal was called the caliga and exposed the toes with a lattice front lacing and a heavy nailed sole. During the Middle Ages, shoes continued to change. The sole and upper were stitched together with thread and the toe became a sharp point, known as scorpion tails. The points on this shoe got longer and became known as pikes, crackowes, or poulaines. The length of the toes on the shoes was an indication of status. The rulers and other royalty had the longest toes on their shoes.

This style was not worn by women. The pointed toe disappeared by the end of the Middle Ages and was replaced by round or square toe shapes. Once again, the toes started to get bigger and bigger. Another popular style was a low-cut shoe with a strap and buckle across the ankle with a square toe. Shoes continued to move back and forth between pointed toes and round toes. Around the late 1500s, heels on shoes started to emerge. By the end of the reign of Queen Elizabeth I, heels on shoes were between two and three inches high. All shoes were made as straights (no left or right foot).

By the seventeenth century, men were wearing shoes and mules (slip on shoes without a back) with square toes. Women had decided that the pointed toe was more feminine. Buckles on shoes became very popular for both men and women's shoes. Women's shoes began to reflect the elaborate pattern found in their dresses by the eighteenth century. Shoes were trimmed with metallic braid, embroidery, ribbons, and intricate designs. On the other hand, men's shoes became plain and were made of black leather with pointed toes and low heels. Shoes for women continued to change. Heels became lower and the cut of the shoe was lower.

Eventually, toward the beginning of the nineteenth century, heels disappeared totally and shoes became very dainty without much structure. Boots were worn by men and women during this era. Boots were made from leather and cloth.

FIGURE 9.3 Men's boots

FIGURE 9.4 Diagram of shoe parts

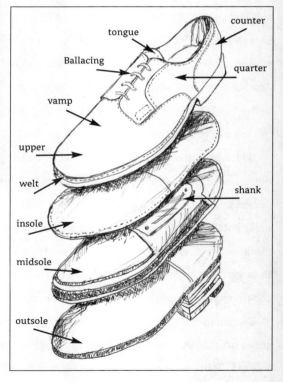

Women also wore court shoes made from a variety of materials such as satin, leather, and reptile skin. Men commonly wore the oxford shoe, which can be described as a low cut shoe with front lacing and a closed toe.

The twentieth century brought lots of variety to the shoe silhouette and designers of shoes became more prevalent. Some examples of styles that have emerged are stiletto heels, platform shoes, utility shoes, athletic shoes, and two-color shoes.

Anatomy of a Shoe

It is important that professionals in the fashion retailing industry understand how shoes are constructed in order to make solid decisions about quality, either for personal use or for the company for which they are selecting product. There are several parts that compose a shoe:

The toe box is the tip of the shoe that provides space for the toes. This portion may be rounded, pointed, or square.

The vamp is the upper middle portion of the shoe, where the laces are commonly placed.

The sole consists of an insole and outsole. The insole is inside the shoe where the foot rests; the outsole is the bottom of the shoe that contacts the ground and helps give the shoe traction. If the sole is soft, the shoe is able to absorb more shock.

The heel of the shoe is the bottom part of the shoe that provides elevation. The higher the heel, the greater the pressure is on the front of the foot. Shoes come in various heel heights.

The part of the shoe that curves in near the arch of the foot is made to conform to the shape of the foot.

The upper is the leather or synthetic part of the shoe that encases the foot. Sometimes a counter may be inserted to stiffen the upper material around the heel and give more support to the foot. A counter is an additional piece of leather or synthetic material.

Shoe Construction

There are more than 100 operations that go into the construction of a shoe. The first and most important step is to create the **last**, a hand-carved wood or molded plastic replica of the human foot. A different last is required for each shoe style. The last is a foot model with dimensions and shape based on the anatomy of the foot. Before mass production of shoes started, shoemakers started the process by taking a footprint outline of the customer's foot. The last was made from wood by whittling the shape from the print. Now, lasts are made from metal or plastic as well as wood. Lastmaking demands great skill and a trained eye for fashion. The modern last is made in three dimensions even though it is not an exact replica of the foot. This process uses more than 35 measurements of the foot in order to construct well-fitting shoes. The important fact to know about lasts is that they do not reflect the exact measurements of the shoe but have some variations that are influenced by the shape and style of the shoe. The shoe is expected to wear well, feel good, keep its shape, and retain its style while allowing for freedom of movement.

The manufacturing of shoes is still labor intensive even with the introduction of technological advances in materials and machinery. The first stage in construction is always to attach the insole to the undersurface of the last. This is done first, no matter what type of construction is being used. Two other operations follow: **Lasting** and Bottoming. Lasting involves shaping the upper sections to the last and insole. In **bottoming**, the sole is attached to the upper. The bottoming process determines the quality, price, and performance of the shoe.

Shoe Classifications and Sizing

There are eight basic styles of shoes: boot, clog, lace-up (Oxford shoe and Derby style), moccasin, mule, sandal, monks, and pumps.

FIGURE 9.5A AND B Shoe lasts

FIGURE 9.6 Basic shoe styles

A Boot is described as any footwear that extends above the ankle.

The clog is a thick-soled wooden shoe that sometimes has a leather upper.

Lace-up shoes have two variations: Oxford shoe and the Derby style. Both of these are fastened by lacings up the front and are low cut.

Moccasins originated from the Algonquin (North American Indian tribe) language and means foot covering. The loafer is a variation of this style.

A mule is a backless shoe or slipper with or without a heel.

A sandal was originally a piece of leather used as a sole and attached to the foot by thongs. Today the sandal has many variations with decorative touches and comes with or without heels. The sandal was actually the first constructed footwear and was made out of necessity to protect the feet and keep them dry and warm depending on the climate of the wearer. Each culture had its own version of the sandal. "Through the ages, sandals have been alternately symbols of prestige or poverty, of chastity or coquetry" (O'Keefe, 1996). During the 1920s, the sandal made a comeback after having been out of style for almost 1,000 years. Sandals became flat and earthy with the arrival of the Birkenstock in the 60s and high heels were added in the 70s.

Monks are similar to Derby shoes style, but with a cross-over section to fasten the shoe with a side buckle.

Pumps are heeled shoes with low-cut fronts and usually have no fastenings. Pumps are always in style. They can be sensible, practical, classic, elegant, yet whimsical, fun, and colorful. Originating in 1553, this silhouette was called poumpe, pompe, or pumpe which is said to be derived from the sound the shoe made when it hit a polished floor. These were practical shoes and were designed as a variation of men's footwear. We will discuss high heels in this section even though heels are now added to sandals, boots, and mules. High heels are peculiar in that they present a paradox. They can make a woman appear taller and more powerful and at the same time, make her appear less powerful and more vulnerable. High heels certainly cause pain and fallen arches but the wearer feels attractive and feminine.

The first recorded wearer of high heels is said to be Catherine de Medici in 1533, who wore them to appear taller. The height of high heels goes up and down based on the whims of fashion and the designers who sell them. The stiletto heel, which is five or more inches high, came into popularity in the 1950s.

Sizing

Shoe sizing systems based on standard measurements have been around for about 100 years, but shoes made in half sizes have been in existence for only about 50 years. For many years, there was no shoe sizing standard for crafting shoes and shoemakers used their own bodies as models for approximating sizes of shoes. The problem with this was that every human is different and nothing was made uniform by using this method. There are currently three sizing systems in use for footwear: They are the American, Continental, and the United Kingdom systems.

FIGURE 9.7 The popular stiletto heel for women

FIGURE 9.8A AND B The classic Roman sandal as imagined in 1934 and again by Balenciaga in 2008.

Handbags

A handbag, commonly referred to as a purse, is defined as a bag held in the hand or hung on the shoulder for carrying valuables and other personal articles. Today, handbags are not only beautiful, but also functional and are designed to help modern women carry and organize the multitude of items necessary for meeting the lifestyle needs of the busy consumer.

History of the Handbag

The ways in which people have carried themselves and their belongings throughout history have reflected the eras in which they lived. In a 1997 article from the National Fashion Accessories Association, the following information is given about the history of handbags.

The earliest historically verifiable handbags—little sacks containing pomanders (scented oranges), flint and money—were carried by gentlemen and known as 'pockets'. By the 1400s, both men and women were wearing purses, and as times prospered and the little sacks got fuller, they were ornamented with gold or elaborate embroidery . . .

By the 1500s, these bags became a status symbol and were in the form of drawstring purses. Fashions changed and women started carrying these bags under their skirts. In 1670, breeches were made with built-in pockets. These were so popular that men stopped carrying their handbags . . .

In the 18th century, pouches for men and women disappeared. After the French Revolution, however, the style of women's clothes was so delicate that it was impossible for them to contain a pocket. Out into the open came the handbag, then known as a reticule (and occasionally a "ridicule" by men whose idea that was of a good joke).

FIGURE 9.9 Ancient handbag

FIGURE 9.10 Embroidered pouch

Skirts became wider and pockets were again made popular. By the 1880s, dresses became tighter and closer to the body, but carrying handbags was slow to return as a dressing trend. Around the turn of the century, with the creation of the hobble skirt, handbags made a definite impact on fashion. Pockets were impossible for the tight-fitting hobble skirt, and very large handbags with long strings or chains became popular. Handbags were tiny and intricately designed with beading and embroidery.

In the 1920s, the handbag became a mainstay for fashion and has remained so through the years. By the 1930s, the clutch handbag silhouette was designed. Between the 1940s and 1950s, handbags were made by various materials and were extravagantly designed. Silks and genuine reptile skins were used during the 1960s and vivid colors were added during the 1970s. In the 1980s, Hermes introduced the "Birkin" bag after celebrity Jane Birkin spoke to the marketing director of Hermes complaining that one of the bags was difficult to open. Consequently, the "Birkin" bag was developed with a wider opening and remains a status symbol today. Handbags are utilitarian as well as decorative and reflect the wearer's personal style.

Twentieth-century technology has allowed manufacturers to produce various textures and materials of handbags. Handbags can be classified by their end use and/or shapes.

There are many popular shapes of handbags:

>> Backpack is a sack that is carried between the shoulders, worn across the back or can be slung on either shoulder.

>> Barrel is a horizontal cylinder shape with a zip top closure, usually on a small scale.

>> Bucket is a stiff shoulder bag basically shaped like a bucket with a wide top opening. The bottom is either round or oval-shaped.

>> Camera is a rectangular-shaped bag with rounded corners. It has a zip top closure and some-times has outside pockets. This bag resembles the shape of cases used in carrying older cameras.

FIGURE 9.11 Basic handbag styles

FIGURE 9.12 (left) A clutch bag

FIGURE 9.13 (right) A Birkin bag

>> Clutch is a small bag with no handles or straps and is carried tucked under the arm or carried in the hand. These styles often have detachable shoulder straps.

>> Double handle is a bag that has double handles, usually worn on the shoulders, and comes in many sizes.

>> Drawstring is a bag that has a cord woven through the opening to gather the top for closing.

>> Facile is a bag that has a covered frame that snaps together as the closure.

>> Flap is a bag with a closure that flaps over. This is usually one piece with the handbag.

>> Frame has a metal top fastening with a snap, knob, or clasp closure.

>> Hobo has a crescent shape and is worn on the shoulder with a zip top closure. This bag is soft and flexible in shape and the bag dips in the center.

>> Luggage Frame resembles the shape and structure of luggage and has a metal frame with a top fastener.

>> Luggage Handle bag has handles that are covered with the handbag material with a hard structure. The handles are cut out of the bag.

>> Satchel is a square or dome-shaped bag with a zip top closure. It has a wide, flat bottom and a gusset. This is a short-handled handbag and is commonly carried over the crook of the elbow. Variations of this bag have slightly longer handles that can be tucked over the shoulder and carried under the armpit.

>> Shoulder handbag has long straps or chains, which enable the wearer to hang the bag from the shoulders or across the body.

>> Tote is a medium to large bag with a wide opening and two handles.

>> Trapezoid is a bag with an A-line shape that is inverted.

>> Wireframe is a zip top bag with wire piping running along the top to hold the framed shape.

Key Terms

Bottoming   Last   Lasting   Shoe

Ideas for Discussion and Application

1. Why is it important to have knowledge about shoes and handbags in the apparel industry?

2. Review current shoe trends and compare them to historical trends. Pick one style and try to determine what period in history your chosen silhouette was copied from.

3. Discuss why you think shoe design has been elevated to an art in current fashion trends.

4. Discuss the evolution of handbags from functionality to status symbol.

5. Review current handbag trends and attempt to predict the trend for next season (color, shape, texture).

6. Why do you think the Chanel quilted handbag has remained a classic?

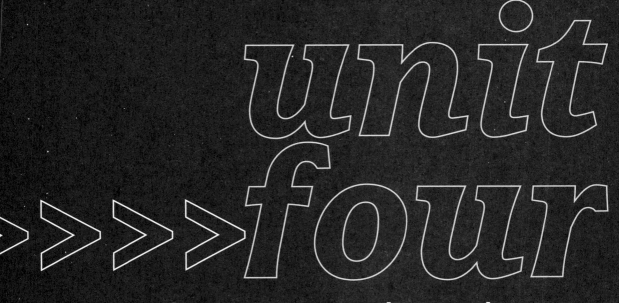

unit four

coordination and marketing

chapter ten

creating a coordinated image: corporate and personal strategies

OBJECTIVES

>> Discuss the elements that contribute to corporate image.

>> Recognize the use of product design and selection; advertising, promotion, and communication; store design and visual merchandising; customer service; branding and product positioning; and perception as contributors to the image of apparel products and services currently on the market.

>> Discuss the elements that contribute to personal image.

>> Recognize the application of self-concept, self-image and the role of communication in the personal image of peers and other consumers.

Creation of a coordinated apparel image occurs at two levels. First, manufacturers and retailers of apparel products construct images to effectively match the needs of consumers and lure them to purchase products. Hence, corporate image refers to the image held by consumers of the specific providers of apparel goods. Second, consumers create apparel-based images for themselves by using apparel and accessory products to match or enhance their personal self-concept or lifestyle.

FIGURE 10.1 Corporate image is carefully constructed to lure consumers to purchase products.

FIGURE 10.2 Ads are powerful tools to create corporate image.

Corporate Image

In much the same way that individuals have characteristics and personalities, it is important for each apparel manufacturer and retailer to develop and present a clear personality and character to potential consumers. In an era of intense competition for apparel dollars and loyalties, retailers and manufacturers seek diligently to identify the needs and wants of their target consumers and then develop an easily identifiable image to entice the identified target consumers to buy. Careful market research, target market selection, and application of effective marketing strategies are imperative. (These are described more fully in Chapter 13.)

In reality, while a corporation may desire to have a specific image, company image is actually created within the mind of the consumer. Image is based on the perceptions of that company held by individual consumers. Collectively and individually, those perceptions form the image of a company. To create favorable perceptions that lead to specific images, companies employ tools such as (1) product design and selection, (2) advertising, promotion, and communication, (3) store design and visual merchandising, and (4) customer service.

Product Design and Selection

Product design and selection forms the foundation for image creation. Knowing the needs and expectations of the consumer with regard to attributes, such as style and quality, are imperative. Having the right merchandise is critical. This can best be achieved by understanding consumer demographics; expectations regarding position within the fashion adoption cycle (innovations, early adopters, mass market, and laggards); and perspectives on the tradeoffs between quality and price. For example, in lingerie, product designs and assortments offered by Victoria's Secret and Wal-Mart contrast sharply based on the retailers' understanding of consumer demographics, adoption cycle position, and expectations regarding price and quality.

FIGURE 10.3A AND B Store design and visual merchandising aid in image creation.

Previous chapters have outlined the processes involved in the design, fabrication, and manufacture of apparel goods. In addition to these specific production steps, consideration of product design and selection also include understanding the foundational elements that underlie the bringing of product innovations to market. These concepts apply in relative amounts to individual fashion articles, which include new or innovative design concepts, new lines of clothing or accessories, creation of an e-tailing website, or entire manufacturing or retailing enterprises.

New ideas or product concepts can be the result of either **market pull** or **market push** conditions. For apparel, market pull is the primary force. Market pull means that a concept emerges to meet a need in the market place. The gradual need for change and consumers' desire for new fashions create a pull situation for apparel producers.

Designers create to meet demand. An example might be consumers' desire for light, flexible, absorbent, and breathable workout attire that "pulls" the creation of specific types of active wear.

Under market push conditions, the apparel industry pushes innovation or change onto the consumer. In its most striking form, developments in textile science or advances in technology push innovation toward consumers. New textile fibers, as they become available commercially, offer new fabric options with new properties. To some extent, the recent growth in e-tailing may have originated as a push condition for consumers. Early evidence seemed to show that consumers were not initially ready to buy online. However, over time, conditions changed and e-tailing options currently operate as both push and pull market participants.

Whether initiated either by push or pull market conditions, apparel innovations can be either evolutionary or revolutionary in nature. By far, most new clothing and accessory products and services are evolutionary. Subtle changes proceed smoothly from season to season and year to year. Often, items from one season bridge easily to the next and, in the case of classics, apparel items can be fashionably worn for years.

Revolutionary change in fashion is less common. While it may seem that runway fashions are starkly different from those seen previously, it is more likely that they are predicated on an earlier season of success. Evolutionary change makes it easier for the consumer to adopt the new product. It's easier to coordinate the new item with existing wardrobe pieces. New designers, manufacturers, or retailers most likely build their concepts on observations of the success of others. Only occasionally does truly revolutionary change occur in the apparel industry. A brave new idea or technology may find either success or failure.

The advent of paper clothing in the 1970s provides perhaps a humorous example of a nearly revolutionary innovation that didn't seem to be successful. While new non-woven fabric technology led to more durable paper fabrics, consumers were unsatisfied with cost, performance, and durability. As apparel providers strategically plan the image they create through the products and services offered, they carefully evaluate the dynamics of push versus pull market conditions and the evolutionary versus revolutionary nature of the product innovations they offer.

One step in determining whether products or services will create the corporate image desired is testing an idea or concept through a feasibility study. Preliminary questions would be: Does the product or service meet a real need? and Are there conditions under which proceeding would be wise or unwise? The primary steps of a feasibility study can include industry assessment, market and customer assessment, product or service assessment, team assessment, and financial assessment. The industry assessment stage considers who the major players in the industry are and whether they are competitors or whether collaborative linkages could be developed.

Next, it looks at the demographics of those potentially involved and the status of the technology.

Additionally, patterns of change within the industry are examined. The market and customer assessment stage identifies target market demographics and customer profiles to determine demand factors. It also investigates potential competitors and weighs the competitive advantages of the new product or service. The new concept may be unique in features, quality, benefits, technology, marketing channel, financial aspects, or the people it targets. The product or service assessment stage looks carefully at features and benefits, status of current products that are similar, licensing or legal requirements, plans for testing and creating samples or prototypes, tasks and timeline requirements, and future products or services that may spin off from the concept.

The team assessment stage considers the team of personnel available to bring the idea to fruition. Current skills, experience, and expertise are considered. Gaps are identified and sources for additional assistance are identified and weighed. Finally, the financial stage evaluates financial background, potential costs and revenues, availability of cash and capital, and price and margin expectations (Allen, 2003).

Creating an appropriate, consistent, and successful corporate image for new and existing products in the dynamic, even dramatic, fashion industry presents special challenges. The market and the culture move rapidly and innovations are expected. To be competitive new products need to be developed and ready for sale quickly with controlled costs.

Allen (2003) recommends action steps: First, put customer knowledge at the core of everything. Talk to the customer during the concept, design, prototype, production, and introduction stages. This can result in giving the customer exactly what they want, avoiding costly redesign processes, building lifelong customer relationships, and achieving competitive advantage.

Second, design right the first time. Whether the design is a concept store or a garment there is an advantage in communicating with all levels of production and management and in creating prototypes early in the process. This results in cost savings by not having to redesign, and a faster time to market which is more likely to meet customer needs and create financial gains. Prototyping and communicating early also allows for a check on whether the image being created is the desired image.

Third, focus on core competencies. Focusing efforts and resources on what is done best and building alliances to gain the benefits of the core competencies of others is wise.

Fourth, think virtual. Forming alliances, or outsourcing, enables taking advantage of the core competencies of others and keeps overhead costs down. As a result, shared resources spread the risk, increase the ability to innovate, and reduce time to market.

Fifth, prepare financially. By having a financial plan at the early stages of product development, the focus can be on product development, rather than on resource development.

Whether a new product involves incremental changes, as in the case of evolutionary innovation, or a breakthrough change, as in the case of revolutionary innovation, the image of the new venture needs careful consideration—not only in terms of product development, but also in terms of achieving customer-oriented growth. Communication with customers must be two-way, especially during the product development stages. Product developers must know how to identify their best customers, what those customers value, and how to provide it.

Special consideration is required for global product ventures. Products, and the image created for them, must meet the needs of the global locality. Business practices such as infrastructure; availability of supplies; currency; competition; and legal, tax, and labor laws are important.

However, a good match to the culture, communication channels, and characteristics of the target market are critical.

Even the business plan prepared in contemplation of a new idea, especially for new stores, lines, or websites, rather than individual garments, requires attention to corporate image. Each component of the plan needs to create or reinforce the desired image. Typically, business plans include a short executive summary; a description of the concept including the product, customer benefit, distribution, and business model; the qualifications of the management team; an industry and market profile including demographics, trends, and customer profile; a management and organization plan; an operations plan; and a marketing plan. Hence, efforts to create a positive and sustainable image permeate all aspects of the business.

Advertising, Promotion, and Communication

An integrated marketing communication program enables apparel providers to deliver a consistent message to current and potential consumers. A coordinated approach means that all messages sent to the consumer are unified in their approach and thereby create a single, solid image for the company. Multiple media, such as print, television, and radio advertising; in-store and community sales promotions; websites; and personal selling can be part of this effort but all messages, while not identical, should be uniform in keeping with the desired image. Such image development is designed to capture the spirit of the brand or retailer on an emotional or psychological level and create an identity that transcends individual seasons.

When accomplished effectively and consistently, consumers can identify the brand even when words are not present. The advertising and promotion creates a clear and identifiable message. Even when flipping quickly through a magazine, driving rapidly past a billboard, or

FIGURE 10.4 Consistent advertising messages in multiple media reinforce corporate images.

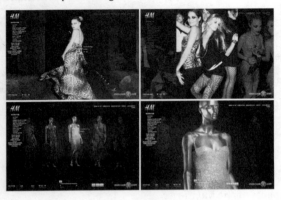

hearing part of a radio or television advertisement, the message is so consistent that it is easily perceived by the consumer who is exposed to it.

The combination of tools used to communicate with prospective buyers, whether at the wholesale or retail levels, is often called the **communication mix**. Regardless of which tools or techniques are used, the goal must be to create a unified image for the item, brand, or company. Each method of projecting or communicating image has unique characteristics that make it an appropriate tool in specific circumstances. In general, elements of the communication mix can be categorized as paid or unpaid, and as personal or impersonal.

Paid, personal methods of influencing image include personal selling; telephone, mail, and e-mail contacts directly to consumers; and public relations. At both retail and wholesale levels personal selling involves individual contact between a seller and a potential buyer. Image is conveyed

Communication Mix Elements for Creating Corporate Image

	Personal	**Impersonal**
Paid	personal selling e-mail personal contacts public relations	advertising sales promotion website store design visual merchandising public relations
Unpaid	publicity	word of mouth Electronic "word of mouth"

one-on-one. Attributes of the seller are highly influential. These can include personal characteristics, including dress, grooming, and mannerisms; product knowledge; presentation style; credibility; and general trust and likeability. Telephone, mail, and e-mail contacts are also means to communicate image to buyers. Tone, clarity, credibility, information, and convenience influence their effectiveness. Public relations includes any activities designed to influence image in the public's eye. While usually impersonal in nature, it can occasionally be designed for personal contact.

Paid, impersonal communication mixes elements include advertising, websites, sales promotions, store design, visual merchandising, and public relations. Each can contribute to a unified image. Advertising uses mass media to reach consumers with a message. Media employed include television; magazines; outdoor venues including billboards, public signage such as bus cards, and electronic and video displays; newspapers; and direct mail.

Similarly, the Internet is exploding as a venue for paid image communications. Pop-up and banner ads are common. Sales promotions can be especially successful as an image tool. For example, a promotion affiliated with a specific sporting event may be very influential on image development in young male consumers. Opportunities to test, try, or receive free goods or services, similarly, can be effective. Store design and visual merchandising set the stage for which merchandise to be seen. The retail space conveys a message which is transferred by the consumer to the goods it contains. Then visual merchandising, effectively executed, extends that image and informs the consumer on how to buy and use products. Finally, public relations includes a myriad of activities orchestrated by the corporation to influence consumers' perceptions.

Publicity and word-of-mouth, both verbal and electronic, form the most influential forms of unpaid communication of image. Each occurs as the result of interpersonal communication without payment. In the case of publicity, media exposure is the result, not of advertising fund expenditures, but usually of news coverage. Store openings, introductions of new products and services, or use of products by celebrities, are common sources of publicity. Generally, a director of fashion, special events, or public relations seeks to influence publicity so that the image projected is consistent with corporate design. Word-of-mouth communication is also unpaid and occurs naturally as part of personal interactions.

Today's technology offers extended conversation venues. Instant messages, blogs, personal websites, and e-mails all provide platforms for the sharing of product perceptions and images.

Store Design and Visual Merchandising

Store design is another tool available to create or reinforce image. It should be created with the needs of the target customer in mind and be consistent with the marketing strategy developed to meet the needs of those customers. In general, good store design should positively influence consumer behavior; consider costs versus value in creation, construction, and maintenance; and be flexible enough to accommodate changes in seasonal needs and future trends (Levy & Weitz, 2004).

FIGURE 10.5 Store design influences consumers' perceptions.

Store layout, use of space, traffic patterns, construction materials, and interior surface finishes create both functional and aesthetic influences on purchasing decisions. Indeed, the decision to enter a retail store (or an online website) is likely to be highly influenced by these important elements.

Within the design of the store, visual merchandising is another means to create image by communicating the fashion and quality messages of the merchandise and store by enticing the customer into the store, showcasing the merchandise for sale, and showing the customer how to wear and adopt the apparel and accessory items.

Visual merchandisers have a wide range of tools and techniques to use to influence buyer behavior. Often, the career choice of creative people, window and in-store displays become the canvas for creative expression with the purpose to sell merchandise. All of the elements and principles of art and design examined in Chapter 5 are applied in creating productive selling environments. Lighting, fixtures, mannequins, props, graphics, and signage can be expertly employed to draw consumers into the store and encourage purchase.

More broadly, **atmospherics** is the current term used to describe the creation of a selling environment using visual techniques, lighting, color, music, and scent to perceptually stimulate customers and ultimately influence their buying behavior. Store design and visual merchandising can effectively create environments that are readily recognizable to consumers. The long florescent-lit chrome racks of apparel in Wal-Mart, for example, send a message which is very different from the wood-toned fixtures in Talbot's or Ann Taylor. The dim lighting of Abercrombie & Fitch, similarly, contrasts with the bright appearance of Forever XXI. A consumer stepping into each of these retail locations is likely to know exactly where they are without needing any signage.

FIGURE 10.6 Atmospherics is the creation of a selling environment using visual techniques, lighting, colors, music, and scent.

Customer Service

Exceptional opportunities for building positive product or store image exist in customer service. In a highly competitive environment, customer service offers a means to provide differentiation and extra value and thus, enhanced image. Knowing what consumers' expectations are regarding customer service further offers the chance to stretch beyond expectations to offer exceptional service. While the list of customer service options is long, examples include gift wrapping, delivery, credit, child care, personal assistance, return privileges, and alterations. It includes both tangible and intangible services.

An extension of customer service that is currently achieving great success is **customer relationship management (CRM).** CRM is a set of strategies designed to identify and build loyalty with a marketer's most valued customers. The goal is to create a base of loyal customers who patronize the company frequently or in large volume. Strategies designed to create an emotional connection between the customer and the retailer or seller are based on providing more value to the very best customers. Increasingly, creating committed customers is a popular marketing strategy. This concept is based on the idea of moving customers from the categories of total buyers, to satisfied buyers, to repeat purchasers, and finally, to committed customers. Those committed customers hold positive images of the company, act upon that image through purchases, and share that image with others.

Sequence to Committed Customers

Total buyers → satisfied buyers → repeat purchasers → committed customers

---

As part of customer relationship management, a study by the IBM Institute for Business Value (Chu & Pike, 2002) highlighted the need to create competitive differentiation among retailers because the success of mega retailers has used superior scale and efficiency to capture the high volume end of the market place. Their findings confirmed that interactions with store employees and elements of the in-store experience were important drivers of customer satisfaction. On a relative scale where a score above 110 indicated significant correlation to level of customer satisfaction, person-to-person experience scored 272 and store experience scored 122. In contrast, pricing and value scored 47, marketing and communication scored 38, and data integration and analytics scored 21. Person-to-person attributes included employee knowledge, helpfulness, and availability. Store experience attributes included high quality merchandise, well-designed stores, and product availability.

Stating that excellent customer-employee (person-to-person) relations were a competitive requirement, Paglucia-Morrison (2005) advised that retailers can additionally differentiate themselves from competitors via store-related factors. Four factors for enhancing the store experience include offering a store experience that evolves with changes in customer expectations, providing a truly convenient shopping experience, developing an integrated view of the customer, and delivering a flexible product or service.

First, creating a store experience that evolves with changes in customer expectations requires methods to identify and keep in touch with customers on a regular basis. Commitment to experimentation and innovation in meeting those changes is also required. In addition, willingness to hire and retain the right staff is needed since employees are often the customer's first, last, or only point of interaction.

Second, providing a convenient shopping experience is important. An environment that requires less time and effort for consumers is more likely to keep them coming back. This involves store navigation via store design and shopping aids such as maps and product locators. Convenience can also be improved by productivity-enhancing tools such as those that provide timely information and promote efficiency and speed in transactions. Consumer scanners to check item prices and efficient point of sale terminals are examples.

Important here is also the need to educate shoppers on how to use the efficiency-creating services. Self service or automated systems without instructions decrease, rather than increase, customer satisfaction and image.

Third, developing an integrated view of the customer entails viewing the customer from all aspects of their experience in the setting. Channels such as websites, departments within stores, and individual sales associates need to be unified to meet customer needs. Consumers, for example, become frustrated when they are required to provide information more than once or upon each transaction. Making purchases needs to be made easy for the consumer.

Fourth, delivering flexible products and services is based on a clear understanding of target customers and necessitates offering variety in shopping experiences. For example, some products and some customers require more or less personal service. Flexible staffing can be used to have the right type of sales personnel on the floor at specific periods. Different types of customers value different traits and skills in the sales associates with whom they interact. Each of these factors (an evolving shopping experience, shopping convenience, integrating the view of the customer, and delivering flexible products or services) can be designed to meet customer needs. In doing so, a corporate image can be successfully created and orchestrated. This image can be easily identified, and even owned by the consumer, which then leads to mutual satisfaction for both the buyer and the seller.

Branding and Product Positioning

From these techniques, and more, the concept of brand emerges. A **brand** is a name, logo, or symbol that identifies a product or service and differentiates it from other offerings in the marketplace. Apparel products and the retailers that sell them are branded. Brands are beneficial to both sellers and buyers as they convey valuable information about the product or service, including related shopping and post-purchase experiences. Loyalty to brands is achieved as consumers become increasingly aware of the brand and form positive emotional ties to it. When this occurs, there is added value for the brand beyond the functional characteristics of the product. This is termed **brand equity**. Brand equity, because it represents increased value, offers the seller the opportunity to increase profit.

FIGURE 10.7 A brand identifies a product or service and differentiates it in the marketplace.

Brand image is at the core of building brand equity. It is a reflection of what people think, feel, and say when they see or hear a brand name. It is developed from consumers' interpretation of product attributes and benefits, usage conditions and situations, consumer base, and marketer characteristics. Brand image is both an objective and emotional response.

Taking on the Big Guys: Brand Equity Helps

Small retailers can leverage strong brand identity in the battle to survive in a competitive market where retail giants are getting bigger. Acquisitions such as that of the May Company by Federated have brought discussions of the replacement of local stores with a more generic, national strategy. Yet, for small retailers, this very consolidation of major retailers offers an opportunity to create strong brand identity and a competitive edge. While many of the large corporate retailers may seek to build sales through low prices, leveraging their sheer size to drive down costs and prices, smaller, independent retailers can counteract the business model built on volume and create brand equity based on competitive attributes other than price and volume. By differentiating their products and services from the giants, independent retails can create lucrative market niches (Hurlbut, 2007a).

From brand image, product position is formed. **Product position** refers to the position, either positive or negative, that a product holds within the mind of the consumer. Product position includes a product's position relative to other similar offerings. Because position attributes are highly influential on purchase decisions, marketers seek to create a specific positive position for their products or services.

The term **product positioning** refers to decisions made by marketers to attempt to achieve a specific perception of the brand or a brand image within the mind of specific target market consumers. Marketing strategies will be described in greater detail in Chapter 11, such as how product design, pricing, promotion and advertising are used.

Apparel products and retailers invest heavily on the development of a brand image and product position. For apparel products, brands are known to consumers by their labels, advertisements, and consumer-to-consumer communications. Increasingly, apparel items are printed or embroidered with the name of the brand to further enhance identification and acceptance. Retailers, too, are recognized brands. Retailers have images and positions that influence consumer patronage. Additionally, retailers often promote branded apparel available only from that specific retailer. The store brand may carry the name of the store or some other identifying name. In either case, the image of the store and the private store brand are intimately connected. Limited Too, in the teen market, and Nordstrom's Smartcare, in menswear, have each created successful private label brand identity.

While the terms *brand image* and *product position* have similar and complementary applications and are often used interchangeably, there is a subtle, yet important, difference. Brand image is most likely to be used to describe the perception of a product or retailer without reference to the competition. Product position, on the other hand, infers a direct comparison to other providers within the marketplace seeking to influence the same or similar target audience. Product position is a relative term, taking into account the attributes of the product or retailer in direct comparison to others.

Both image and position rely heavily on the creation of a clear identity. Apparel providers must first have a firm understanding of their mission and target market before attempting to build and communicate that identity in the form of merchandise, service, clientele, promotion, and support. For apparel marketers especially, critical factors include consumers' expectations regarding fashion adoption cycle stage, quality, pricing, sizing, and related services. Since the apparel industry is highly competitive, both manufacturers and retailers must differentiate

Shopping the Competition

One tool to develop a positive market position is to shop the competition. Scanning, visiting, and studying the competition can illuminate key factors such as: What makes the competition tick? How do consumers perceive the competition? What does the competition do well? What can be learned from the competition?

Learning why their customers, your potential customers, view you as a preferable source is valuable. For example, when visiting a competitor, questions such as the following are useful.

>> Who is their target customer and how do they entice them?
>> Is the visual presentation compelling? What message do they convey with the first impression?
>> What is the product niche? What level of service and product knowledge do their customers expect?
>> How are customers led through the physical layout of the site?
>> What are their most important products or categories? Where are they located in the store?
>> What is the pricing strategy? Are they competing directly on price or on other attributes?
>> What type of staffing is used and how knowledgeable is the staff?
>> Is this a fun place to show? Is buying part of an overall experience?
>> Is the site well maintained?
>> How effective is the signage?
>> Is the visual merchandising innovative and compelling?
>> How fast does it appear that the inventory turns?
>> What appears to be the markdown strategy?
>> What are customers buying and in what quantities?
>> What can I learn from this competitor and apply to my own business?

(Hurlbut, 2007b).

> **Influences on Apparel Product and Store Identity**
> Merchandise Attributes
> Service
> Clientele
> Promotion
> Ambience
> Post-Purchase Support

themselves from the competition. In today's marketplace, it is impossible to be all things to all people. Successful apparel marketers select a specific market segment that, based on solid market research, is likely to produce a profitable return, and then apply marketing strategies to create image and position that yield success.

Perception

Since brand image and product position, both powerful forces in successful apparel marketing, are based on the perception of consumers, discussion of the creation of consumer perception is merited. Hawkins, Mothersbaugh, and Best (2007) characterize the creation of perception as comprised of three steps: (1) exposure, (2) attention, and (3) interpretation. As part of daily human life, these functions, while described here as sequential, actually occur rapidly and simultaneously in an interactive manner.

Exposure occurs when a stimulus enters the range of an individual's ability to receive it. Whether the individual does, indeed, receive it is based on multiple factors. In some cases, individuals can select or choose to receive a stimulus. In other cases, individuals can choose to avoid a stimulus. In still other cases, a stimulus is received without conscious focusing of attention. Which of these occurs is highly important to apparel marketers. Individuals have the capability to either accept or screen out stimuli that they perceive as meeting their needs.

Attention occurs when the stimulus is allowed to become active and is sent to the brain for further processing. Attention is situational and can be influenced by specific attributes, including size, intensity, repetition, attractiveness, color, movement, relative position, contrast, and quality.

FIGURE 10.8 Exposure occurs when a stimulus enters the range of an individual's ability to receive it.

Interpretation is the third step in perception. The characteristics of the stimulus, the individual, and the situation are combined as the individual makes sense of the incoming message. Hence, the sequence of exposure, attention, and interpretation yields the creation of perception that for apparel consumers becomes brand image and product position (Hawkins, Mothersbaugh, & Best, 2007).

Creating Perception:
Exposure → Attention → Interpretation → yields → Perception

Personal Image

The creation of personal image has two primary aspects. First, image exists in the way individuals see themselves. Second, image is created in the eyes of others based on the use of apparel as a communication form.

Self-Concept, Self-Image

The way individuals see themselves is called self-concept. Self-concept was described in Chapter 2 as being composed of consumers' attitudes, formed as a result of self-evaluation (including evaluation of self in the context of the social setting). Multiple components, including physical body, personality, environment, and others combine to form personal image. This personal image, in turn, is a strong influence on apparel selection.

Self-esteem, a reflection of the positive or negative self-concept held, can further influence apparel choices. Fashion as a cultural symbol can serve to express self-esteem when self-esteem is high. Correspondingly, clothing can be used as a means of gaining social acceptance and bolstering self-esteem.

The theory of self-concept product image congruence and models of self-image product congruence (Hawkins, Mothersbaugh, & Best, 2007 and Solomon & Rabolt, 2004) predict that individuals will select apparel products when their attributes match those of the individual's self-concept. This is reflected in statements such as "that shirt looks just like you" or "that is just your brand." In both cases, the image of the shirt and the brand matched the self-concept or image of the individual.

Alternatively, self-concept product image congruence, or lack of, is evident when an apparel gift doesn't match the image of the recipient and is left to languish, unused, in the closet. In some cases, when consumers find themselves uncomfortable in retail settings, self-concept product image may be in play. A conservative middle-aged female in a funky teen boutique may find herself uncomfortable because the designs, fabrications, lighting, and music that contribute to the store image do not match her self-concept. More positively, when the store's physical attributes, atmospherics, merchandise, and personnel are in sync with the self concept of shoppers they are more likely to feel comfortable, linger, and make purchases.

Perceived physical appearance represents one major contributor to an individual's self-concept. Body image is a subjective evaluation of one's physical attributes, usually within the context of the social environment. Hence, conformity or discrepancy with cultural standards or perceived cultural standards may influence body image. As a result, clothing choices are likely to be impacted.

Under the influence of body image and self-concept, individuals create, both consciously and unconsciously, a personal apparel image. A clear personal image can result in wardrobe planning and selection that is unified and consistent while allowing for diversity in occasions and settings. A poorly or ill defined personal image results in a disparity of apparel images and a wardrobe that does not project a consistent image for the wearer.

FIGURE 10.9 Self-concept influences personal image which, in turn, influences apparel selection.

Occasionally, rising politicians, as they first hit the campaign trail, offer illustrations of the mismatch between personal apparel images and career aspirations. In such cases, voters can't clearly read their image and may perceive the candidate as either not fit for, or even competent, for the position to which they aspire. Once seeking higher office, such cases are usually remedied by consultation with an image advisor. As a result, voters often see red "power" ties with dark suits worn during debates, and softer blue ties, or even casual jackets when the candidate wants to appear friendly and approachable.

Communication of Personal Image

Apparel is a highly effective form of non-verbal communication. Clothing and accessories communicate personal and social attributes such as age, gender, economic status, self-esteem, opinions, attitudes, values, and even marital status. Such communication, especially in the early stages of interaction, allows the formation of judgments about people. First impressions are based predominately on apparel cues. The personal image projected via apparel, in large measure, influences what people think about and remember about individuals they meet.

Clothing is a silent language with signs, cues, and icons that send messages regarding an individual. The symbols of clothing express meanings including those that tell what kind of person the wearer is, what that person thinks of himself, and what kind of a person the wearer would like to be. As a strong and effective tool, apparel can help project attitudes, interests, and capabilities and to invite and encourage others to become better acquainted with the wearer. Apparel and the personal image it projects can be instrumental in achieving social and professional goals.

Additionally, levels of conformity or individuality as components of personal image can be seen in apparel choices. Such evidence includes actions, such as rejection or acceptance of

FIGURE 10.10 First impressions are based on apparel symbols that communicate meaning.

fashion styles that may be unflattering, wearing or refraining from wearing styles or brands just because others wear them, choosing to wear a favorite color or style on a consistent basis, creating a personal or signature look, or being known as the first or last to try fashion innovations.

Key Terms

Atmospherics	Attention	Brand
Brand equity	Brand image	Communication mix
Customer relationship management (CMR)	Exposure	Interpretation
Market pull	Market push	Product position
Product positioning		

Ideas for Discussion and Application

1. Select five branded apparel products. Then interview five individuals to identify the product position for each individual and each product. What differences do you find? Why do you think there are differences? What can the marketers do to influence the product position for each of the products?

2. Review the concepts of market pull and market push conditions. Make a list of evidence of market pull for apparel products. Make a list of evidence of market push for apparel products.

3. Visit a mall or shopping area. Identify 10 cases where atmospherics are influential. Do you believe that contemporary consumers have expectations regarding atmospherics? What are they?

4. Select five print advertisements. Identify which, if any, of the three steps of creating perception (exposure, attention, and interpretation) were in operation for you as you first viewed the ad.

5. Observe five apparel ads that attract your attention. Which of the influences identified in this chapter (size, intensity, repetition, attractiveness, color, movement, position, contrast, and quality) contributed to your attention?

6. Visit the websites of three apparel brands you wear. Do the websites reflect the images of the brands as you perceive them? What have the marketers done to create the brand images you hold?

7. Select three products. For each, observe two advertisements in either print, broadcast, or Internet for each product. Describe whether the image created is consistent for each advertisement pair.

8. Interview three people you know well about their favorite items of clothing. In what ways do you feel these "favorites" illustrate self-concept product image congruence?

9. Think about a job interview you anticipate having in the not-too-distant future. How can the concepts of self-concept, self-image, first impressions, and self-concept product image congruence influence your apparel selection for the interview?

>> *chapter eleven*

marketing apparel products

OBJECTIVES

>> *Define marketing.*

>> *Discuss the influences of marketing on individuals.*

>> *Identify marketing strategies.*

>> *Recognize the roles of the traditional and contemporary marketing mix components.*

>> *Identify and apply the four roles assumed by individuals in consumer behavior including initiator, influencer, buyer, and user.*

>> *Differentiate between market aggregation and market segmentation strategies.*

>> *Discuss the values and challenges associated with market aggregation or segmentation strategies.*

>> *Discuss the global nature of the apparel market.*

>> *Identify areas in which changes in technology create changes in the apparel industry.*

The American Marketing Association defines **marketing** as "an organizational function and a set of processes for creating, communicating, and delivering value to customers and for managing customer relationships in ways that benefit the organization and its stakeholders" (American Marketing Association, 2007b). A traditional definition adds the detail that marketing is the "process of planning and executing the conception, pricing, promotion, and distribution of ideas, goods and services to create exchanges that satisfy individual and organizational objectives" (*AMA*

329

Board Approves New Marketing Definition, 1985) (see box below). This comprehensive definition, appropriate for apparel marketing, includes the multiple steps involved in creating and promoting goods and services that meet the needs of both sellers and buyers. It outlines marketing as including multiple factors of product/service design, creation, and manufacturing; establishing optimum price structures; selecting promotional appeals and media; and utilizing appropriate inventory, transportation, and sales outlet strategies. It is an active, rather than passive, process. Key words of this definition are "create exchanges" and "satisfy objectives," which suggest that marketing has been successfully accomplished only when exchanges, or transactions, have been made that meet the needs or objectives of both the seller and the buyer. In most cases, the needs and objectives are to make a profit on individual sales or to contribute to the total profitability of the enterprise.

Marketing apparel products and services exert powerful forces in today's society in two primary ways. First, apparel marketing has the power to influence consumer consumption, and second, it has the power to influence how consumers think of themselves. While consumers generally hold a finite amount of money, credit, or resources, to invest in apparel items, marketers

---

Definitions of Marketing

Current: "An organizational function and a set of processes for creating, communicating, and delivering value to customers and for managing customer relationships in ways that benefit the organization and its stakeholders." (American Marketing Association, 2007b).

Traditional: "Process of planning and executing the conception, pricing, promotion, and distribution of ideas, goods and services to create exchanges that satisfy individual and organizational objectives." (*AMA Board Approves New Marketing Definition,* 1985).

Marketing Summary

Marketing = Planning/Executing → to Create Exchanges → yields → Satisfaction

have powerful tools to influence them to part with these resources. Magazine, television, radio, direct mail, Internet, and display ads bombard consumers with images and messages designed to tell consumers they "need" specific items. Store layouts, interior displays, and product websites are effective tools to expose consumers to products and encourage purchases by making items appear desirable. Additionally, consumer-to-consumer interactions exert strong consumption pressures as peers adopt apparel items and then influence others to do the same.

In addition, apparel marketers have power to influence how consumers actually feel about themselves. As marketers select and promote specific images they mold and influence consumers' perceptions. For example, the current exposure of extremely thin models promotes that as a desirable body type. Consumers then view that image and compare it to their own perceived body type. This can lead to both positive and negative self-concept attributes. Hence, marketers can influence how the consumer feels about himself by providing images of the "ideal" look, which either comply or contrast with the actual or current image. Such comparison, then, provides powerful motivation for consumption.

Marketing Strategies

To accomplish the creation of exchanges that meet the needs of sellers and buyers, apparel marketers employ specific marketing strategies. **Marketing strategies** are specific managerial decisions to affect the probability or frequency that exchanges will occur.

FIGURE 11.1 Marketing can influence how consumers feel about themselves.

Apparel Marketing Strategies Yield Huge Sales Volumes

The US Census Bureau reports the following estimates of sales for 2005 (reported in millions of dollars sold).

Clothing and clothing and accessories stores	201,896
Clothing stores	146,315
Men's clothing stores	9,465
Women's clothing stores	36,948
Family clothing stores	77,510
Shoe Stores	25,488
Jewelry stores	28,216

Note: Other retail store types may sell apparel and accessory items. (U.S. Census, 2007b).

To accomplish their goals, apparel marketers can create a coordinated mix of strategies, traditionally termed the "marketing mix" by selecting variables associated with key factors, including product, price, promotion, and place or physical distribution. In simple terms, the traditional marketing mix is called the 4 P's. By making calculated decisions regarding these four variables, apparel marketers endeavor to influence the frequency or probability that satisfying exchanges will occur, or that profit will result.

Components of the Marketing Mix

Traditional Marketing Mix = Product + Price + Promotion + Place

FIGURE 11.2 Components of the Marketing Mix

Product

A product, by general interpretation, includes almost anything that somebody is willing to sell and somebody else is willing to buy. Products can include either physical objects or services. Thus both a garment and the alteration services for that garment are products. The value of apparel products from the consumer's perspective is based on the usefulness or utility of the product. Such value depends on both psychological and physical factors. Indeed, products usually represent a group of values that can satisfy multiple physical and psychological needs.

Branding of products is an attempt to identify a product within a product category that includes many similar products by distinguishing it from the similar products made by others. Brand names are designed to generate consumer recognition and identification of a specific product. Usually a trademark, including a design, symbol, or name, is used to further legally protect the product's identity. Another tool that is popular within the apparel industry is the creation of private labels. Often owned by the distributor or retailer rather than the manufacturer, a private label is affixed to apparel items that are then sold only through outlets owned or supplied by that particular distributor or retailer.

Price

Price is the second "P" of the marketing mix. Demand for apparel products is a measure or prediction of how many, or how much, of that product can be sold. Customer-related factors that affect demand include personal taste and income, while product-related factors include competition and price. Of these four factors, price is the most easily controlled or influenced by the manufacturer. The other "P's" of the marketing mix (product, promotion, and place) can also impact demand.

When the demand for a product varies inversely with its price, the demand is said to be **elastic.** In such cases, as price increases, demand decreases; or as price decreases, demand increases. Generally, sales quantity and total sales revenue go up as price goes down; or quantity and revenue go down as price goes up. Contrastingly, when a price change pushes total revenue in the same direction, demand is said to be **inelastic.** Hence, when the price is increased, sales revenue also increases.

In most cases, when demand is graphically plotted with price on one axis and number of units on the other axis, a curve rather than a straight line is created. This is because the change in demand related to the number of units purchased is not constant for all prices. For example, a two dollar price change on an accessory item priced at $5 may have dramatically different results than a two dollar price change on the same item priced at $10. Factors that affect the elasticity or inelasticity of demand based on price include such things as availability of substitutes, competition or competitive advantage, and product and consumer characteristics.

Pricing Strategies

Pricing Strategies:	Specific Return on Investment
	Maximize Profits
	Specific Rate of Growth
	Market Share

When establishing price for apparel products, multiple strategies may be used. These might be based on pricing policies designed to (1) create a specific percentage return on invested capital, (2) maximize profits, (3) establish or maintain a specific rate of growth for the company, or (4) maintain or increase the company's share of the market.

Promotion

Promotion is the third "P" of the marketing mix. It is communication from a seller to prospective customers and may include anything done by a manufacturer or retailer to get people to buy. Promotion can include four basic types of communication: advertising, sales promotion, personal selling, and publicity or public relations.

Types of Promotion
Advertising
Sales Promotion
Personal Selling
Publicity/Public Relations

Advertising is mass selling via a medium, such as radio, television, or direct mail to a large number of people. The American Marketing Association includes in its definition "the placement of announcements and persuasive messages in time or space purchased in any of the mass media by business firms, nonprofit organizations, government agencies, and individuals who seek to inform and/or persuade members of a particular target market or audience about their products, services, organizations, or ideas" (American Marketing Association, 2007a).

FIGURE 11.3A AND B Well designed advertisements attract the consumer's attention, arouse their interest, strengthen their motivation to buy, and prepare them for the sale: (a) Product ads and (b) Institutional ads.

FIGURE 11.4 Sponsorship of events, loyalty plans, premiums, and in-store demonstrations are examples of sales promotions.

FIGURE 11.5 One-to-one communication in personal selling is a strong influence on consumer apparel behavior.

Three main types of advertisements are (1) product, (2) institutional, and (3) reminder. Generally, product ads ask for something to be done, like buying a specific product, while institutional ads are designed to improve the sponsor's image in the community and the market. Reminder ads simply remind the consumer of something, usually a product or a message previously received. Expertly designed advertisements will attract the consumer's attention, arouse their interest, strengthen their motivation to buy, and then prepare them for the sale.

Sales promotion includes any activity or device used to promote a sale. Sponsorship of events, customer loyalty plans, premiums, and in-store demonstrations are examples of sales promotions. In-store displays, utilizing effective visual merchandising techniques, can be effective sales promotion tools. Sales promotions, in general, can create an environment that encourages sales.

Personal selling is one-to-one communication between the seller and the potential buyer. Since the salesperson is most often face-to-face with the customer, feedback can be immediate and direct. Sales associates in retail settings engage in personal selling as they share the attributes of specific apparel items with customers.

Publicity involves unpaid communication offered by a third party, such as a magazine or newspaper, while public relations includes any strategy used by a company to influence its image in the eyes of potential consumers. Sponsorship of events or support of community causes can lead not only to coverage by the mass media, but can also result in an enhanced community image.

Selection of the promotional strategies to be used usually results in a blend of advertising, sales promotion, personal selling, and publicity/public relations based on the nature of the product, target market, stage of the product in its life cycle, and promotion budget.

Place

Place, or physical distribution, can be divided into two primary components. The first, physical distribution, includes the physical flow of materials including transportation, warehousing,

FIGURE 11.6A AND B
Publicity is unpaid communication offered by a third party, such as *Vogue* magazine.

protective packaging, and materials handling. The second, channels of distribution, includes the selection of marketing institutions such as wholesalers, retailers, or other middlemen to enable the product to reach the target market. Functions covered by physical distribution include those such as buying, selling, storing, inventorying, grading, shipping, financing, risk taking, and providing market information.

Distribution channels include the chain of marketing institutions, including distributors and retailers, which carry a product from the manufacturer to the end consumer. While vertical integration is sometimes used whereby a single corporation assumes all or most of the roles from manufacturer to the point of sale, more frequently, this sequence involves multiple participants. Factors that affect the choice of the distribution channel include the nature of the target market including its size, geographical dispersion, and preferences, the nature of the product, and the kinds of middlemen and services available.

Luxury Fashion Industry is Embracing E-Commerce Distribution

"Place" in the marketing mix for many luxury apparel goods providers is seeing a shift toward embracing e-commerce. While some, such as Rolex, continue to refuse to sell their products online and even actively pursue Internet sites selling its watches by tracking suppliers via serial numbers, others such as Valentino, Burberry, Jimmy Choo, Louis Vuitton, Boucheron, and Giogio Armani have recently announced online ventures.

With annual sales of $259.2 billion in 2007, e-commerce merits notice. By 2010, luxury products alone are expected to generate $7 billion. While still a small percentage of total retail sales, online sales are projected to be the fastest growing segment for luxury fashion brands (Brass, 2007). For example, Coach reports that sales at Coach.com grew 51 percent. The 60 million online site visits were more traffic than in all North American full-priced Coach stores for the same period.

Additional Marketing Mix Components

In addition to the traditional 4 P's of the marketing mix, contemporary marketing techniques include careful consideration of additional factors. These can be characterized as the 5 C's and include customer, company, competition, collaborators, and context components (Hauser, 2005). Customer

focus includes consideration of customer needs, market segments to be targeted, and consumer behavior, in terms of both general shopping and consumption patterns, as well as those specific to the apparel product being offered. Company skills refer to the attributes of the apparel firm. These can include brand name, company and brand name image, production capability, financial strengths and weaknesses, organizational structure, and talent pool. Competition encourages the marketer to recognize the market environment and to realize that actions among competitors are interrelated. For example, changes in products offered, prices, or advertisements usually impact other sellers in the area. Collaborators are the component that recognize the advantage or opportunities presented by working cooperatively with downstream whole-

Loyalty Retailing: Making Friends

Since retaining only five percent more customers can increase profits by 25 to 125 percent, building consumer loyalty is an important strategy. Yet, beyond loyalty programs designed to lure repeat customers, a strategy of "making friends" can set retailers apart from the competition. Smart retailers seek to develop relationships where customers desire to return again and again, like visiting a good friend. Getting to know their customers and listening to their needs establishes loyal and long-lasting friendships. Key elements in developing friendships include privacy, information, personalization, interaction, and respect (Vargas, 2007).

salers or retailers and upstream suppliers. Context refers to factors such as culture, politics, regulations, and social norms which can impact and be used for success.

Consumer Behavior

Consumer behavior includes the decision-making processes and physical activities individuals engage in when evaluating, using, or disposing of goods and services. Key elements in this definition include the concept that consumer behavior is both a process and an activity, either physical or mental, and that it includes the full scope of activities from evaluation through disposal of goods or services. In simple terms, consumer behavior examines "why people buy." The value of answering that question lies in the belief that if marketers understand why people buy, they will be better positioned to develop strategies to encourage the purchase of specific products or brands.

Consumer behavior is a subset of the larger field of human behavior. As such, it draws upon the research and wisdom from multiple fields, including psychology, sociology, social psychology, economics, and anthropology. Consumer behavior issues can be examined from each of these perspectives and/or a multidisciplinary approach can be taken. In most cases, a multidisciplinary approach is needed. For example, strategic planning to market a summer dress targeted toward a teen market would need to include economic aspects related to price, social components related to peer acceptance and norms, and psychological factors including teen self-concept, as well as many others.

Consumer behavior is an especially challenging field of study because, while some aspects are visible to the researcher or marketer, others occur within the thought process of the consumer. For example, while it is rather easy to observe and track traffic patterns within a store, noting when consumers stop, touch, or seek more information regarding products in a retail setting, it is nearly impossible to know what they are thinking as they do so. Because consumer behavior is so multi-faceted, the number of variables that can impact a single apparel purchase can be huge.

Another factor that impacts the study of consumer behavior is that consumers assume multiple roles. These roles include (1) **initiator**: the person who identifies a need or want, (2) **influencer**: the individual who either intentionally or unintentionally by word or action provides influence, (3) **buyer**: the one who actually makes the purchase transaction, and (d) **user**: the person most involved in the use or consumption

| Consumer Roles |
| Initiator |
| Influencer |
| Buyer |
| User |

of the product. Each of these roles can be held by one or more persons or a single person may perform in each of the roles. Because of the complexity of studying consumer behavior, models have been developed to slow down aspects of the consumer behavior process and isolate specific variables. These will be examined in Chapter 12.

Obtaining and applying consumer behavior knowledge enables utilization of a consumer oriented marketing plan. An integrated strategy can be developed to identify and satisfy consumer needs and wants while at the same time meeting company objectives. Components of such a plan may include market opportunity analysis, target market selection, and marketing mix.

Market opportunity analysis means the process of identifying, within the marketplace, consumer needs or wants that are not currently being satisfied. Essentially, market opportunity analysis seeks to find the "hole" in the market. **Target market selection** identifies the group or groups of consumers most likely to purchase a product.

Market Aggregation and Market Segmentation

When marketers choose to sell the same product or service to all consumers, it is called **market aggregation** because all consumers have been aggregated, or put together, to form a single market. For this strategy, consumers are judged to be sufficiently alike to be likely to respond to a product or service offered in a similar manner. Otherwise, when there is enough variation within

a market such that subdividing it into smaller groups with similar characteristics appears to have benefits, the strategy is called **market segmentation**. In this case, from the heterogeneous market more homogeneous subgroups are formed conceptually. Then, products, services, and promotions are designed to appeal to that specific subgroup or segment. While market aggregation may at first glance appear to have the benefit of increased profits based on the principle of economy of scale, which takes advantage of economies based on volume, it is likely that over time, a well-designed segmented strategy will prove more successful for a larger range of products.

Apparel items are especially likely to benefit from segmented strategies. Benefits of market segmentation include the ability to detect trends more readily, to design products that truly meet demand, to create the most effective advertisements, to promote via the right media, and to promote at the right times.

Decisions regarding the selection of appropriate market segments are based on consumer and market characteristics and the potential to make a profit. Selected segments should exhibit measurability, accessibility, substantiality, and congruity (Blackwell, et al, 2006). Measurability requires that it is possible to obtain information about the size, nature, and behavior of the segment. Accessibility refers to the degree to which the segment can be reached via retail and media channels. Substantiality requires that the segment generate sufficient volume to support research and development, production, marketing, and distribution costs. Congruity denotes that the segment must have members who are similar enough in characteristics that correlate to consumption behaviors. In today's marketplace, the overwhelming majority of products and services employ market segmentation.

APPAREL APPLICATIONS

1. Apparel products can exhibit either elastic or inelastic demand based on consumer, market, and product characteristics.

2. The marketing mix, including the 4 P's and the 5 C's are tools that apparel marketers can use to successfully develop marketing strategies to meet the needs of both consumers and the apparel firm.

3. Apparel products marketing typically employs market segmentation strategies.

The Global Apparel Market

While historically apparel products and marketing efforts were largely geographically confined to specific regions, this is no longer the case. Barriers created by distance, transportation, economics, and politics are diminishing. The result is an increasingly global blending of ideas, talents, materials, technologies, and production. Garments are no longer designed, manufactured, and sold in a single country. Instead, a garment may have material and construction components from multiple locations. **Imports** and **exports** create the framework for this global market network.

Importing occurs when goods are purchased from another country. Exporting occurs when goods are sold to another country. Often, importers and exporters work with intermediaries (customs agents for imports, export trading companies for exports) to facilitate the multiple aspects of international transactions. Both assist not only with the business and logistics of the sale, but also with the important aspects of understanding differences in culture, customs, laws, business practices, distribution and communication channels, and values.

Currently, the United States imports substantially more apparel articles than it exports. Computed from U.S. Department of Commerce figures in U.S. dollars, the United States currently imports nearly 22 times as much apparel and accessories than it exports (TradeStats Express, 2007). Total textiles and apparel import value in U.S. dollars for the period ending August 2007 was nearly $96.5 billion (Office of Textiles and Apparel, U.S. Department of Commerce, 2007b) (see Table 11.1).

TABLE 11.1 Apparel & Textiles Imports to the US in Millions of Dollars from Selected Countries

Group	Countries	Import value in Millions of US Dollars
ASEAN (Association of Southeast Asian Nations)	Brunei, Cambodia, Indonesia, Laos, Malaysia, Burma, Philippines, Singapore, Thailand and Viet Nam.	15,619,703
ANDEAN	Beneficiary countries for purposes of the Andean Trade Preference Act (ATPA): Bolivia, Colombia, Ecuador, and Peru	1,385,000
CBI (Caribbean Basin Initiative)	Antigua, Aruba, Bahamas, Barbados, Belize, British Virgin Islands, Costa Rica, Dominica, Dominican Republic, El Salvador, Grenada, Guatemala, Guyana, Haiti, Honduras, Jamaica, Montserrat, Netherlands Antilles, Nicaragua, Panama, St. Kitts-Nevis, St. Lucia, St. Vincent/Grenadines, and Trinidad and Tobago	8,788,424
CAFTA (Central American Free Trade Agreement)	El Salvador, Guatemala, Honduras, Nicaragua, Costa Rica, and the Dominican Republic	8,256,091
EU12	Belgium, Denmark, France, Germany, Greece, Ireland, Italy, Luxembourg, Netherlands, Portugal, Spain, and United Kingdom	4,205,753
EU15	Imports from above plus Sweden, Finland, and Austria	4,302,274
OECD (Organization for Economic Co-Operation and Development)	Members of the OECD: Australia, Austria, Belgium, Canada, Czech Republic, Denmark, Finland, France, Germany, Greece, Hungary, Iceland, Ireland, Italy, South Korea, Luxembourg, Netherlands, New Zealand, Norway, Portugal, Spain, Sweden, Switzerland, Turkey and the United Kingdom. Note: Japan and Mexico are members of the OECD, but are not included in the OECD totals.	9,611,997

Group	Countries	Import value in Millions of US Dollars
	TABLE 11.1 (*continued*)	
SUB-SAH	Sub-Saharan African Countries: Angola, Benin, Botswana, Burkina, Burundi, Cameroon, Cape Verde, Central African Rep., Chad, Comoros, Congo (Brazzaville), Congo (Kinshasa), Djibouti, Eritrea, Ethiopia, Gabon, Gambia, Ghana, Guinea, Guinea-Bissau, Ivory Coast, Kenya, Lesotho, Liberia, Madagascar, Malawi, Mali, Mauritania, Mauritius, Mozambique, Namibia, Niger, Nigeria, Rwanda, Sao Tome and Principe, Senegal, Seychelles, Sierra Leone, Somalia, South Africa, St Helena, Sudan, Swaziland, Tanzania, Togo, Uganda and Zambia, Zimbabwe	1,350,600
T,K,HK	Taiwan, Korea, and Hong Kong	4,949,514
C,T,K,HK	China, Taiwan, Korea, and Hong Kong.	36,649,304
Total		**95,118,660**

Source: Office of Textiles and Apparel, U.S. Department of Commerce, 2007b

Worldwide, imports and exports are controlled and regulated by multiple factors including consumer demand, market economies, technology, material resources, human resources, and market interventions, such as quotas, tariffs, duties, and customs fees. Quotas are limits placed on the quantity of items that can be imported, while tariffs, duties, and customs fees are taxes or fees levied on imported goods.

To manage and create the systems of rules that govern trade between nations, key organizations have evolved. For example, the International Harmonized Commodity Description and Coding System (HS) is administered by the World Customs Organization in Brussels, Belgium.

The Harmonized Tariff Schedule of the United States (HTS) is based on the international system (HS) and provides a hierarchical structure for listing duties, quota, and statistics by product categories (United States International Trade Commission, 2007). Another example is the World Trade Organization (WTO). Created in 1995 as the successor to the General Agreement on Tariffs and Trade which was established and the end or World War II, the World Trade Organization has as its main function to ensure the free flow of trade. Its 151 member countries account for over 97 percent of the world's trade. Its objectives include administering trade agreements, providing a forum for trade negotiations, settling trade disputes, reviewing trade policies, assisting developing countries, and cooperating with other international organizations (World Trade Organization, 2007).

Currently, several factors contribute to the global nature of the apparel market. Among others, these include issues of cost reduction, the popularity of licensing agreements, the blurring of regional market divisions, and free trade versus fair trade debates. Cost reduction is a powerful driver of global sourcing and contracting. Factors that encourage offshore production include an abundance of labor, reasonable wages, and the availability facilities, machinery, and transportation. These can converge to allow creation of the best garment at the lowest price. Three methods are most commonly used when garments or accessories are produced either completely or partially offshore. First, nearly the entire process can be accomplished in a foreign country. A complete production package, including sketches, sample garments, sizing standards, and specifications, can be provided. The contractor can then order fabric and trims, make the patterns and markers, cut, assemble, finish, label, and ship the garments. Design and marketing may be the only processes accomplished onshore. Secondly, materials may be sent from the home country or from another international location. Patterns and markers are, also, provided by the home country. Then the garments are cut, sewn, finished, and labeled in the contractor's location. The third arrangement is where only the sewing is done offshore. All other steps are accomplished onshore.

Licensing agreements are another factor in the global nature of the apparel and accessories market. Licensing affords a designer, or brand, the opportunity to increase its consumer audience without heavy capital investment or responsibility for production. Licensing agreements are contracts that give permission to use a designer's name, brand name, trademark, or logo to a manufacturer in exchange for a fee. Thus, many items that carry a famous or brand name are not really designed or manufactured by the brand, but instead are produced through a licensing agreement. Accessories, fragrances, and home furnishings are often manufactured using licensing arrangements. Examples of licensed names found on apparel include Looney Tunes characters, Calvin Klein, Coca-Cola, Lifesavers, and the Houston Astros.

Finally, the debate of free trade versus fair trade is an issue in the current global environment. In the United States, as well as in other countries, the fundamental issue is whether it is better to support domestic businesses by protecting them via legislated tariffs and quotas or to let an open market economy develop. Proponents of fair trade support the protection of key industries, including textiles and apparel manufacturing, in order to maintain vibrant industries that contribute to a strong national economy. They cite the challenges faced by lower cost imports, which cause the closure of domestic manufacturing sites and the loss of jobs and revenues. Free trade advocates favor removing restrictions to international trade in order to create an open global marketplace. Within the global marketplace, free trade advocates anticipate that providers and producers will find lucrative niches based on human and natural resources, and the needs of the global marketplace.

Technology: Influences on Marketing

Monthly, if not daily, new technologies and applications emerge to aid in the creation and marketing of apparel. A summary of some of the current and developing innovations is useful to understand the current apparel marketing environment and to prepare for future developments. Selected categories of technology applications included here are database marketing; communications; buying, inventory, and receiving management; manufacturing; quick response; and customer interface.

Database Marketing

The information age offers incredible opportunities for apparel marketers. The ability to apply technology to gain, store, manipulate, analyze, and apply information about consumers, markets, and sources is amazing. Examples of computerized data collection include Internet-based surveys; computer-assisted interviews; electronic recording of field data; and electronic scanning of company records, online blogs, journal articles, and website content. Data can instantly be stored electronically and can be readily retrieved when needed. Diverse processes are available for the storage and retrieval of data via large corporate-based computers located in centralized offices, laptops, and hand-held electronic devices. Software programs allow for easy retrieval and manipulation of data to meet the needs of the user.

Statistical analyses, including easy-to-read and share charts and graphs, facilitate understanding of the data gathered and facilitate knowledge-based decision-making. Records, comparisons, and files can be updated instantaneously, as required by the dynamics of the fast-paced apparel industry. Market research, apparel design, manufacturing, financial and merchandise planning, buying, logistics, receiving, inventory control, and retail operations all depend on data collection and application.

Database marketing has increasingly become a cornerstone of current practice. The collection and storage of massive amounts of data, retrievable by very narrow attributes, allows apparel providers to benefit from large resource files, but also to access detailed data pertinent to unique needs.

Data mining is the term used to describe this practice of gathering and selecting, from large data sets, that information which will be most beneficial for decision-making. While data mining can be accomplished in-house, much of it is outsourced or done on a contract or licensed basis by specialized firms. The practice of buying and selling consumer and market information has spawned an entire new industry, where the product is data or information and the service is access and analysis for that data.

Communications

Various modes of technology, including computers, offer avenues for instantaneous communication. Intranet systems, the Internet, and advanced communication channels are growing fields. Closed Intranet systems offer companies safe and secure systems for internally linking and sharing information among personnel in various departments, offices, branches, or stores. Employees can share data, records, opinions, plans, prototypes, and discussions within a secure environment. On a much larger scale, and without the security of an Intranet, the Internet allows public access. Through a vast system of interconnecting networks the Internet offers searchable access to vast amounts of information within seconds and offers sophisticated communication tools.

Communication channels, including those afforded via the Internet, are expanding rapidly both in quality and access. Both Intranets and the Internet offer companies the ability to communicate with personnel through videoconferencing and training, exchanging and sharing information, conducting virtual staff meetings, and one-on-one audio and video conversations. Communications with customers are enhanced by technology as well. Advertising media are improving sound, graphics, video, and print qualities to capture and hold the consumer interest. Additional means of exposure are now available, such as electronic display panels on the sides of buses and buildings. Advertising messages now appear in unexpected locations. For example, the use of pop-up ads on the Internet is both a blessing and a plague. The expanded use of television infomercials and on-demand TV has also brought changes.

Fiber-optic cables now carry digital signals that enhance interactive shopping via telephone, while the use of websites to sell goods is expanding exponentially. Catalog, TV, and Internet sales are all forms of direct marketing that are greatly enhanced by technology.

E-commerce, the establishment of retail sites in cyberspace using the Internet, is an expanding field. Websites offer both large, established brands and small emerging brands the opportunity to communicate with potential customers and afford retailers the option to reach consumers without the cost of opening a physical store. However, E-retailing ventures that are supported by traditional "bricks and mortar" stores have been more widely well received. Online retail sales continue to increase, allowing customers to shop anytime and at any place across the globe.

Electronic Data Interchange

In this environment of such vast amounts of information, **Electronic Data Interchange** (EDI) systems have emerged as a means to facilitate the efficient and expedient exchange of data among specific interested parties. EDIs can be tailor-made or adapted to meet specific needs. Key elements include ease of use, speed, flexibility, and security. For example, electronic data interchange systems can be installed to speedily exchange product or inventory data between textile producers, manufacturers, or retailers. An EDI system could enable an apparel manufacturer to have access to retail sales or inventory data in order to trigger materials ordering, cutting, sewing, and shipping of replacement goods as part of an automatic replenishment agreement with the retailer. In similar cases, inventory information can reduce wait time for ordering and distribution. Bar codes, now familiar on products, are part of electronic data interchange. Price tags that include a **Universal Product Code** (UPC) contain black lines and spaces that translate to digits that encode information about the product, including style, color, size, retail price, and fabric.

Buying, Inventory, and Receiving Management

Merchandise information systems (MIS) and inventory management systems (IMS) facilitate tracking the planning, production, inventory, distribution, and sale of apparel goods. An inventory management system, for example, can record sales, receipts, additions to stock, subtractions to stock, and stock transfers. A terminal at the point-of-sale can not only record the sale, but also delete the item from inventory and enter the sale in the financial ledger. A unit control system, as part of an MIS, can be used to record the number of units purchased, on order, received, in stock, and sold. By keeping track of consumer demand via units sold, it can facilitate automatic reordering when markdowns are not

FIGURE 11.8 UPC symbol

planned and demand is expected to remain high. Such automatic replenishment systems allow the manufacturer to ship goods automatically when inventory levels reach predetermined low levels. The system informs the retail buyer of the need to replenish stock and stimulates the manufacturer to cut, produce, and ship the goods.

Receiving systems are also being propelled by technology. Standardization of information systems is central to these innovations. Standardized purchase orders, bar-coded shipping labels that can be scanned at retail distribution centers without opening the box, pre-ticketing of merchandise by the manufacturer, and advance shipment notices from the manufacturer alerting the receivers of the shipment all utilize cutting-edge technology to contribute to efficient receiving.

Manufacturing

Computer-integrated manufacturing (CIM) employs computers to regulate and manage the production process. Such computer driven programs enable increased speed, accuracy, and quality throughout the manufacturing process including design, patternmaking, grading, marker making, spreading, cutting, sewing, and pressing. While each individual process is computer executed, employing the use of sensors to monitor progress, the overall system is then orchestrated via linked computers. The apparel and textiles industry as a whole, while drawing upon a long history of machinery and tradition, is achieving solid progress in the application of technology to its processes. Computer-aided yarn spinning, fabric design, weaving, knitting, dyeing, and finishing processes are evidence of this application of technology.

Laser systems are becoming increasingly sophisticated for use in cutting tools and processes. **Computer-aided design** (CAD) programs not only provide great flexibility in the creative processes of design, but also allow for digitizers to be used to record pattern shapes, which are translated directly into patternmaking capability. Computerized power looms and knitting machines allow patterns to be seen, changed, or adjusted on computer screens without creating a physical sample.

Mass customization is a growing area, based on the ability to efficiently scan a customer's body and create a custom-fitting garment. One system, developed by the Textile/Clothing Technology Corporation, uses digital technology to capture a three-dimensional body image in less than six seconds and then produce a scaled 3D body model within minutes. This model can then be automatically sent for laser cutting of a garment and construction to the specifications. The Textile/Clothing Technology Corporation is a not-for-profit organization of member companies designed to provide research and demonstration of emerging technologies applicable to the apparel industry (Textile/Clothing Technology Corporation, 2007).

Fabric testing kits that enable 3D visualization of fabric properties for designers and patternmakers, male and female avatars to be used in virtual sampling and testing processes; advanced computer drivers for printing and cutting applications; ecologically friendly yet economical fabrics for direct and transfer printing; fashion lifecycle management software; automatic cutting, patternmaking, and grading tools; advanced textile pigment printing systems; 3D design and communication software; and improved label printing solutions are all emerging technological advances in the industry (Textile/Clothing Technology Corporation, 2007).

Quick Response

Quick response (QR) and **just in time** (JIT) strategies were born of two primary components. First, technology provided the opportunity. Second, shortening the business cycle between raw materials and consumers was seen as a way to gain competitive edge, both from competing international providers and also from domestic firms who did not, or could not, adopt the strategy. The underlying concept of QR and JIT is reduction in the time required for production and delivery. Computers enable increased efficiency in planning, procurement, production, transportation, and receiving. Time is not wasted between steps and inventory is not held until needed when utilizing these innovations. Partnerships are formed and information is shared among suppliers and retailers to more efficiently meet customer demand.

Customer Interface

Advances in technology also substantially impact how consumers interface with apparel marketing efforts. Direct response systems provide instant sales opportunities via 1-800 telephone numbers, direct mail to home or office, and online websites. These forms prompt or allow consumers to act on the impulse to buy quickly before intervening variables occur that divert attention from the sale.

While the advent of E-retailing is perhaps the most substantial change in customer interface in recent years, other technology-based innovations are also having impact. For example, interactive videos are now available to show customers how to use a product, entice them to buy it, or show them its location in the store. Gift registries are shared electronically with ease among branch stores and electronic scanning of product codes makes it easy for consumers to point and record items they would like to receive. Incentive programs electronically record consumer purchase levels and reward those who shop frequently or in large volume. In-store electronic kiosks provide opportunities to promote or demonstrate goods, as well as the chance to order online items, which may not be in stock at that particular location.

Visual merchandising, one way to interface with consumers, is also impacted by technology. Videos can show merchandise in use and add excitement and energy to display windows and sales floors. Technology allows the centralized creation and dissemination of visual presentation plans by administrators for use in multiple locations. Such visual merchandising packages can include instructions for floor set-up and displays as well as photos to guide and reinforce uniformity so that all stores create the same look and image. Teleconferencing can also be used to share visual ideas. Computer mockups can be created and shared electronically. Graphics, text, sound, and moving images can be incorporated.

Key Terms

Advertising	Buyer
Computer-aided design	Computer-integrated manufacturing
Consumer behavior	Data mining
Elastic	Electronic data interchange
Exports	Imports
Inelastic	Influencer
Initiator	Just in Time
Market aggregation	Market opportunity analysis
Market segmentation	Marketing
Marketing strategies	Personal selling
Publicity	Sales promotion
Target market selection	Universal Product Code
User	

Ideas for Discussion and Application

1. What do you think about the statements that apparel marketing has the power to influence consumer consumption and the power to influence how consumers think about themselves? Identify aspects of your own self-image (or that of someone you know well) that have been influenced by marketing messages.

2. Select a purchase you made recently. Which of the 4 P's of the marketing mix were most influential in your purchase decision?

3. Identify a product you purchased for which place or physical distribution was a major factor.

4. Identify two or more apparel products that compete in the marketplace. How are the actions of marketers of these products interrelated among competitors?

5. Reread the definition of consumer behavior. Think about a recent apparel purchase you made. Identify both physical and mental activities and processes that led to the purchase.

6. Identify some of the multidisciplinary aspects of selling jeans to 10- to 12-year-old girls. How do the fields of psychology, sociology, and economics apply?

7. Recall an item you purchased recently. Identify who assumed each of the consumer roles of initiator, influencer, buyer, and user.

8. Identify five branded apparel items for which you feel a market segmented strategy is being used. What do you think the characteristics of the targeted market segment(s) are for each item?

9. Visit a local retailer. Select three branded items. First, investigate the labels attached to each garment to identify as much information as possible regarding the country of

origin for the fabric(s). Identify the country in which it was manufactured. Then, visit the Internet site for the brand. What can you learn about the global nature of the manufacturer?

10. Select three technology-based processes currently in use in the apparel industry. Project how you expect them to change in the next five years.

unit five

decision making

personal choices

OBJECTIVES

>> Discuss the value of models.

>> Identify four primary steps in the decision-making process.

>> Describe the states that lead to problem recognition.

>> Differentiate between internal and external search.

>> Discuss four influences on the amount of external search engaged in by consumers.

>> Discuss the social and personal motivations for shopping.

>> Identify influences on apparel outlet selection.

>> Define post purchase dissonance and discuss strategies for lessening its occurrence.

At an individual or household level, apparel consumers are confronted by a barrage of choices and decisions. Because each decision involves a complex network of variables there is benefit in slowing down the decision-making process and examining some of the individual components. Models provide a means of accomplishing this. A **model** is a simplified representation of something. It enables time to be paused at a particular point and variables to be isolated so that they can be considered more carefully.

Models are especially useful in examining consumer decisions regarding apparel because of the complexity of the process. Specifically, consumer apparel behavior is challenging to understand because: (1) It involves multiple variables many of which are not directly observable such as attitudes and predispositions; (2) Variables interact with each other canceling and magnifying their effects; and (3) Behavior is subjective and therefore open to interpretation. Models can serve to reduce the complex to make it easier to follow the process, to organize knowledge for easier learning, and to develop theories of how apparel consumption occurs.

Many models have been developed to attempt to illustrate the decision-making process for consumers. Three popular comprehensive models are shared here. These and others share three primary components. Common to each of these models are the elements of internal influences on the decision-making process, external influences on the decision making process, and the decision making process.

Simplified Apparel Decision Making Model
Internal Influences + External Influences + Decision Making Process =
Apparel Consumption Behavior

FIGURE 12.1 Consumer decision process model

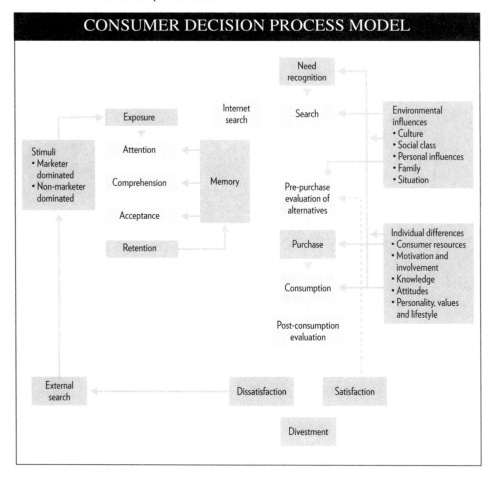

FIGURE 12.2 Decision process for consumer behavior

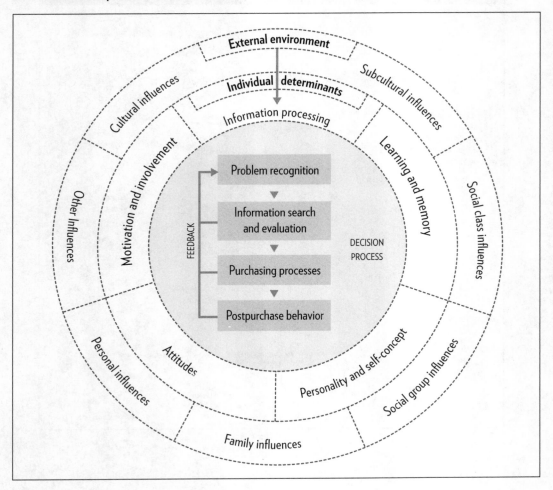

FIGURE 12.3 Consumer behavior model

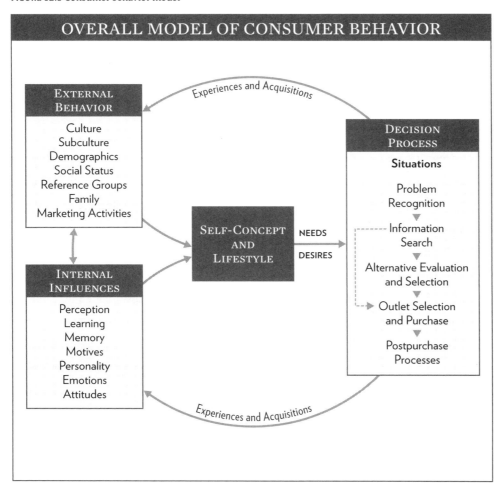

OVERALL MODEL OF CONSUMER BEHAVIOR

Experiences and Acquisitions

EXTERNAL BEHAVIOR

Culture
Subculture
Demographics
Social Status
Reference Groups
Family
Marketing Activities

INTERNAL INFLUENCES

Perception
Learning
Memory
Motives
Personality
Emotions
Attitudes

SELF-CONCEPT AND LIFESTYLE

NEEDS

DESIRES

DECISION PROCESS

Situations

Problem
Recognition

Information
Search

Alternative Evaluation
and Selection

Outlet Selection
and Purchase

Postpurchase
Processes

Experiences and Acquisitions

Since many of the internal and external components of these models, such as culture, subculture, social class, social group, family, personality, self-concept, involvement, motivation, and learning style were discussed in Chapter 2, this chapter focuses on the steps of the consumer decision-making process as it applies to apparel decision-making. The four primary steps in the decision-making process are problem recognition, search and evaluation, outlet selection and purchase, and post-purchase processes.

Problem Recognition

Problem recognition occurs for apparel consumers when they recognize a difference between their desired state and the current state. This can occur in many ways, for example, when an apparel item becomes worn or dated or when something new and desirable appears on the market. Problem recognition is created by judgment of depleted or inadequate apparel stock, discontentment with existing stock, changing personal or environmental circumstances, changing financial situations, and marketing activities.

Depletion may occur when an apparel item has been discarded or lost. Inadequacy may be seen when items are worn, poorly fitting, or not suitable for specific occasions. Discontentment may result when apparel items exist but are not viewed favorably. Changing circumstances, such as a new job or social involvement, may lead to problem recognition and the need to be properly attired, and changing finances may mean there is more money to be spent on apparel or that resources need to be conserved more strictly. Finally, well designed marketing efforts may introduce the notion that a specific item or items are required or that a new trend should be followed.

Not all problem recognition requires action within the same timeframe. In some cases, the recognition of a problem is **evolving**, while no immediate solution is required. At other times, a

FIGURE 12.4 Changing personal circumstances such as a new job or a new baby lead to product need.

Timeframes for Problem Recognition

Timeframes for Problem Recognition
>   Evolving
>   Anticipated
>   Emergency
>   Routine

problem is **anticipated,** but perhaps an immediate solution is still not needed. However, in some instances, immediate solutions are required. An **emergency** situation may arise unexpectedly and require an immediate response. At other times, a **routine** need may be expected and may also require immediate attention.

Recognition and understanding, not only of the types of problem recognition, but also their source and temporal aspects, is useful to both apparel consumers and marketers. Consumers can use this information to manage their consumption and make better use of apparel acquisition resources. Astute marketers can use this information to attempt to judge and influence consumers' readiness to buy. One classic model of a portion of the consumer behavior process suggests that consumers' intent to buy, likely linked to problem recognition, then creates purchases (Fishbein & Ajzen, 1975).

Earlier work (Wells, 1961) created a foundation for understanding by outlining a range of consumer's predispositions to buy, which included six categories: (1) firm and immediate intent to buy a specific brand; (2) positive intention without definite buying plans; (3) neutrality: might buy, might not buy; (4) inclined not to buy the brand but not definite about it; (5) firm intention not to buy the brand; and (6) never considered buying the brand.

Understanding the attributes of problem recognition for consumers has important implications for apparel marketers. Since problem recognition is the first step in the potential buying process, marketers can substantially benefit by being able to respond appropriately to problems recognized by offering solutions in the form of products or services that meet the needs of consumers.

Apparel marketers can strive to actually activate problem recognition, thus creating or driving a need for products. Critical avenues for activating problem recognition in apparel consumers include influencing the desired state, perceptions of the actual state, and the timing of problem recognition. By influencing consumers' perceptions of the desired state, marketers can actually create a need. This may be accomplished by introducing new products or promoting new trends. The consumer is exposed to new concepts or products which they may find desirable, thus triggering problem recognition. To influence perceptions of the actual state, contrast is a positive tool. Terms such as "new," "current," or "seasonal" can be used to cause the consumer to see their existing apparel stock as being old, outdated, insufficient, or inappropriate. By influencing the timing, marketers can accelerate the immediacy of the need, thus driving the consumer closer to action. Such movement may actually increase the frequency of buying by diminishing the time interval between purchases, thus increasing the volume of purchases over time. Influencing the timing of problem recognition can have positive effects by presenting a trigger to problem recognition at or near the point of transaction to decrease the chances for intervening circumstances to come between the recognition of the problem, intention to buy, and actual purchase. Advertising messages such as "look younger," "new for spring," and "10 days 'til Christmas" are based on these concepts.

APPAREL APPLICATIONS

1. Apparel marketers can select appropriate consumer decision-making models as tools to use in strategy development.
2. Apparel producers and marketers can apply consumer behavior models to focus on specific aspects of the process for apparel consumers, thus facilitating better design and sales related decisions.

3. Consumer behavior models can be used as tools for maximizing profit in apparel marketing by allowing better understanding of apparel choice behaviors.
4. By understanding the situations that lead to problem recognition apparel marketers are more capable of manipulating the 4 P's of the marketing mix to meet consumers' needs.
5. Apparel marketers can capitalize on strategies for activating problem recognition by influencing the desired state, perceptions of the current state, and the timing of problem recognition.

Search and Evaluation

After recognizing a problem, apparel consumers begin the process of seeking and evaluating information to assist them in meeting their need. **Internal search** is likely to be the first step in this process. At this stage, consumers begin scanning their stored memory for information previously obtained. This may include previous experiences with specific products or brands, as well as conversations held or overheard, printed or electronic matter read, advertisements exposed to, and promotions encountered. Either after or simultaneous to this internal search, **external search** follows.

External search includes seeking information from any source other than that stored within the consumer. Sources may include marketer-dominated sources, consumer-dominated sources, and neutral or third-party sources. Examples of marketer-dominated sources are magazine, newspaper, radio, television, direct mail, and Internet advertisements; window and in-store displays; catalogues; and sales associates, personal shoppers, and wardrobe consultants. Examples of consumer-dominated sources include conversations with friends, colleagues, and acquaintances; and observations of others in both public and private settings. Examples of neutral or

FIGURE 12.5 External search includes seeking information from any source other than that stored as consumer experience.

unbiased third-party sources include communications, such as print or Internet, which are not paid for by the product or service being examined, and are designed to present objective commentary on the product. A feature in a fashion magazine that mentions, discusses, or presents the designs of a particular manufacturer without any financial compensation is considered a third-party source. Similarly, an Internet source designed to present objective review or recommendations on specific products without support from those products is a third-party source.

In general, consumers follow a **cost-benefit model** for determining how much search, particularly external, they need to do. In simplest terms, this means that apparel consumers seek information on which to base their decisions when the benefits of acquiring the information exceed the costs of obtaining it. So, as long as consumers feel that the benefits of more information will meet their personal needs, including making better decisions, and the costs of obtaining that information is not excessive in relation to its value, the search will continue.

More specifically, there are categories of influences on the amount of external search engaged in by consumers. These influences include: The market environment, situational variables, product variables, and personal attributes. First, the nature and complexity of the market environment is a factor in how much external search consumers will engage in. Elements of this environment include the number of viable alternatives, both product and outlet, available to the consumer; the complexity of the product and the alternatives; the marketing mix being used by alternatives; the presence of new alternatives; and the availability of information. For example, an apparel product, such as a fashion shoe, for which there are numerous alternatives including new options, is more likely to spawn greater search activity than the purchase of a more routine item available most easily via one outlet.

Second, situational variables, including circumstances such as ease of access to information sources, time pressure, current physical and mental condition of the consumer, and financial and social pressures, influence the amount of external search considered appropriate. For example, the less effort consumers are required to expend to get information, the more likely it is that they will seek that information. Similarly, situation plays a part when a problem is time driven. For example, external search for information regarding a Christmas gift may be much greater during the month of November than on the 24th of December. Situational variables related to the retail environment are also factors. Store conditions, such as crowding with people or merchandise, similarity among stores, distance between stores, and store preferences and loyalty make a difference.

FIGURE 12.6 Situational variables such as time and store crowding influence the amount of external search.

FIGURE 12.7 Involvement with the product and the pleasure of the shopping experience increase the amount of external search.

FIGURE 12.8 The evoked set includes alternatives judged favorably by the consumer.

Third, variables related to the product and its attributes influence the amount of external search consumers are likely to engage in. These include such aspects as the importance of the product class, the number of critical attributes, price, social visibility, and perceived risk. Risk may include several types of real or perceived types including psychological, social, physical, performance, or financial. Where risk is judged to be high, search will be greater.

Additionally, consumers may seek greater information to accommodate strategies to deal with, or reduce, the risks of consumption. Such strategies may include buying a brand the consumer has bought before, buying a well-known brand, buying the most expensive or elaborate brand or model, or buying a product that has been tested or approved or has a money-back guarantee. For example, a consumer who is concerned about obtaining a new pair of shoes that are comfortable may reduce his risk by selecting a brand purchased previously that was comfortable. Money back guarantees and liberal return policies further reduce risk.

Fourth, personal attributes can influence the amount of external search consumers engage in. Income, education, and occupation are influential demographic variables. Personality and lifestyle variables include self-confidence, openness to new experiences, and time management as constraints. Involvement with the product and the enjoyment of shopping either in general or for a specific product class are factors as well. In addition, training, historical shopping patterns, and the ability to process information make a difference. Finally, consumers' knowledge and experience with products and services play a major part in the amount of search engagement. Previous information held as stored knowledge, product loyalty and preferences, as well as brand satisfaction and usage rate influence the amount of search.

During and following the search process, consumers use evaluation tools. Consumers categorize the available alternatives based on their search, both internal and external, into one of three sets. These sets are critical for the success or failure of apparel marketers. The **evoked set** is comprised of those alternatives judged favorably by the consumer. The **inert set** includes alternatives for which the consumer has neither a positive or negative opinion. The **inept set** includes the alternative evaluated negatively by the consumer.

For apparel marketers, the challenge is to move consumers with products in the evoked set to the point of purchase, to provide influence on consumers with products in the inert set to move their perception into the evoked set, and to drop or redesign products in the inept set.

Because apparel products are comprised of multiple attributes they present a particularly challenging situation to consumers. Each consumer creates individualized criteria for evaluation and systems may have great fluidity across time and circumstance. Common elements in such evaluation systems include aesthetics, fit, economy, use, usefulness, appropriateness, compliance with personal style, quality of construction, quality of materials, and image including perceptions by others and self. In addition, specific attributes are likely to be judged more or less favorably than others.

Non-compensatory decision rules are in effect when a low score on an important or critical feature cannot be overcome by a high score or rating on another attribute. For example, in apparel, size is usually a highly critical factor. Hence, the fact that a garment doesn't fit well cannot be compensated by it being a favorite color or a reasonable price. On the other hand, when the shortcomings of one attribute can be overcome by a more favorable rating on a second attribute, the decision rule is **compensatory**. For example, a second choice in the color of a sweater may be judged as satisfactory when the price is lower. One attribute can "compensate" for another.

APPAREL APPLICATIONS

1. Apparel manufacturers can benefit by recognizing that the best way to capitalize on consumers' internal search is to create a product and experience for the consumer that will be remembered favorably.

2. Apparel markets can develop strategies to provide easy access for consumers to marketing messages. This will reduce the costs of information search and increase the likelihood that information will be available for decision making.

3. Careful attention to apparel design and marketing strategies are necessary to facilitate evaluation of apparel products by consumers as part of their evoked set.

Outlet Selection and Purchase

The next step in the consumer decision-making process, following information search and evaluation, is outlet selection and purchase. As a foundation for understanding how consumers select an outlet through which to make their purchase, it is useful to first understand the variety of

FIGURE 12.9 Consumers select specific outlets for multiple reasons.

reasons why people shop. Tauber (1972), more than 30 years ago, outlined both personal and social motives for shopping. While the channels through which consumers can shop have changed greatly in that time, the reasons why people shop continue to be consistent. Tauber's personal motives include role playing, diversion, self-gratification, learning about new trends, physical activity, and sensory stimulation. His social motives include social experience outside the home, communication with others with similar interest, peer group attraction, status and authority, and pleasure of bargaining. Understanding motives can enable apparel marketers to select and create purchase venues that will meet the needs of potential customers.

Why People Shop

Personal Motives

Role Playing: Shopping activities are expected as part of one's role

Diversion: Shopping offers diversion or recreation

Self-Gratification: Shopping provides emotional gratification or reward

Learning about Trends: Shopping provides information about what is new or current

Physical Activity: Shopping can provide exercise

Sensory Stimulation: Looking, listening, smelling, and touching provide sensory stimulation

Social Motives

Social Experience Outside the Home: Interaction with others is available in the shopping environment

Communication with Others with Similar Interests: Consumers and salespersons with similar interests can share and communicate

Peer Group Attraction: Shopping environments provide meeting places

Status and Authority: Being waited on can provide a feeling of status or power

Pleasure of Bargaining: Getting a good deal or bargaining can be rewarding

Source: Loudon, D., & Della Bitta, A. J. (1988). *Consumer Behavior Concepts and Applications* (3rd ed). NY: McGraw-Hill, Table 20-1, p. 633.

Personal Shopping Motives

Role playing motivates shopping behavior when the "job" of shopping has essentially been assigned to an individual because of their role within the household or family unit. A mother, for example, because of her role as caretaker of children, may take responsibility for back-to-school apparel purchases. Diversion may be a motivating force toward shopping to provide a change from daily routines. For some, shopping may provide self-gratification or a means of rewarding self through actual purchases or the indulgence of spending time seeking information and evaluating alternatives.

Similarly, learning about new trends is a shopping motivation. This allows the shopper to view what is offered and what is new and thereby to become more knowledgeable. The opportunity for physical activity is a motivator for some. Indeed, many malls have calculated distances and plotted walking routes to encourage those who desire the physical activity of shopping. Added steps mean more consumer exposure to merchandise. The final personal motive for shopping is sensory stimulation. Retail, Internet, and direct mail environments provide rich opportunities for sensory stimulation. Strategic planning of elements such as color, texture, and content as well as auditory and olfactory factors are carefully orchestrated to create an alluring mix.

FIGURE 12.10 Sensory stimulation is a motivation for shopping.

FIGURE 12.11 Social interaction can be a strong motivation for shopping.

FIGURE 12.12 Online shoppers are often motivated by finding the best prices or hard-to-find items.

Social Motives for Shopping

For some consumers, the opportunity to have social experiences outside of the home is a motivator to shop. Conversation within the retail environment with other consumers or staff provides social experience. Additionally, shopping may also provide the opportunity to communicate with others who hold similar interests.

Handbag or shoe enthusiasts may enjoy the opportunity to voice their opinions among others who share their interest. In some cases, peer group attraction provides motivation to shop. For example, the presence of groups of teenage girls shopping together is strong evidence of this phenomenon.

For some consumers, there is status and authority in shopping. In the role of a shopper, the ability to weigh alternatives and make purchases represents power. Sales personnel are likely to extend kindness, courtesy, and information because of the shopper's role. Finally, some consumers are motivated to shop because of the pleasure of bargaining or the "thrill of the hunt." Satisfaction can be gained by getting a good deal or by finding just the right thing.

> **A Creative Option**
> *Bag, Borrow or Steal* represents a creative option for consumers wanting to carry the latest designer handbags. By paying a monthly fee, members can select and borrow up to five handbags at a time. Fees for each bag vary by category (couture, diva, princess, and trendsetter) from $20 to $175 per month. The steps involved include selecting an item, receiving it by post, borrowing the next item, and returning the first item by post. Frequency of borrowing is left up to the consumer (www.bagborroworsteal.com).

Outlet Selection

Multiple outlets for consumer activity exist. Consumers can choose from retail stores, Internet sites, direct markets, and other shopping environments. Indeed, in the course of their decision-making, consumers may browse and use many channels.

Multiple factors determine outlet selection whether electronic, telephone, mail, or retail store. Then, even after an outlet type is selected, the consumer must select a specific vendor. While some differences exist in choice making with regard to outlet type, such as electronic versus retail store, many factors that influence choice are the same. These can include: location (including ease of access), outlet design (including physical facilities or consumer logistics such as ease of navigation through the shopping experience either in person or electronically), merchandise (especially the appropriateness of the assortment to meet the consumer's needs), advertising and promotion, personnel (including likeability), credibility, and ease of access, customer services, image and atmosphere (both internal and external), and trust.

Outlet Selection Factors
Location
Outlet design
Merchandise
Advertising and promotion
Personnel
Customer services
Image and atmosphere
Trust

Knowing the reasons why people shop and the factors that influence outlet choice, apparel marketers can design strategies to influence the location, volume, and rate of purchase. Several techniques are available. Store layout and traffic patterns can be effectively used to increase shoppers' exposure to, interaction with, and opinion of merchandise. Visual merchandising techniques can be used to promote specific items, create a positive image, instruct the shopper, and encourage selection. Point-of-purchase media techniques can be used to remind consumers of their need for particular items or to remind them of previous media exposure, such as a magazine spread featuring a particular apparel item. Store fixtures, such as shelving and rack units, are critical tools in creating consumer interest and easing the selection process.

Packaging and pricing strategies are also highly influential. Finally, personal selling in retail stores can greatly enhance the shopping experience by providing competent knowledge, easy access to goods, social support, and ease of transaction.

FIGURE 12.13 Store layout and visual merchandising techniques can provide strong cues to encourage sales.

1. Since multiple types of outlets exist for apparel products marketers must give careful consideration to matching the type of outlet (i.e., electronic versus retail store) to the needs of the target market.

2. In designing a retail store, Internet site, or direct mail program, apparel marketers should seek specific means to provide fulfillment of the multiple motives that propel consumers to shop.

3. Consumer logistics or the ease of access to and progression through the shopping experience is important for apparel marketers using either retail store or electronic strategies.

Post-Purchase Evaluation and Disposition

Consumer satisfaction, dissatisfaction, or some feeling in the middle of the spectrum follows apparel transactions. For satisfied customers, the likelihood of future purchases from the same vendor or site follows when a similar need exists or is triggered. From a marketer's perspective, this is ideal. Some of those satisfied customers will become repeat customers. Even better, some of those repeat customers will find such value in the product that they become loyal customers. Astute apparel marketers work hard to develop such customer relationships. Consumer loyalty programs that reward committed consumers are currently popular.

Customer dissatisfaction triggers **post purchase dissonance**. Post purchase dissonance is the state where the consumer feels a state of discontentment because of a difference in the post purchase state of affairs and the consumer's expectations regarding the purchase. The consumer is unhappy with the purchase or some aspect of it. Generally, post purchase dissonance is likely to be heightened when the purchase is large or important, the ability to alter the decision is less, the choice between alternatives is difficult, the individual is prone toward anxiety, and there is little or no confirmation that a satisfactory purchase was made.

Customer Satisfaction/Loyalty Relationship
Satisfied Customer – Repeat Customer – Loyal Customer

Coping with post purchase dissonance is the responsibility of both the consumer and the marketer. First, in general, marketers can decrease the occurrence of post purchase dissonance by paying attention to important factors prior to the sale. These include considerations such as matching the product to the need of the consumer, encouraging reasonable expectations regarding the outcomes of the purchase, providing easy to use care and use information, providing a quality product, and creating a customer-friendly system for consumer complaints or redress.

Together, after the purchase, consumers and vendors can seek to lessen post purchase dissonance by seeking and providing new information, confirming expectations, changing attitudes, altering product evaluations, reinforcing buyers, and providing reasonable methods for communication and redress.

Out with the Old

After purchase and primary use, the final step in the consumption process is product disposition. In general consumers can keep the item, get rid of it temporarily, or get rid of it permanently. In keeping it, the item can be retained for its original use or it could be given a new use or purpose. Alterations may or may not be required for the new use. Ways to get rid of an item temporarily could include renting it or lending it to someone else.

APPAREL APPLICATIONS

1. Post purchase dissonance can be a serious problem for apparel marketers. Well designed strategies, including the elements of the marketing mix, are required prior to offering products or services to the market.
2. Apparel product disposition offers opportunities for a second level of apparel entrepreneurship. Second-hand retail sites and other means of redistributing apparel goods offer new business opportunities.

Resale Yields Global Market for Vintage Apparel

Quality vintage and period clothes are hitting international markets as sought-after items. Big trading companies operating in Europe, the U.S. and Japan scour the international scene and then ship apparel in five-ton lots to resellers around the globe. Hot items include classic designer labels such as Karl Lagerfeld, Chanel, Dior, and Yves Saint Laurent. Retail stores and online sites are meeting this niche market (Kermond, 2007).

Personal Shopping Checklist

The following are tips to maximize the success of personal shopping:

1. Think about personal image and lifestyle.
2. Analyze personal physical attributes. Plan to use the elements and principle of good design to maximize attributes, minimize flaws.
3. Inventory and analyze the current wardrobe.
4. Create a plan for apparel and accessory purchases.
5. Know the many sources for apparel and accessory products.
6. Seek product and style information before seriously engaging in the shopping process.
7. Use the telephone, Internet, and other sources to ease the information search process.
8. Prepare to shop. Don't shop when hungry, tired, rushed, or overly influenced by others. Dress neatly but comfortably.
9. Create a shopping plan, listing best outlet to search.
10. Watch for quality indicators.
11. Try on if possible. Watch for good fit.
12. Match potential purchase(s) with the apparel purchase plan.
13. Purchase/non-purchase.
14. Try on at home. Check coordination with existing wardrobe contents.
15. Hang, fold or store properly for extended life and optimum visual appeal.

Key Terms

Anticipated problem recognition

Cost-benefit model

Evoked set

External search

Inert set

Model

Post purchase dissonance

Routine problem recognition

Compensatory decision rules

Emergency problem recognition

Evolving problem recognition

Inept set

Internal search

Non-compensatory decision rules

Problem recognition

Ideas for Discussion and Application

1. Study Figures 12.1, 12.2, and 12.3. Select an apparel purchase you made recently. Follow the components of each of the three models for the purchase you made. Explain the application of one of the models for your purchase to a student peer.

2. Think of an apparel purchase you made recently. Review in your mind the internal search involved in that purchase. What information stored in your memory did you access and review?

3. It is likely that situational variables influenced a recent apparel purchase you made. Describe how the market environment, situational variables, product variables, and personal attributes influenced your external search.

4. Working with a partner, identify five branded apparel products. For each, determine whether it is part of your evoked set, inert set, or inept set. Do your responses match those of your partner? Why might they be the same or different?

5. Review the box on page 378, "Why People Shop." Identify which of these circumstances and motives for shopping apply to you. Can you identify the motives of someone you know well?

chapter thirteen

organizational decisions: retail choices

OBJECTIVES

>> *Define merchandise management.*

>> *Apply a structure for organizational decision-making.*

>> *Identify internal and external sources for consumer and market research.*

>> *Discuss the process of conducting original consumer and market research.*

>> *Describe the role and components of a six-month plan in financial planning.*

In general terms, making apparel choices at the manufacturing, wholesaling, and retailing levels follows much the same sequence as making personal choices, including the steps of problem recognition, search and evaluation, outlet selection and purchase, and post-purchase activities. Important differences, however, include changes in terminology, purchase volume, and planning and implementation strategies. This section, while focusing on retail decisions, presents strategies appropriate for manufacturers and wholesalers as well.

Merchandise management, often performed by a team within a merchandising division, is the process used to meet a company's financial goals by meeting the needs of the customer by offering the right merchandise, in the right quantity, to the right customer, at the right time, and in the right place (Smykay et al, 1971).

Merchandise management seeks to obtain profit by offering:
The right *merchandise*
In the right *quantity*
To the right *customer*
At the right *time*,
And in the right *place*.

A Structure for Retail Decision-Making
Consumer and Market Research
Financial Planning
Merchandise Planning
Vendor Selection
Product Selection
Performance Evaluation

Retail is Big Business

Retail, including apparel, is the second largest U.S. industry by employment and number of establishments. It generates $3.8 trillion annually in U.S. retail sales and employs about 11.6% of the U.S population.

Globally, retail also represents a major market component. The two largest retailers are U.S.-based Wal-Mart with more than $312 billion (USD) annual sales and French-based Carrefour with sales of 97.24 billion euros annually from 12,500 stores (Vargas, 2007).

Because of all these variables and the fact that both large and small retailers make timely decisions regarding thousands of individual apparel items offered by hundreds of vendors or manufacturers, a structure for decision-making is useful. This structure includes consumer and market research, financial planning, merchandise planning, vender or source selection, product selection, and performance evaluation.

Consumer and Market Research

Apparel buyers and merchandise managers engage in a constant process of seeking information on which to base their assortment decisions. They must be able to obtain and integrate information on consumer needs and wants, and market conditions. To do so, they access information sources both internal and external to their companies.

Internal Information Sources

Internal sources can include sophisticated electronic records, input from personal conversations, and competitive observations. Electronic records can provide details of past performance including success or failure rates of each style, color, price point, and vendor. Personal conversations can solicit valuable employee feedback. This type of feedback has particular merit because of the close relationship employees have with both consumers and merchandise. "Want slips" from consumers who seek products they don't find can also be valuable. Additionally, observations of the merchandise assortments of competitive retailers and the responses of their consumers can prove beneficial.

External Information Sources

While dramatic international runway collection openings and line releases for new seasons of fashion, as well as market weeks, offer opportunities for retailers and the press to view and evaluate designer's and manufacturer's new seasonal offerings, the need for solid foundational research usually begins much earlier with a variety of sources. Either during or after collecting and analyzing internal information sources, apparel merchandisers look to a diverse array of external information sources. These include fashion consultants and information services, trade

FIGURE 13.1 Collection openings and runway shows serve as information sources.

associations and trade shows, trade publications, resident buying offices, consumer information sources, and original research.

Numerous types of fashion and consulting firms and organizations offer services that provide trend analysis, forecasting, market research, consumer research, collection reporting and analysis, sourcing, design, promotion, advertising, importing, product development, and buying related services. These services are usually provided on a subscription, contract, or fee basis. A listing of examples of fashion consultants and information services is given in the box below.

Fashion Consultants and Information Services (selected)

BrainReserve (Faith Popcorn)	Kurt Salmon Associates
Carlin International	L. A. Colours
The Color Box	Management Horizons
The Color Marketing Group	Margit Publications
Color Portfolio	Nigel French
Colorplay	ORizzonti
Concepts in Color	Pantone Color Institute
Deloitte and Touche	Pat Tunsky Inc.
Dominique Peclers	Promostyl
Ernst & Young	Retail Management Consultants
ESP Trend Lab	Retail Reporting Corporation
Essential Colours and Colorance	State Street Research
Fashion Box	Tobe' Associates (The Doneger Group)
Here & There	Trend Union
Huepoint	Walter F. Loeb
International Colour Authority	WSL Strategic Retail
Kurt Barnard	

TRADE ASSOCIATIONS AND TRADE SHOWS

Apparel related trade associations offer members the opportunity to promote specific aspects of the industry and to share information. Through publications, websites, conferences, conventions, seminars, and trade shows, members of trade associations share information useful to those involved in a particular segment of the apparel industry and to those who use their goods or services. A listing of examples of influential trade associations is included on pages 398 and 399.

Membership in trade organizations can be either by invitation or open to anyone with an interest in the field depending on the organization. By banding together, individuals, usually representing specific businesses, increase their capabilities to promote their field, increase their knowledge, and expand profit potential. Professionals often find it beneficial to join more than one trade organization related to their field. In some cases, student memberships are available to encourage the development of new talent. Conferences and trade shows afford the opportunity through attendance at lectures, forums, demonstrations, and seminars to expand knowledge and to develop networks with others. Often, trade organizations use their collective strengths to foster or encourage legislation, which is beneficial to their industry. Students and new professionals can learn about trade organizations from industry peers, professional publications, and the websites of the trade organizations.

TRADE PUBLICATIONS

Both domestic and international trade publications provide current, easily accessible information on specific aspects of the apparel trade. Published daily, weekly, monthly, or quarterly, they can provide a well-respected basis on which to inform decision-making. Trade publications can be sponsored by trade associations or independent publishing firms.

FIGURE 13.2 Trade shows afford an opportunity to see what is new and communicate with suppliers or customers.

FIGURE 13.3 *WWD* is a well-known and valued trade publication.

Trade Associations (selected)

Acrylic Council
American Apparel Manufacturers Association
American Association for Textile Technology, Inc.
American Association of Textile Chemist and Colorists
American Fiber Manufacturers Association
American Fur Industry
American Leather Accessory Designers
American Management Association
American Printed Fabrics Council
American Textile Machinery Association
American Textile Machinery Association
American Textile Manufacturers Institute
American Wool Council
American Yarn Spinners Association
Associated Corset & Brassiere Manufacturers Inc.
Camel Hair and Cashmere Institute of America
Carpet and Rug Institute
Chambre Syndicale
Clothing Manufacturers Association
Color Association of the United States
Cotton Incorporated
Council of Fashion Designers of America
Crafted with Pride in the USA
Eastern Mink Breeders Association
The Fashion Association
Fashion Footwear Association of New York
The Fashion Group International Inc.
Fashion Jewelry Association of America
Fe'de'ration Franca'ise de la Couture
Footwear Industries of America
Fur Farm Animal Welfare Coalition, Ltd.
Headwear Institute of America

Infants', Children's & Girls' Sportswear & Coat Association, Inc.
International Association of Clothing Designers
International Linen Promotion Commission
International Silk Association
International Swimwear & Activewear Market and the Swimwear Association
The Intimate Apparel Council
Jewelers of America
Leather Apparel Association
The Leather Association
Leather Industries of America
Men's Apparel Guild of California
Mohair Council of America
National Association of Fashion and Accessory Designers
National Association of Hosiery Manufacturers
National Association of Men's Sportswear Buyers
National Association of Milliners, Dressmakers, and Tailors
National Cotton Council of America
National Fashion Accessories Association
National Knitwear & Sportswear association
National Mass Retail Association
National Retail Federation
National Shoe Retailers Association
National Women's Neckwear and Scarf Association
Neckwear Association of America
Polyester Council
Shoe Retailers League
Sunglass Association of America
Underfashion Club Inc.
United Infants' & Children's Wear Association
United Textile Association
Wool Bureau Inc.
Young Menswear Association

Trade Publications (selected)

Accessories Magazine
Advertising Age
American Demographics
American Dyestuff Reporter
America's Textiles International
Apparel (formerly Bobbin)
Apparel Industry Magazine
Apparel Manufacturer
Brandweek
California Apparel News
Chain Store Age
Children's Business
Communication Arts
Daily News Record
Discount Merchandiser
Discount Store News
Display & Design Ideas
Earnshaw's Infants, Girls, and Boys Wear Review
Fashion Extras
Fashion Forecast
Fashion International
Fashion Record
Fashion Showcase Retailer
Fashion Update
Fashion Weekly
Fashionews
Femme Ele'gante
Fiber World
First View
Footwear News
Gap
Hosiery News
Inspiration

International Textiles
Italian Design Fashion
Knitting Times
Lighting Dimensions
Marketing News
Mode
Nonwovens Industry
Retail Ad World
Retail Control
Retail Design & Visual Presentation
Retail Forward
Retail Intelligence
Retail Merchandiser
Retailing Today
Sales & Marketing Management
Salon News
Shopping Center World
Shuz
Sport & Street
SportStyle
Sportswear International
Sposabella
Stores
Style
Textile Arts Council Newsletter
Textile Forecast
Textile Hi-Lights
Textile Organon
Textile Technology Digest
Textile View
Textile World
Textiles Suise
Visual Merchandising and Store Design
Women's Wear Daily

Historically formed for the primary purpose of buying merchandise in major apparel markets, resident buying offices have evolved to become buying, merchandising, and product development organizations with greatly expanded roles. While buying remains a mainstay of their functions, other services are similar to those provided by consulting and information services. These include activities such as order coordination and follow-up, market week facilitation for buyers, trend reporting, strategic planning, source selection, importing, and product development. For example, one buying office offers services for retailers and services for manufactures and designers. Services for retailers include market research, group buys, fashion forecasting, buying, order follow-up, market appointments, vendor listing, trend and market updates, photo packs, feasibility consultation, retail check-ups, open-to-buy planning, and sales training. Services for manufacturers and designers include consultation, design direction, fabric and trim buying, market research, forecasting, product development, brand placement, sample shopping, tradeshow planning, and factory and production sourcing (Global Purchasing Companies, 2007).

Buying offices can be independent or owned by a store or group of stores. Independent offices typically represent a group of non-competitive retailers. Each retailer pays an annual fee for the services. Store owned offices can either be owned by a group of privately owned retailers (an associated or cooperative office) or they can be owned by a single parent organization (corporate owned or syndicated office) to provide services for its stores or divisions. A sample listing of resident buying offices is provided in the box to the right.

> **Resident Buying Offices (selected)**
> Alper International
> Associated Merchandising Corporation
> The Doneger Group
> Federated
>   Federated Merchandising
>   Federated Product Development
> Marshall Kline Buying Service

CONSUMER INFORMATION SOURCES

Consumer information sources serve not only apparel consumers, but also those involved professionally in the field. They provide an excellent means of learning and following the pulse of the consumer. Apparel related publications and websites, as well as general consumer sources, are excellent resources. A listing of consumer publications related to apparel is included in the box below.

Consumer Publications (selected)

Amica	*Line a Italiana*
Baby Fashion	*L'Officiel Collections*
Brigitte	*L'Officiel Hommes*
Burda International	*Lucky*
Carina	*Madam*
Collections	*Men's Club*
Dansen	*McSister*
Details	*Moda*
Donna	*Moda In*
E'le'gance	*Moda Viva*
Elle	*Mode et Mode*
Fashion Guide	*Mondo Uomo*
Fashion Yearbook	*Non-no*
Flair	*Rendez-vous*
GQ	*Sposa*
Harper's Bazaar	*Style*
Hi Fashion	*Teen*
In-Style	*Vogue*
Jeune et Jolie	

General consumer sources provide access to a means of general lifestyle scanning, which is important in interpreting and predicting consumer needs and shopping behaviors. By understanding current political and social thought, business and financial trends, family dynamics, consumer demographics, and lifestyle components, apparel merchandisers can plan more effectively.

While numerous sources of information do exist, in some cases, original research may be the best option. Original research can be conducted either in-house or it can be contracted out to an entity such as a research firm, consultant, or advertising agency.

Consumer and marketing research is the systematic gathering, recording, and analyzing of data about consumers or the market. There are two fundamental strategies which are best classified by their goal. First, research can be **conclusive**. This is research designed to enable a conclusion to be drawn as an aid in making a decision. Second, research can be **exploratory**. Exploratory research usually has as its goal the formation of a hypothesis. The results of exploratory research are designed to provide a starting point and to offer direction for further thought or consideration. Consumer suggestion cards and focus groups are typical data collection methods for exploratory research.

Research data can be either primary or secondary. **Primary data** is gathered firsthand for the purpose of the current research being done. An exit survey of retail store customers would be primary data. Customer response cards, telephone interviews, and mall intercept interviews are other sources of primary data. **Secondary data** is information that has been gathered for some purpose other than the current investigation. However, if the data is judged to match the needs of the current study, it can be used—to save both time and money. The key is whether the secondary data is appropriate, especially whether it answers the research question posed in terms of subjects, time period, and information gathered. The U.S. Census is an example of secondary data that may be appropriately used.

Regarding the timeframe of consumer and market research studies, they can be either cross-sectional or longitudinal. In **cross-sectional research,** data is gathered at a single point in time. For example, if consumer shopping behaviors are recorded for a single week or month, the study is cross-sectional. **Longitudinal research** is conducted over a period of time. It may be collected at timed intervals and allows for comparison and observation of change over time. If consumer shopping behaviors were recorded for each of the 12 months of the year to enable comparisons during the year, the study would be longitudinal.

Numerous methods exist for the design of research and the collection of data. The most popular methods are observations, experiments, and surveys. Observations can include multiple means of making and recording observations including visual, mechanical, and electronic methods. A simple example would be a field study where the researcher visually observes the physical movements of consumers on a retail selling floor. A more sophisticated observation example would be the monitoring of consumers' eye movements using highly sophisticated technologies, while being exposed to television commercials. Hidden cameras recording traffic patterns within malls and stores, as well as counters on websites are additional observational research methods.

Experimental methods can be conducted either in the field or in a laboratory. Textile product testing for wear or abrasion would be a laboratory method, while the use of test markets to investigate consumer responses to new products or advertisements would be a field method. Research using surveys include questionnaires and interviews. Typically, questionnaires can be administered in person or via the Internet or mail. Interviews can be in person or via telephone or the Internet.

To aid in decision-making, consumer and market research can focus on diverse types of data. Consumer characteristics can include demographics, activities, and cognition. Demographic information, such as consumer age, gender, income, and occupation, can be valuable in formulating plans for apparel merchandising. Cognitive studies, including motivations, attitudes, and information processing, are also a critical part of understanding consumer behavior. Motivational research can help explain why consumers make apparel selections as they do. Attitudinal research examines how consumers form and change attitudes about apparel products. Information processing measures focus on the process consumers use to arrive at apparel decisions.

Financial Planning

Based on the market research, the next step is the development of a financial plan. Merchandise is usually grouped into categories and classifications to facilitate planning and buying. Financial plans usually begin with a historical view of the organization, including past performance, such as sales and profits. Plans can be either short- or long-term but most commonly include a 6-month period. Financial plans are based on a company's financial objectives and provide sales projections that are used to aid in planning the amount of money to spend on specific categories of merchandise to achieve the desired profit goal.

A 6-month plan forms a financial blueprint for the selection and purchase of goods to be sold. Two 6-month plans are created to plan the calendar year. Typically, one covers spring and summer (February–July) and the other covers fall and winter (August–January). Each 6-month

6-Month Merchandise Plan Calculations

Merchandise costs: Expenses of obtaining merchandise, including the merchandise purchase and associated transportation and inventory costs.

Markup: The amount added to the cost of the merchandise to establish the selling price.

Markdown: An adjustment to the retail price downward.

Gross margin: The dollar difference between net sales and the net cost of merchandise.

Operating expenses: Costs incurred in daily operation of the business such as rent, utilities, and supplies.

Expected profit: Anticipated difference between total revenue and total expense.

Turnover or stock turn: The number of times stock is sold and replaced.

Stock/sales ratio: Relationship between stock on hand and sales volume for a period.

Shrinkage: Inventory loss from shoplifting, employee theft, or clerical errors.

Open-to-buy: The amount of funds available for purchases by classification each month.

Simple Open-to-Buy Formula

    Planned Sales

\+   Planned Markdowns

\+   Planned End of Month Inventory

−   Planned Beginning of Month Inventory

=   Open-to Buy (Walters, 2007)

---

plan is the result of planning (1) retail sales for the period, (2) amount of inventory to be on hand at the beginning of each month, (3) reductions to be taken such as markdowns, employee discounts, theft, etc. and (4) markup or retail price versus cost. This plan then facilitates the planning of purchases to meet the projected sales and inventory levels. While detailed description is beyond the scope of this text, calculations available for the creation of the plan include merchandise costs, markup, markdown, gross margin, operating expenses, expected profit, turnover or stock turn, stock/sales ratios, shrinkage, and open-to-buy.

> **Did you know?**
> **Shrinkage Protection: Source Tagging Technologies**
> Worldwide retail shrinkage, sometimes called shortage, currently exceeds $70 billion annually! About 40 percent or $28 billion of that is the result of shoplifting. Electronic Article Surveillance (EAS) is an aggressive measure to curb this loss. With the high demand from retailers for floor-ready merchandise, this is increasingly being done at the manufacturing level. EAS systems usually have two parts: (1) tags or labels are attached to or hidden within merchandise and (2) a set of detectors is installed at the retail exit point to identify tags that were not removed or desensitized at the point-of-sale. Currently, two non-compatible EAS technologies are dominant. Swept Radio Frequency (RF) and Acousto-Magnetic (AM) systems are most commonly manufactured in North America, Europe and Asia and shipped for application worldwide. Since retailers typically adopt one technology or the other, it is important at the point of manufacture to know where the item is headed so that the tag applied will match the retail system. An emerging practice is to create tags that employ both popular EAS technologies (Prime Newswire, 2007, October 10; KMA Global Solutions, 2007).

Merchandise Planning

Based on the financial plan, the merchandise or assortment plan is created. The calculated beginning of the month (BOM) and end of the month (EOM) figures from the 6-month plan enable planning to ensure that adequate merchandise will be available to meet planned sales.

Because of the great diversity in apparel products, the planning and buying processes are typically organized by categories. A **category** can be an assortment of items seen by the customer as reasonable substitutes for each other, such as girls' apparel, boys' apparel, or infants' apparel

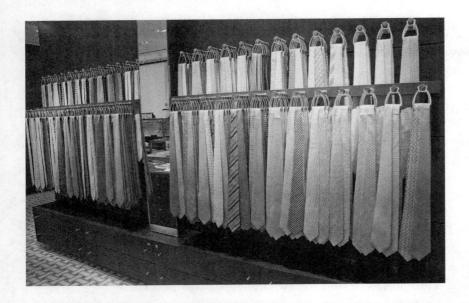

FIGURE 13.4 A merchandise or assortment plan attempts to insure that appropriate and adequate stock will be on hand to enable planned sales.

FIGURE 13.5 Basic stock does not change greatly from season to season or year to year.

(Levy & Weitz, 2004). In some cases, retailers may define their categories in terms of specific brands, such as Tommy Hilfiger or Polo/Ralph Lauren (Levy & Weitz, 2004). The term **category management** is used to describe the process of making strategic decisions to maximize the sales and profits of a category for a company.

Within each retail organization, whether large or small, a buying organization is designed to enable efficient buying processes. Large entities may employ many buyers to cover the various types of merchandise, yet within small companies, a single person may have responsibility for many product types. While each company may have its own system for classifying and working with merchandise, the National Retail Federation offers a standard scheme that includes merchandise groups, departments, classifications, categories, and stock keeping units (SKUs) (Levy & Weitz, 2004). These divisions enable merchandise managers and buyers to focus on and examine merchandise attributes and company needs by using sequentially smaller groupings.

A **merchandise assortment** is the range of goods that is determined to best meet the needs of consumers and the retailer. It is developed to ensure that the styles, colors, sizes, and prices can meet the planned financial goals by having appropriate and sufficient stock in the right proportions. One technique to create the merchandise assortment is the **model stock plan**. A model stock plan is a quantitative listing or inventory of styles, sizes, colors and fabrics, and price points needed. An effective model stock plan includes consideration of four key features: quantities required, quality and other qualitative variables including trends and consumer demand, available resources or sources, and timing. Development of a model stock plan for fashion goods is considerably more difficult than for basic or staple goods. **Basic or staple goods** are those that do not change substantially from season-to-season or year-to-year. Men's dress socks are an example of a basic, or staple, stock. The fluctuations and volatility characteristic of fashion goods substantially increases the challenges of developing a model stock plan for these goods.

Product Lifecycles

One aspect of an apparel product that requires careful consideration is its life cycle. Typically, products move, over time, through the stages of (1) introduction, (2) growth, (3) maturity, and (4) decline (Levy & Weitz, 2004). These stages match almost exactly with the categories of product innovators (2.5 percent of the market), early adopters (13.5 percent of the market), early majority (34 percent of the market), late majority (34 percent of the market), and laggards (16 percent of the market) (Hawkins, Mothersbaugh, & Best, 2007). Of special interest is the fact that apparel products do not move through these cycles at the same rate. Fads, for example, rise and fall in popularity rapidly, often within a single season. Classics stretch the cycle over several seasons or years.

Variety, Depth, and Breadth

During merchandise planning, decisions are made not only regarding the dollar value and types of merchandise selected for resale, but also regarding the number of choices and product availability to be supported. Assortment breadth and depth are aspects that are considered. Breadth, or variety, refers to the number of different choices available for the consumer. A **broad assortment** will contain more styles and colors than a narrow assortment and allows the consumer variety in selection. A **deep assortment** will contain multiple items in a single size, color, and style. This may enable a customer to find his or her specific size in a desired item. A shallow assortment, on the other hand, is likely to result in a "stock out" situation, where the item wanted by a specific customer is out of stock or not available. Since the financial resources to invest in inventory are usually finite, there are constant tradeoffs between positions of depth and breadth.

FIGURE 13.6 The fashion life cycle

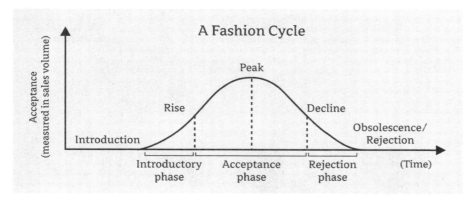

FIGURE 13.7 A broad assortment contains many styles and colors, allowing the consumer variety in selection.

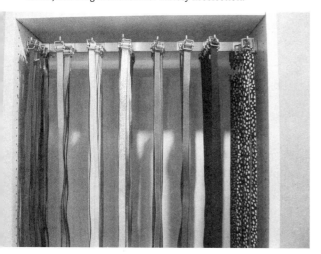

FIGURE 13.8 A deep assortment contains multiple units of a single size, color, or style.

FIGURE 13.9 Manufacturers, wholesalers, and middlemen are common types of sources.

Vendor or Source Selection

Sourcing describes the process of deciding from where goods will be obtained. Retailers have a variety of options. **Manufacturers**, wholesalers, and middlemen are common types of sources. Manufacturers produce goods and then offer them for sale. The terms vendor, supplier, or manufacturer (in this context) are used interchangeably. **Wholesalers** typically purchase goods in large quantities and then resell them in smaller quantities. **Middlemen** act as agents between manufacturers and retailers by adding some service in between. Middlemen may finish garments in some manner, arrange shipment of goods to a retailer, or serve as a broker or negotiator between the retailer and manufacturer. Middlemen may or may not actually own or take possession of the goods.

Increasingly, in today's market, **vertical integration** is a trend. Vertical integration is the term that describes the arrangement where the manufacturer also serves as the retailer for the finished goods and where the retailer creates goods for sale in their stores. "Company stores" and private labels are examples of this practice. Macy's Charter Club and Victoria Secret's Pink brands are examples.

Since multiple sources exist to meet the needs of both manufacturers and retailers, and materials and finished goods are available from diverse suppliers, both domestic and global, sourcing is a complex task. Apparel marketers are keenly aware of the characteristics of their target consumers and seek to secure products that will meet their needs, leading both to customer satisfaction and company profit. Important considerations in the selection of sources include the merchandise offered, and factors related to distribution, promotion, shipping, inventory, price, contract terms, timing, and exclusivity.

Sourcing Factors
Merchandise
Distribution
Promotion
Shipping
Inventory
Price
Contract Terms
Timing
Exclusivity

International Sourcing

Apparel consumers and the producers and retailers that support them have come to enjoy and expect the diversity and variety provided by imports. Thus, buyers cover the world seeking to satisfy consumer wants. In addition, textile and apparel producers engage in offshore production allowing foreign workers to complete one or more of the steps of production. This is accomplished via company-owned factories abroad, contracts with foreign owned factories, or joint ownership ventures. Attributes that encourage international sourcing include cost, uniqueness,

Global Labor Practices Under Fire

Child labor, harassment, abuse, discrimination, health and safety, freedom of association, collective bargaining, wages and benefits, hours of work, overtime compensation, and environmental protection are hot topics related to global labor practices. Manufacturers who operate internationally and those who contract for production offshore are under pressure from consumers and social groups to curb harmful and unfair practices.

While many manufacturers show little effort to improve working conditions, others, such as Eddie Bauer and Gap, are setting standards and requiring their manufacturing partners to comply. While not owning or managing any factories, Eddie Bauer and Gap select partners who share their commitment to ethical practices and agree to standards of conduct. They, like many others, seek compliance through a global labor practices program that monitors adherence to a supplier code of conduct. In addition, many companies (Adidas AG, Asics Corp., Liz Clairborne, H&M, Hennes & Mauritz AB, Fossil Inc., Nike, Nordstrom Inc., Phillips-VanHeusen, Puma AG, and Umbro Plc. elect to participate in organizations designed to promote fair labor practices globally. For example, the Fair Labor Association (FLA) (www.fairlabor.org/) is made up of apparel and footwear companies, human and consumer groups, and colleges and universities dedicated to improving working conditions. It operates an accredited compliance program that provides assurance that accredited manufacturers follow fair practice codes (Eddie Bauer, 2007; Fair Labor Association, 2007; Gap, 2007).

quality, and variety. While foreign sourcing is desirable because of lower costs and higher profit possibilities, it is a complex business that requires intricate knowledge of local and international laws and customs, transportation and logistics systems, labor force characteristics, tax systems, monetary exchange rates, and export/import regulations including tariffs and quotas. The United States is both an exporter and importer of apparel products with the balance of trade substantially on the side of imports.

FIGURE 13.10 Cost, uniqueness, quality, and variety are factors that encourage international sourcing.

While some buyers comb foreign markets independently to procure goods, more commonly, store-owned foreign buying offices, agents, import fairs, and importers are used. For large retailers, company-owned buying offices in foreign markets survey the market, offer recommendations, supervise purchases, and follow-up. Independent agents serve smaller retailers by

---

Designer Sources Seek Strategies to Limit Copies

Domenic Dolce and Stefano Gabbana showed evidence in the presentation of the Spring 2008 show of their high-end Dolce & Gabbana line, a strategy to limit copies of their work. While the runway introduction and backdrop screened a video of artists carefully hand-painting Impressionist-style flowers, models arrived in ensembles bearing oversized flowers on pencil skirts, dresses, and voluminous ball gowns as if they had just been hand painted. This detailing was designed to be hard to copy. As knockoffs have multiplied and become mainstream many high-end designers are employing complex shapes and detailing to thwart copying (The Wall Street Journal, 2007).

offering similar services. Import fairs held in the United States enable buyers of small to mid-sized stores to have access to foreign goods. Finally, importers are firms that purchase foreign goods and offer them for resale to small retailers.

Vendor Relationships

Productive partnerships between retailers and their suppliers yield increased success for both parties. Cooperation and collaboration are key as vendors recognize that promoting the success of the retailer ultimately results in success for the vendor. Hence, both are engaged in seeking and employing strategies that will gain competitive advantage for the retailers. In addition to the application of sound business practices, such as honoring contracts with regard to product, quality, price, delivery, and exclusivity, many vendors also provide other initiatives. These include substantial sales staff training, in-store promotions (including fixtures and signage), cooperative advertising, and other strategies designed to sell merchandise. Technology further enhances the collaborative relationship among vendors and retailers. With speed being a key element in success, technology based systems such as Electronic Data Interchange (EDI) and Collaborative Planning, Forecasting, and Replenishment (CPER) (Levy & Weitz, 2004) offer solutions. Strong vendor/retailer relationships can be fostered by developing faith in common goals, mutual trust, credible communication, and commitment to partnership as evidenced by action and follow through.

Vendor/Retailer Relationships
Positive Vendor/Retailer Relationships **Yield** ▶ Higher Profits

---

Product Selection

The buying or merchandise selection process requires a delicate balance between analytical and creative skills. The abilities to analyze consumer demographic and psychographic data, local and global market indicators, and sociocultural trends must be coupled with the capability to think creatively, consider new options, and take risks. Based on the planning accomplished during the development of the financial and merchandise plans, the role of the buyer or buying team is to procure the merchandise necessary to accomplish those plans.

After extended research using sources and techniques described earlier in this chapter—financial planning, and merchandise planning—the next step in the decision-making process is the selection of the actual merchandise to be offered for sale. This step occurs simultaneously with vendor selection.

The buying function can be either centralized or decentralized based on the size and philosophy of the organization. In **centralized buying,** all procurement functions are focused in a central location. Even though there may be numerous retail locations, all buying is done in one place. This is the mode of operation for many of the largest retail chains. This system allows for efficiency and economy of scale. In contrast, **decentralized buying** systems allow the buying function to be performed at the regional, local, or even store level. The advantage of this method is that it allows the buying staff to make purchases respectful of the needs of the local customer.

Resident buying offices, discussed previously as an information source for buyers, also function to buy merchandise. Usually located in a specific geographic market center or area, they can serve as the retailer's market representative in procuring goods. Resident buying offices can be either store owned or independent. Store-owned offices are owned and operated by a retailer or a retail group. Independent offices are operated under separate ownership and serve the needs of specific retailers. In addition to buying functions, resident buying offices also provide services related to forecasting, contracting, financing, advertising, promoting, and personnel development.

Often, a sales representative acts as the link between the retailer and the manufacturer. Company reps work exclusively for one vendor while independent reps may represent and be employed by more than one supplier. Retail buyers can interact with representatives and their merchandise in several ways in order to see, evaluate, and buy apparel goods. The term "market" is commonly used to describe a concentration of vendors in a centralized location, either geographically or over the Internet. These may include permanent wholesale market centers (usually in dedicated buildings or groupings of buildings), temporary trade shows, or Internet exchanges. In addition, sales representatives can visit buyers' offices.

Permanent wholesale market centers are established market centers that house the offices of multiple vendors. Typically, these market centers are open throughout the year to provide access for buyers. In the United States, examples include The Fashion Center in New York City, which encompasses several blocks of buildings known as the Garment District, and the Dallas Market Center, a complex where more than 26,000 manufacturers and importers offer their products. Other prominent U.S. merchandise marts include those in Atlanta, Chicago, Los Angeles, and Miami. Trade shows, often called merchandise shows or market

FIGURE 13.12 Permanent merchandise marts offer buyers access to vendors year around.

International Market Events

January

Pitti Uomo and Uomo Italia (men's)	Florence
Milano Collezioni Uomo (men's)	Milan
Designer Men's Wear Collections	New York
Hong Kong Fashion Week	Hong Kong
NAMSB—National Association of Men's Sportswear Buyers Show	New York
Haute Couture collections (women's, spring)	Paris
Market Week (women's ready-to-wear)	New York
Los Angeles Market	Los Angeles
Pitti Bimbo (children's wear)	Florence
Salon de la Mode Enfantine (children's wear)	Paris
Prêt-á-Porter Paris (women's ready-to-wear)	Paris
Premiere Classe (accessories)	Paris
SIHM—Salon Internationade l'Habillement Masculin (men's)	Paris

February

CPD (Collections Premieren Düsseldorf) Woman - Man	Düsseldorf
FFANY—Fashion Footwear Association of New York and National Shoe Fair	New York
WSA—Shoe Show	Las Vegas
Mercedes Benz Fashion Week (7th on Sixth) and Market Week	New York
Prêt-á-Porter Designer Collection Shows	Paris
Milano Moda Donna and MilanoVendaModa (women's ready-to-wear)	Milan
London Fashion Week	London
MAGIC (men's and women's)	Las Vegas
The Super Show (sporting goods)	Las Vegas

March

Montreal Fashion Week	Montreal
MIDEC—Mode Internationale de la Chaussure (shoes)	Paris
MIPEL (leather accessories)	Milan
MICAM (shoes)	Milan
NAMSB Show (men's wear)	New York

April

American Designer Collection Shows (women's ready-to-wear)	New York
Los Angeles (women's market)	Los Angeles

May

The Accessories Show and Accessories Circuit	New York

June

Moda Prima (knitwear)	Milan
Milano Collezioni Uomo (men's designer collections)	Milan
Pitti Uomo and Uomo Italia (men's wear)	Florence
NAMSB Show (men's wear)	New York

Market Week (women's ready-to-wear)	New York
Los Angeles women's market	Los Angeles
FFANY—Fashion Footwear Association of New York and National Shoe Fair	New York

July

Mode Enfantine (children's wear)	Paris
Designer Men's Wear Collections	Paris
SIHM—Salon International de l'Habillement Masculin (men's)	Paris
Haute Couture Collections (fall–winter)	Paris
Hong Kong Fashion Week	Hong Kong
Market Week (women's ready-to-wear)	New York

August

CPD Woman—Man	Düsseldorf
The Accessories Show and Accessories Circuit	New York
Los Angeles Ready-to-Wear market	Los Angeles
MAGIC	Las Vegas
FFANY—Fashion Footwear Association of New York and National Shoe Fair	New York
WSA Shoe Show	Las Vegas
Salon de la Mode Enfantine (children's wear)	Paris

September

MIDEC—Model Internationale de la Chaussure (shoes)	Paris
MICAM (shoes)	Milan
MIPEL (leather accessories)	Milan
Mercedes Benz Fashion Week (7th on Sixth and Market Week)	New York
Prêt-á-Porter Paris (women's ready-to-wear)	Paris
Première Classe (accessories)	Paris
Milano Moda Donna and MilanoVendaModa (women's ready-to-wear)	Milan
London Fashion Week (women's ready-to-wear)	London
Montreal Fashion Week	Montreal

October

NAMSB Show (men's wear)	New York
Market Week (women's ready-to-wear)	New York
The Accessories Show, Accessories Circuit, and Accessories Market Week	New York

November

| Los Angeles Market (women's ready-to-wear) | Los Angeles |

December

| Moda Prima (knitwear) | Milan |
| FFANY—Fashion Footwear Association of New York and National Shoe Fair | New York |

Adapted from Frings, G. S. (2005). *Fashion from Concept to Consumer* (8th ed). Upper Saddle River, NJ: Pearson Prentice Hall.

weeks, may be hosted within permanent market centers or can be located in convention centers or exposition halls. These are typically held at specific times of the year. The boxes on pages 420 and 421 lists several of the national and international market events. Retail Internet exchanges are electronic marketplaces to facilitate the buying and selling of merchandise via the Internet.

Among the choices available to retailers are those related to branding. **Manufacturer brands or national brands** are designed, manufactured, and marketed by a vendor who also has the responsibility to develop the image of the brand. Since the manufacturer invests heavily in promoting the brand image, the retailer can benefit from customer loyalty, resulting in enhanced store traffic, image, and sales. However, if more than one retailer within a market offers the same national brand, then competitive advantage is lost and store loyalty may be damaged.

FIGURE 13.13 Manufacturer or national brands are designed, manufactured, and marketed by a vendor.

FIGURE 13.14 Licensed brands result when the owner of a brand contracts with a manufacturer to produce and sell the brand.

Similar to national brands, **licensed brands** result when the owner of a well known name brand contracts with a manufacturer to produce and sell the brand. This practice is increasingly popular and has seen great success, for example, in the licensing of designer names for accessory products. The challenges inherent in national or licensed brands being sold by competing retailers can be circumvented by the adoption of **private-label or store brands**. These are products designed and sold exclusively by the retailer and are manufactured by a contractor. Benefits of private label merchandise include exclusivity, manufacturing and quality control, and the opportunity to build store loyalty. Negative attributes include increased design, promotion, and advertising costs; additional training needed to help staff sell the unknown private label; and the inability to return unsold units to the vendor.

FIGURE 13.15 Private label or store brands are designed by and sold exclusively by a retailer.

> ***Zara's Vertical Integration Model Brings Global Success; Avoids Sweatshop Labor Issues***
> As the flagship chain for the Spanish Inditex Group, Zara has a unique vertically integrated business model which includes design, manufacturing, and retailing components. Because it makes the clothes itself, Inditex is able to react quickly to changing market trends and complete successfully with rivals such as Gap and H&M. More than 3,000 stores in over 65 countries (with 4,000 locations projected by 2009) represent rapid expansion (*Business Week*, 2006). In-house design and manufacturing not only reduces the time to develop a new product to two to four weeks rather than nine months, but also avoids the use of manufacturing sub-contractors. The use of sub-contractors, particularly in underdeveloped countries, opens the issue of sweatshop labor. Zara, with control of labor and manufacturing conditions, has been recognized as a positive industry example (CNN.com, 2001). Zara launches thousands of new designs annually. Another diversion from common industry practice is Zara's avoidance of advertising. Zara's parent company spends only about 0.3 percent of revenue on advertising compared to the industry average of 3.5 percent. They do, however, offer a catalogue and website (CNN.com, 2001).

Performance Evaluation

Evaluation of the performance of retail units, goods, and suppliers facilitates not only knowing the relative success of financial, merchandising, and marketing strategies but also enables improved planning for the future. Numerous tools, calculations, and methods are available for evaluation. Technology-based merchandise information systems and point-of-sale data systems enable sophisticated and timely data presentation and analysis. Merchandising teams can, in many cases, have almost instantaneous feedback on how merchandise is selling and contributing to the business enterprise.

While anecdotal and conversational feedback from consumers is extremely valuable, especially in knowing what the consumer desires but did not find, most evaluation tools use mathematical calculations based on the collection of quantitative data. Examples of popular

Career Paths in Merchandising and Stores

Many major retailers recruit regularly for highly qualified individuals to prepare for careers in merchandising and store operations via executive development or training programs. These programs vary in length but typically provide an orientation to the retailer and the functions therein and then set the trainee on a path designed to provide integrated experience in planning, buying, and store operations to facilitate flexibility in career progression. An example of career progression includes an assistant buyer or assistant merchandise planner, department manager or senior merchandise planner, senior merchandise planner, buyer or manager of merchandise planning, store merchandise manager or manager of merchandise planning, and vice-president of merchandise management, vice-president store general manager, or director of merchandise planning (The Neiman Marcus Group, 2007). While titles vary, the progression is through new experiences and greater dollar volume responsibility.

Job roles of the entry positions following an executive training program may resemble the following:

Assistant buyer
  Vendor support
  Store communication
  Marketing events and advertising
  Recap and analysis of sales
  Assist buyer achieve sales and gross margin plans
  Product receipt
  Assist buyer with product selection
  Manage buying office operations
Assistant merchandise planner
  Locker stock and replenishment programs
  Recap and analyze sales
  Purchase order mechanics
  Assist buyer in achieving sales and gross margin plans
  Inventory management
  Strategic plans, budgets, and recaps
  Manage buying office operations (The Neiman Marcus Group, 2007)

calculations include sales in dollars, sales in units, year-to-year comparisons, comparisons to merchandise plan, stock turnover, average gross sales per customer, sales per square foot, sell through percentage, gross margin, and profit and loss comparisons.

By combining this information in a variety of ways, retailers can obtain a useful picture for specific aspects of their operation as well as for overall performance. For example, vendor analysis or the creation of a vendor matrix can provide a clear image of the individual and comparative contributions of vendors or suppliers. Sales, markdowns, returns, sell-through percentages, and gross margins can be calculated for each vendor and compared to other vendors to identify the most successful sources. These may be good opportunities for increased purchases of stock in future periods. Rankings by vendor can provide input for relative allocation of future merchandise dollars. In general, retailers seek multiple tools or calculations to examine and evaluate the diverse aspects of apparel merchandise performance.

Contrasts in Personal and Organizational Buyer Behaviors

Strategies for decision-making have been presented in this and the previous chapter. Chapter 12 includes a decision-making model for the consumer's personal apparel choices. This chapter

Through 2014 Apparel Employment Outlook Is Strong

The U.S. Department of Labor, Bureau of Labor Statistics projects strong growth in apparel related occupations through 2014. Selected projections, based on 2004 employment statistics are shown below. Many categories include apparel and non-apparel products.

Employment Title	Employment		Percent Change
(Bureau of Labor Statistics) (in thousands)	2004	2014	
First-line supervisors/managers of retail sales workers	1,667	1,731	3.8
Retail sales workers	8,445	9,382	11.1
Retail salespersons	4,256	4,992	17.3
Sales representatives, wholesale and manufacturing, except technical & scientific	1,454	1,641	12.9
Models	2	3	15.7
Textile, apparel, and furnishings occupations	929	768	−17.3*
Advertising, marketing, promotions, public relations, and sales managers	646	777	20.3
Wholesale and retail buyers, except farm products	156	169	8.4
Fashion designers	17	18	8.4
Merchandise displayers and window trimmers	86	95	10.3

*Note trend toward offshore production
(U.S. Department of Labor, 2007)

includes decision-making strategies for businesses in making apparel-related choices for resale. Both have the same primary components: (1) determining needs and formulating a plan, (2) seeking alternatives, (3) making selections, and (4) evaluating purchases. While fundamentally the same, a few key differences must be noted. Typically, organizations are likely to have relatively more objective and clearly articulated criteria for profit maximization that guide the decision-making process. Second, organizational purchases are less likely to have impact upon

> **Selected Performance Evaluation Tools**
>
> **Sales in dollars:** The amount, in dollars, of merchandise sold.
>
> **Sales in units***:* The amount, in units, of merchandise sold.
>
> **Year-to-year comparisons:** Data comparisons from one year to another.
>
> **Comparisons to merchandise plan:** Actual data compared to planned amounts.
>
> **Stock turnover***:* The number of times stock is sold and replaced.
>
> **Average gross sales per customer:** Total sales divided by number of transactions.
>
> **Sales per square foot:** Sales divided by store or department square footage.
>
> **Sell through percentage:** The percentage of merchandise sold during a specific period.
>
> **Gross margin:** The dollar difference between net sales and the net cost of merchandise.
>
> **Profit and loss comparison***:* Summary of financial data that tells whether there was a net profit or loss.

other members of the organization than personal purchases have on other household members. Other than the need for coordination to create a store image or enable customers to match garments and accessories, departmental choices may have less impact on each other. Third, businesses often develop strong reciprocal alliances with their suppliers that go beyond the relationship developed between individual consumers and providers. They are proactive in encouraging or even requiring sources to develop products that meet their specific needs. Private labels are an extreme example of this relationship.

In sum, the processes for both personal and business decision making are remarkably similar including determining needs and planning, seeking alternatives, making selections, and evaluating purchases. Yet, unique differences exist based on whether purchases are made for personal use or corporate resale (see Table 13.1).

TABLE 13.1 Comparison of Personal and Corporate Decision Making

Personal Strategies	Corporate Strategies
Determining Need and Planning	
Problem Recognition	Consumer & Market Research
Recognizing a difference between desired and current states	Systematic gathering & analyzing market data
	Financial Planning
	Provide sales projections to aid planning of expenditures to meet profit goals
	Merchandise Planning
	Assortment plan to ensure adequate merchandise to meet planned sales
Seeking Alternatives	
Search & Evaluation	Vendor Selection
Internal & external information search	Decide where goods will be obtained
Making Selections	
Outlet Selection & Purchase	Product Selection
Store or outlet selection & purchase	Buy merchandise to meet financial and merchandise plans
Evaluating Purchases	
Post Purchase Evaluation & Disposition	Performance Evaluation
Assessment of satisfaction or dissonance; disposition of used goods	Assessment of financial, merchandise, and marketing strategies

Key Terms

Basic or staple goods

Category management

Consumer and marketing research

Deep assortment

Longitudinal research

Merchandise assortment

Model stock plan

Secondary data

Wholesalers

Broad assortment

Centralized buying

Cross-sectional research

Exploratory research

Manufacturer brands or national brands

Merchandise management

Primary data

Sourcing

Category

Conclusive research

Decentralized buying

Licensed brands

Manufacturers

Middlemen

Private-label or store brand

Vertical integration

Ideas for Discussion and Application

1. Visit the websites of at least three of the trade associations listed in the boxes on pages 398 and 399. For each, identify their purpose, membership requirements and fees, and services offered.

2. Find three of the trade publications listed in the box on page 400. Describe the types of articles each contain. Compare the three publications.

3. Find three of the consumer publications listed in the box on page 402. Briefly summarize three articles or features in each. What do you notice about the target audience for each publication?

4. Visit two local apparel retailers. Identify 20 brands as national, licensed, or private label. You may need to augment your findings with information from sales personnel or websites.

5. Compare and contrast the differences and similarities between personal and corporate buying strategies.

glossary

Advertising: Communication to a large number of people with the goal of selling via a medium such as radio, television, or direct mail. *Ch. 11*

Amictus: Clothing wrapped or draped around the body in Roman costume. *Ch. 1*

Analogous schemes: Color schemes that use adjacent colors from the color wheel such as green and blue or red, orange, and yellow. *Ch. 5*

Anticipated problem recognition: A need that is expected but does not require an immediate solution. *Ch. 12*

Apparel fashion: Apparel or accessories worn during a specific time period by a majority or large number of people. *Ch. 5*

Asymmetrical balance: An informal balance where the elements on either side of an imaginary center line are different but have equal visual weight. *Ch. 5*

Atmospherics: The creation of a selling environment using visual techniques, lighting, colors, music, and scent to perceptually stimulate customers and ultimately influence their buying behavior. *Ch. 10*

Attention: The second step in perception when a stimulus is allowed to become active and is sent to the brain for further processing. *Ch. 10*

Attitude: The positive or negative feelings consumers have toward objects. *Ch. 2*

Autonomic: A power structure where an equal yet separate number of decisions are made by two household heads. *Ch. 2*

Average gross sales per customer: Total sales divided by number of transactions.

Balance: The perception that the elements in a design are equal in visual weight. *Ch. 5*

Basic or staple goods: Those products that do not change substantially from season-to-season or year-to-year. *Ch. 13*

Bias Grain: An exact 45-degree angle between the warp and filling yarns across the face of the fabric. *Ch. 6*

Bottoming: The process of attaching the sole of the shoe to the upper part. *Ch. 9*

Brand: A name, logo, or symbol that identifies a product or service and differentiates it from other offerings in the marketplace. *Ch. 10*

Brand equity: The added value for a brand beyond the functional characteristics of the product achieved through customer awareness of the brand and positive emotional ties to it. *Ch. 10*

Brand image: The reflection of what people think, feel, and say when they see or hear a brand name. *Ch. 10*

Breeches: Also known as braies, these were basic garments for men; ankle-length trousers. *Ch. 1*

Broad assortment: An assortment of merchandise that contains numerous style and color choices for the consumer. *Ch. 13*

Buyer: A consumer role where a person actually makes a purchase. *Ch. 11*

Calasiris: A sheath dress or tunic worn by ancient Egyptians. *Ch. 1*

Category: An assortment of items seen by the customer as reasonable substitutes for each other. *Ch. 13*

Category management: The process of making strategic decisions to maximize the sales and profits of a category. *Ch. 13*

Cellulosic fibers: Fibers made from natural plant cellulose and require minimum chemical steps. *Ch. 6*

Centralized buying: A system where all procurement functions are focused in a central location. *Ch. 13*

Chiton: A tunic worn by Grecians, very similar to the calasiris and worn by both men and women. *Ch. 1*

Classic: A garment that takes decades to move through the fashion cycle. *Ch. 7*

Classics: Items that move extremely slowly from one category to the next of the fashion adoption stages. *Ch. 2*

Codpiece: A padded, protective triangle of fabric worn by men to protect and emphasize the groin. *Ch. 1*

Color: The sensation aroused when the eye is stimulated by light waves. *Ch. 5*

Color schemes: The ways colors are used together. *Ch. 5*

Communication mix: The combination of tools used to communicate with prospective buyers including personal selling, advertising, publicity, public relations, store design, and visual merchandising. *Ch. 10*

Comparisons to merchandise plan: Actual data compared to planned amounts. *Ch. 13*

Compensatory decision rules: The case when the shortcomings of one attribute can be overcome by a more favorable rating on a second attribute. *Ch. 12*

Complementary schemes: Color schemes that use colors that are opposite on the color wheel such as violet and yellow or red and green. *Ch. 5*

Computer aided design (CAD): A design process accomplished with the assistance of a computer. *Ch. 11*

Computer-integrated manufacturing (CIM): Manufacturing that is controlled by computer. *Ch. 11*

Conclusive research: Research that is designed to enable a conclusion to be drawn as an aid in making a decision. *Ch. 13*

Conspicuous consumption: The practice of making purchases or obtaining goods or services primarily to be seen by others for their symbolic meaning or indication of wealth and status. *Ch. 2*

Consumer and marketing research: The systematic gathering, recording, and analyzing of data about consumers or the market. *Ch. 13*

Consumer behavior: The decision processes and physical activities individuals engage in when evaluating using, or disposing of goods and services. *Ch. 11*

Continuous line: The use of either real or suggested lines to lead the eyes in the creation of rhythm. *Ch. 5*

Cost-benefit model: A plan where consumers seek information on which to base decisions when the benefits of acquiring the information exceed the costs of obtaining it. *Ch. 12*

Costing: The process of estimating and then determining the total cost of producing a garment. *Ch. 7*

Cross-sectional research: Research where data is gathered at a single point in time. *Ch. 13*

Cultural myopia: Cultural nearsightedness or making decisions as if one's culture is the only one to be considered. *Ch. 2*

Culture: A distinctive way of life for a group of people. *Ch. 2*

Customer relationship management (CRM): A set of strategies designed to identify and build loyalty with a marketer's most valued customers. *Ch. 10*

Data mining: Accessing and analyzing collected data to extract useful information. *Ch. 11*

Decentralized buying: Systems where the buying function is performed at the regional, local, or even store level. *Ch. 13*

Declining phase: A stage in the fashion cycle where styles are still being worn but are purchased by fewer consumers and at lower prices. *Ch. 7*

Deep assortment: An assortment that contains multiple items in a single size, color, and style. *Ch. 13*

Design ease: The extra fabric needed to create a visual effect. *Ch. 5*

Discrimination: The ability of consumers to distinguish he differences between two stimuli. *Ch. 2*

Doublet: Covers the male torso; usually had sleeves and sometimes padded. *Ch. 1*

Drafting: A method of creating patterns by using the body measurements of a typical target customer. *Ch. 3*

Draping: A method of creating patterns that involves fitting a muslin on a mannequin or on a real body. *Ch. 3*

Dyeing: The process of imparting color to fibers, yarns, and fabrics. *Ch. 6*

Ecological design: A technique to modify behavior by using physical surroundings. *Ch. 2*

Ego: The Freudian term for the portion of self that mediates the demands of the id and the prohibitions of the superego. *Ch. 2*

Elastic: Elastic demand is the condition when the demand for a product varies inversely with its price. *Ch. 11*

Electronic data interchange (EDI): A system to share data for to achieve common purposes. *Ch. 11*

Emergency problem recognition: An unexpected need that requires an immediate response. *Ch. 12*

Emphasis: A focal point or center of interest. *Ch. 5*

Evoked set: Alternatives judged favorably by the consumer. *Ch. 12*

Evolving problem recognition: A need that was not anticipated and for which no immediate solution is required. *Ch. 12*

Exploratory research: Research that is designed to provide a starting point or to offer direction for further thought or consideration. *Ch. 13*

Export: A good sold to another country. *Ch. 11*

Exposure: The first step in perception when a stimulus enters the range of an individual's ability to receive it. *Ch. 10*

External search: The step in the decision making process when consumers begin seeking information from sources other than those stored within the consumer. *Ch. 12*

Extinction: A condition where consumers unlearn behavior that is not reinforced. *Ch. 2*

Fabric: The textile material from which most ready-to-wear garments are made. *Ch. 6*

Fad: A fashion trend that has a short life in the fashion cycle. *Ch. 7*

Fads: Items that move with extreme rapidity through the fashion adoption stages from innovators to laggards. *Ch. 2*

Farthingale: A narrow understructure which held out the skirt of the gown and was made from willow twigs, cane, or whale bone sewn into the fabric. *Ch. 1*

Fibers: The most basic unit of fabrics. *Ch. 6*

Figure: The shape of a woman's body. *Ch. 5*

Filament fibers: Long, continuous strands that are measured in yards or meters. *Ch. 6*

Findings: All other materials in a garment besides the fabric that is essential in making the garment. *Ch. 6*

Forgetting: Loss of learning due to non-use or interference from other learning. *Ch. 2*

Gradation: See *progression*. *Ch. 5*

Grading: The process of increasing and decreasing pattern dimensions to reflect the various sizes produced. *Ch. 7*

Grain: The lengthwise and crosswise yarns in a woven fabric. *Ch. 5, 6*

Gross margin: The dollar difference between net sales and the net cost of merchandise. *Ch. 13*

Harmony: A pleasing visual effect created when all design elements work together. *Ch. 5*

Himation: A Greek cloak worn in cold weather. *Ch. 1*

Hue: The name of a color such as red, yellow, or blue. *Ch. 5*

Human behavior: Behavior of Man, including a broad spectrum of actions and activities. *Ch. 2*

Id: The Freudian term for the portion of self driven toward immediate gratification of desires. *Ch. 2*

Import: A good purchased from another country. *Ch. 11*

Indumenta: Garments that were slipped over the head in Roman costume. *Ch. 1*

Inelastic: Inelastic demand is the condition when the demand for a product varies in the same direction as a change in price. *Ch. 11*

Inept set: Alternatives evaluated negatively by the consumer. *Ch. 12*

Inert set: Alternatives for which the consumer has neither positive nor negative opinions. *Ch. 12*

Influencer: A consumer role where a person either intentionally or unintentionally by word or action provides influence. *Ch. 11*

Initiator: A consumer role where a person identifies a need or want. *Ch. 11*

Intensity: The brightness or dullness of a hue. *Ch. 5*

Interfacing: Extra layers of fabric placed between the garment and the facing to add shape or body to the garment. *Ch. 6*

Interlinings: The method of using one fabric as a backing for another fabric. *Ch. 6*

Internal search: The step in the decision making process when consumers begin scanning their stored memory for information previously obtained. *Ch. 12*

Interpretation: The third step in perception when meaning is assigned to a stimuli. *Ch. 10*

Introductory phase: The first stage in the fashion cycle where new silhouettes are worn by trendsetters and fashion innovators. *Ch. 7*

Jabot: An early lace necktie for men. *Ch. 1*

Jerkin: A man's garment, equivalent to the modern suit jacket. *Ch. 1*

Just in time (JIT): A strategy to reduce inventory costs and cut time from production to delivery. *Ch. 11*

Last: A foot model with dimensions and shape based on the anatomy of a foot. *Ch. 9*

Lasting: The process of shaping the upper sections of the shoe to the last and insole. *Ch. 9*

Licensed brands: Brands that result when the owner of a well know name brand contracts with a manufacturer to produce and sell the brand. *Ch. 13*

Line: A continuous mark, that functions to measure the distance between two points, indicate shape, provide movement, and determine direction. *Ch. 5*

Lining: An extra layer of fabric used to prevent stretching and to finish off the inside of the garment. *Ch. 6*

Longitudinal research: Research that is conducted over a period of time. *Ch. 13*

Manufacturer brands or national brands: Brands that are designed, manufactured, and marketed by a vendor who also has the responsibility to develop the image of the brand. *Ch. 13*

Manufacturers: Companies that produce goods and then offer them for resale to the consumer. *Ch. 13*

Marker making: A step in the manufacturing process that diagrams the precise arrangement or layout of pattern pieces for a specific garment and the number of sizes to be cut from a single spread of fabric. *Ch. 7*

Market aggregation: The strategy where all consumers are judged to be sufficiently alike to be likely to respond to a product or service in a like manner. *Ch. 11*

Market maven: An opinion leader who serves across a broad spectrum of product categories. *Ch. 2*

Market opportunity analysis: The process of identifying within the marketplace consumer needs or wants that are not currently being satisfied. *Ch. 11*

Market pull: The condition where a need in the marketplace drives the introduction of a new product or service. *Ch. 10*

Market push: The condition where industry innovation or technology drives the introduction of a new product or service. *Ch. 10*

Market segmentation: The strategy that recognizes sufficient diversity within a market to merit subdividing it into smaller groups with similar purchasing characteristics. *Ch. 11*

Marketing: The process of creating, communication, and delivering value to create exchanges that satisfy customer and organizational objectives. *Ch. 11*

Marketing strategies: Specific managerial decisions to affect the probability or frequency that exchanges will occur. *Ch. 11*

Material components: The physical substances used and changed by individuals who form a culture. *Ch. 2*

Matriarchal: A power system where the female head of household predominates in the decision making process. *Ch. 2*

Merchandise assortment: The range of goods that is determined to best meet the needs of consumers and the retailer. *Ch. 13*

Merchandise management: The process used to meet a company's financial goals by meeting the needs of the customer by offering the right merchandise, in the right quantity, to the right customer, at the right time, and in the right place. *Ch. 13*

Middlemen: Agents between manufacturers and retailers who offer some service such as finishing garments, arranging shipment, or negotiating. *Ch. 13*

Model: A simplified representation of something. *Ch. 12*

Model stock plan: A quantitative listing or inventory of styles, sizes, colors, fabrics, and price points needed. *Ch. 13*

Modeling: A method of changing behavior by allowing the consumer to observe the behavior of others and the consequences of that behavior. *Ch. 2*

Monochromatic schemes: Color schemes that use tints, shades, and intensities of a single hue. *Ch. 5*

Motive: An unobservable inner force that stimulates a consumer toward making a specific choice. *Ch. 2*

Muslin: A term used in the United States that means the first fabric garment made after the pattern has been finalized; a kind of test garment; also referred to as a toile. *Ch. 3*

New Look: Created by Christian Dior in 1947, this look had narrow shoulders, a defined waist, and emphasis on the bust with a wide skirt in a longer length. *Ch. 1*

New wool: Wool fibers that have never been manufactured or used. Also called virgin wool. *Ch. 8*

Non-cellulosic fibers: Fibers made from molecules of carbon, hydrogen, nitrogen, and oxygen. *Ch. 6*

Non-compensatory decision rules: The case when a low score on an important or critical feature cannot be overcome by a high score or rating on another attribute. *Ch. 12*

Non-material components: Cultural attributes such as words, ideas, customs, beliefs, and habits. *Ch. 2*

Off-the-peg: A term used to describe ready-to-wear apparel being sold at retailers. Not custom made garments. *Ch. 1*

One-sided message: A communication structure that presents only the positive aspects of a product or service being promoted. *Ch. 2*

Outsourcing: See sourcing. *Ch. 3*

Passive search: The process by which individuals acquire information without trying but as a normal process of everyday living. *Ch. 2*

Patriarchal: A power system where the male head of household predominates in the decision making process. *Ch. 2*

Peak phase: A phase in the fashion cycle where garments are widely accepted and worn by the mass market. *Ch. 7*

Personal selling: One-to-one communication between a seller and a potential buyer. *Ch. 11*

Physique: The shape of a man's body. *Ch. 5*

Post purchase dissonance: The state where a consumer feels a state of discontentment because of a difference in the post purchase sate of affairs and the consumer's expectations regarding the purchase. *Ch. 12*

Primary data: Data gathered firsthand for the purpose of current research. *Ch. 13*

Private-label or store brands: Products designed and sold exclusively by a retailer. *Ch. 13*

Problem recognition: Recognition of a need created by a difference between a desired state and a current state. *Ch. 12*

Product position: The position, either positive or negative, that a product holds within the mind of the consumer. *Ch. 10*

Product positioning: Decisions made by marketers to attempt to achieve a specific perception of the brand or a brand image within the minds of specific target market consumers. *Ch. 10*

Profit and loss comparison: Summary of financial data that tells whether there was a net profit or loss. *Ch. 13*

Progression: The use of a gradual increase or decrease of a single design element such as color or shape. *Ch. 5*

Proportion: The relation of the size of the parts of a design to the whole and to each other. *Ch. 5*

Psychoanalytic theory: The Freudian idea that personality is derived from interaction of the id, ego, and superego. *Ch. 2*

Psychographics: A technique to measure lifestyle, including such components as consumer activities, interests, and opinions. *Ch. 2*

Publicity: Unpaid communication offered by a third party that influences the image of a company in the eyes of potential consumers. *Ch. 11*

Quality of apparel: Defined as the whether or not the garment meets the expectations of the consumer. *Ch. 8*

Radial balance: A balance formed when the major elements of a design radiate from a central point. *Ch. 5*

Radiation: The creation of visual movement from a central point outward. *Ch. 5*

Reinforcement: A reward provided for specific behavior. *Ch. 2*

Repetition: Repeating lines, shapes, colors, or textures. *Ch. 5*

Reprocessed wool: Also called recycled wool. These fibers result when wool has been woven or felted into a wool product have not been used by the consumer, and are now being converted back to a fibrous state. *Ch. 8*

Reused wool: The resulting fiber when wool or reprocessed wool has been spun, woven, knit, or felted into a wool product and has been used by the consumer and is now being converted back to a fibrous state. *Ch. 8*

Rhythm: The creation of a fluid path of motion for the eyes by allowing them to begin with a dominant feature and then move in an easy progression from that dominant point to subordinate areas. *Ch. 5*

Routine problem recognition: An expected and recurring need that requires an immediate solution. *Ch. 12*

Ruff: An extremely high decorative collar created on upper garments by using a drawstring. *Ch. 1*

Sack: Also called the "sacque," this is a shapeless dress with small box pleats in the back. *Ch. 1*

Sales in dollars: The amount, in dollars, of merchandise sold. *Ch. 13*

Sales in units: The amount, in units, of merchandise sold. *Ch. 13*

Sales per square foot: Sales divided by store or department square footage. *Ch. 13*

Sales promotion: Any activity or device used to promote a sale. *Ch. 11*

Scale: The relationship between the size of one shape compared to another. *Ch. 5*

Schenti: A simple kilt worn by Egyptian men which wrapped around the hips with the ends hanging down in the front of the body. *Ch. 1*

Secondary data: Data gathered for some purpose other than a current investigation yet judged to be appropriately matched to the needs of a current study. *Ch. 13*

Self-concept/product image congruence: A theory that suggests that individuals purchase products and services which match or are congruent with their self-concept. *Ch. 2*

Self-concept: Self image or the way a consumer sees himself. *Ch. 2*

Sell through percentage: The percentage of merchandise sold during a specific period. *Ch. 13*

Selvage: The tightly woven edge of a woven fabric; found on both edges of the fabric. *Ch. 6*

Shade: A darker value of a color created by adding black to a hue. *Ch. 5*

Shape or form: The outer contour of an object or garment. *Ch. 5*

Shaping: A method of changing behavior by reinforcing sequential behaviors that gradually moves the consumer toward a desired behavior. *Ch. 2*

Shoe: Commonly called footwear, defined as a mechanism capable of holding the foot in the heel of the shoe and facilitates support for the foot during push off in walking. *Ch. 9*

Silhouette: The outline of a shape or form. *Ch. 5*

Sizing: The classification of the dimension of garments. *Ch. 8*

Slashing: A practice of cutting slits in the material of garments and pulling the lining through for a decorative effect. *Ch. 1*

Social class: A strata formed from a group of individuals who have approximately equal position in a society. *Ch. 2*

Social theories: Personality theories that suggest that individuals develop personality and modes of behaving based on their social interactions with others. *Ch. 2*

Sourcing: Refers to the process of selecting raw materials or components and also choosing contractors to produce the garments. *Ch. 3, 13*

Split complementary schemes: Color schemes that combine three colors where one color is combined with the two colors on the sides of its complement such as red combined with blue-green and yellow-green. *Ch. 5*

Spreading: The process of superimposing lengths of fabric on a cutting table in order to prepare for the cutting step. *Ch. 7*

Staple fibers: Short fibers that can be measured in inches or centimeters. *Ch. 6*

Stimulus generalization: The use of one response for similar stimuli unless the stimuli (products) are differentiated in some way. *Ch. 2*

Stimulus-response theories: Personality theories that focus on the relationship between behavior, consequences, and future behavior. *Ch. 2*

Stock turnover: The number of times stock is sold and replaced. *Ch. 13*

Stola: Ankle-length garments with full sleeves worn by Roman women. *Ch. 1*

Style: The lines, cut, colors, or other attributes that make garments distinct from one another. *Ch. 5*

Subculture: A segment within a culture which shares distinguishing values and patterns of behavior that are different from the overall culture. *Ch. 2*

Superego: The Freudian term for the portion of self that represents social or individual norms and exerts a constraining force. *Ch. 2*

Symmetrical balance: A formal balance where the elements on either side of an imaginary center line are identical. *Ch. 5*

Syncratic: A power structure where most decisions are made together by both the female and male heads of household. *Ch. 2*

Target market selection: Identification of a group or groups of consumers most likely to purchase a product. *Ch. 11*

Texture: The surface quality of an object including not only the visual aspect but also the feel or drape of the item. *Ch. 5*

Thread: A fine yarn used to hold fabric sections together by way of seams. *Ch. 6*

Toga: Considered the national dress of ancient Rome, a semi-circular one-piece garment. *Ch. 1*

Trait and factor theories: Personality theories that use standardized inventories to identify interrelated variables. *Ch. 2*

Two-sided message: A communication structure that presents both the positive and negative attributes of a single product or presents the positive aspects of both the promoted product and a comparable competitor. *Ch. 2*

Underlining: A method of using one fabric as a backing for another fabric. The two fabrics are treated as one piece in the construction process. *Ch. 6*

Universal Product Code (UPC): A laser readable black and white bar code system that records product information such as style, color, size, price, and fabric. *Ch. 11*

User: A consumer role where a person uses or consumes a product or service. *Ch. 11*

Value: The lightness or darkness of a color. *Ch. 5*

Vanity sizing: Often used by designers and manufacturers where the garments are cut larger to appeal to the vanity of consumers who like to think of themselves as smaller. *Ch. 8*

Vertical integration: The arrangement where a manufacturer also serves as the retailer for the finished goods or where the retailer creates goods for sale in their stores *Ch. 13*

Weaving: The process of interlacing two sets of yarns at right angles. *Ch. 6*

Wholesalers: Companies that purchase goods in large quantities and then resell them in smaller quantities. *Ch. 13*

Yarn: A strand of natural or man-made fibers or filaments that are twisted or grouped together for weaving or knitting in constructing fabric. *Ch. 6*

Year-to-year comparisons: Data comparisons from one year to another. *Ch. 13*

references

Chapter 1

Boucher, F. (1987). *20,000 years of fashion: The history of costume and personal adornment* (expanded edition). New York: Harry N. Abrams, Inc.

Breward, C. (1995). *The culture of fashion*. Manchester, U.K.: Manchester University Press.

Cosgrave, B. (2001). *The complete history of costume and fashion: From ancient Egypt to present day*. New York: Checkmark Books.

Laver, J. (1969). *The concise history of costume and fashion*. New York: Harry N. Abrams, Inc.

Lester, K.M, & Kerr, R. N. (1967). *Historic costume*, (6th ed.). Peoria, IL: Chas. A. Bennett Co., Inc.

Tortora, 2005

Wilcox, C. & Mendes, V. (1991). Modern fashion in detail. London, 20.

Chapter 2

Affinity. (2007). *Interesting facts about fashion*. Retrieved October 10, 2007, from http://ioframe.com/en/interesting_facts_about_fashion.

Bellis, M. (2007). The history of pantyhose? *About.com: Inventors*. Retrieved October 10, 2007, from http://inventors.about.com/library/inventors/blpantyhose.htm.

Blackwell, R. D., Miniard, P. W., & Engel, J. F. (2006). *Consumer behavior* (10th ed.). Mason, OH: Thomson South-Western.

Claritas. (2007). Understanding psychographics. Retrieved September 21, 2007, from www.claritas.com/claritas/psychographics.jsp

Coleman, R. P. (1983, December). The continuing significance of social class in marketing. *Journal of Consumer Research,* p. 267.

Hale, T. (2007, September). The African-American consumer: Is the cultural divide breaking down? *Consumer Insight Magazine.* Retrieved September 21, 2007, from http://nielsen.com/consumer_insight/ci_story4.html.

Fishbein, M., & Ajzen, I. (1975). *Belief, attitude, intention and behavior,* Reading, MA: Addison-Wesley.

Gilbert, D. (1998). *The American class structure.* NY: Wadsworth.

Hawkins, D. I., Mothersbaugh, D. L., & Best, R. J. (2007). *Consumer behavior building marketing strategy* (10th ed.). New York: McGraw-Hill.

Loudon, D., & Della Bitta, A. J. (1988). *Consumer behavior concepts and applications* (3rd ed.). New York: McGraw-Hill.

Maslow, A. H. (1970). *Motivation and personality.* New York: Harper & Row.

McGuire, W. J. (1976, March). Some internal psychological factors influencing consumer choice, *Journal of Consumer Research, 2,* 302–319.

Murry, A. H., (1938). *Explorations in personality.* NY: Oxford University Press.

Nielsen BuzzMetrics. (2007). *Nielsen BuzzMetrics.* Retrieved September 21, 2007, from www.nielsenbuzzmetrics.com

Rokeach, M. (1973). *The nature of human values.* NY: Free Press.

Scott, J. & Leonhardt, D. (2005, May 15). Shadowy lines that still divide: How class works, *The New York Times.* Retrieved October 14, 2007, from www.nytimes.com/packages/html/national/20050515_CLASS_GRAPHIC/index_01.html.

The Nielsen Company. (2007, September 12). Majority of Americans believe pressure to look good escalating. Retrieved September 21, 2007, from www.nielsen.com/media/pr_070912.html.

Thompson, W., & Hickey, J. (2005). *Society in Focus.* Boston, MA: Pearson.

Veblen, T. (1899). *The theory of the leisure class.* NY: Macmillan.

Vegetarian Shoes and Bags. (2007). Vegan shoes: Materials. Retrieved October 10, 2007, from www.vegetarianshoesandbags.com/htmls/material.aspx.

Webster's seventh new collegiate dictionary. (1971). Chicago, IL: B. & C. Merriam Co.

Chapter 3

Jones, S. J. (2002). *Fashion design.* New York: Watson-Guptil Publications.

Breward, C. (2003). *Fashion.* Oxford: Oxford University Press.

Brown, P., Rice, J. (2001). *Ready-to-Wear Apparel Analysis*, (3rd ed.). Upper Saddle River, NJ: Prentice Hall.

Cassin-Scott, J. (1994). *The illustrated encyclopedia of costume and fashion.* London: Brockhampton Press.

Weber, J. (1990). *Clothing-fashion-fabrics-construction*, (2nd ed.). Peoria, IL: Glencoe/McGraw-Hill.

Seeling, C. (2000). *Fashion-The century of the designer 1900–1999.* English edition. Cologne: Konemann Verlagsgesellschaft mbH.

Chapter 4

Dias, L. (2008). *Core concepts in fashion.* New York: McGraw-Hill Irwin.

The fashion book. (1998). New York: Phaidon Press Limited.

Seeling, C. (2000). *Fashion: The century of the designer, 1900–1999.* English edition. Cologne: Konemann Verlagsgesellschaft mbH.

Chapter 5

Beauty by Jeanique. (2007). Welcome to beauty by Jeanique. Retrieved October 26, 2007, from www.bfas.com/index.html.

Brown, P., & Rice, J. (2001). *Ready-to-wear apparel analysis* (3rd ed.). Upper Saddle Hill, NJ: Prentice Hall.

Burns, J. B. (2007, September 22). Apocalypse wow. *The Age*. pA2.

Color Me Beautiful. (2007). Retrieved October 26, 2007, from

Color Wheels, Color Systems. (2007). Retrieved March 28, 2007, from http://www.uwgb.edu/heuerc/2D/ColorSystm.html.

Fenner, A. & Bruns, S. (2004). *Dress smart: A guide to effective personal packaging* (2nd ed.). New York: Fairchild Publications.

Jackson, C. (1980). *Color me beautiful: Discover your natural beauty through the colors that make you look great and feel fabulous*. Washington, DC: Acropolis.

Johnson, J. G., & Foster, A. G. (1990). *Clothing image and impact* (2nd ed.). Cincinnati, OH: South-Western.

Nicholson, J., & Lewis-Crum, J. (1986). *Color wonderful*. New York: Fantom Books.

Nix-Rice, N. (1996). *Looking good: A comprehensive guide to wardrobe planning, color and personal style development*. Portland, OR: Palmer/Pletsch.

Oprah.com (2007, October 10). *Jesse and Joe clean Gayle's closet*. Retrieved October 10, 2007, from www:oprah.com/foodhome/home/housekeeping/home_20041109_closet.jhtml.

Pegler, M. M. (2006). *Visual merchandising and display*. NY: Fairchild Publications.

Rasband, J. (1996). *Wardrobe strategies for women*. Albany, NY: Delmar.

Silverstein, R. (2007). Personal wardrobe consultant. *Careers: You do What?* Retrieved October 10, 2007, from http:/www.collegeclub.com/article/view/1705.

Stylemakeovers.com. (2007). Color makeover: Find your colors. Retrieved October 26, 2007, from www.stylemakeovers.com/colortest/color-module.htm.

Associated Content. (2007). Strange but true fashion facts. (2007). Retrieved October 10, 2007, from www.associatedcontent.com/article/9551/strange.html.

Wallace, J. (1983). *Dress with style*. Old Tappan, NJ: Revell.

Chapter 6

American Home Economics Association. (1969). *Textile handbook,* (3rd ed.). Washington, DC.

Brannon, E. (2006). *Fashion forecasting*, (2nd ed.). New York: Fairchild Publications.

Brower, D. (2002). Natural wonders-linen. *Butterick Home Catalog Summer 2002*, pp. 20–24.

Brown, Ruth. (2000*). History of silk*. Stone Creek Home Page. Accessed April 5, 2004, from www.stonecreeksilk.co.uk.

Butterick Home Catalog

Humphries, M. (2004). *Fabric reference,* (3rd ed.). Upper Saddle River, NJ: Pearson Prentice Hall.

Kadolph, S., Langford, A., Hollen, N. & Saddler, J. (1993). *Textiles,* (7th ed.). New York: Macmillan.

Price, A., Cohen, A., & Johnson, I. (2005). *J.J. Pizzuto's fabric science*, (8th ed.). New York: Fairchild Publications.

Vogue Patterns November/December 1992, 36–37.

Wingate, I. & Mohler, J. (1984). *Textile fabrics and their selection,* (8th ed.). Englewood Cliffs, NJ: Prentice Hall.

Chapter 7

Brown, P. & Rice, J. (2001). *Ready-to-wear apparel analysis,* 3rd edition. Upper Saddle River, NJ: Prentice Hall.

Dias, L. (2008). *Core concepts in fashion*. New York: McGraw-Hill Irwin.

Gary, S. & Ulasewicz, C. (2001). *Made in America: The business of apparel & sewn products manufacturing,* (3rd ed.). Sebastopol, CA: GarmentoSpeak.

Glock, E. & Kunz, G. (2005) *Apparel manufacturing: Sewn product analysis,* (4th ed.). Upper Saddle River, NJ: Pearson Prentice Hall.

Kunz, G. & Garner, M. (2007). Going global: The textile and apparel industry. New York: Fairchild Publications.

Tate, S. (2004). *Inside fashion design,* (5th ed.). Upper Saddle River, NJ: Pearson Prentice Hall.

Chapter 8

Ajzen, I. & Fishbein, M. (1980). Understanding attitudes and predicting social behavior. Englewood Cliffs, NJ: Prentice Hall.

American Home Economics Association. (1969). *Textile handbook,* (3rd ed.),. Washington, DC.

Brown, P., & Rice, J. (2001). *Ready-to-wear apparel analysis,* (3rd ed.). Upper Saddle Hill, NJ: Prentice Hall.

Glock, R. & Kunz, G. (2005). *Apparel manufacturing: Sewn product analysis,* (4th ed.). Upper Saddle River, NJ: Prentice Hall.

Size conversions for American, British, and European clothing and shoes. Retrieved January 26, 2006 from www.fashion-411.com/Size_Conversions.htm.

Price, A., Cohen, A., & Johnson, I. (2005*). J.J. Pizzuto's fabric science,* (8th ed.). New York: Fairchild Publications.

Seleshanko, K. (August, 2002). Fashion firsts. *Sew News*, 52–53.

Chapter 9

Amethyst Handbag Library. (2005). Handbag shapes. Retrieved June 12, 2007, from
http://thehandbagresource.com/library/amethyst-handbag-library/index.ptp

Johnson, A. (2002). *Handbags: The power of the purse.* New York: Workman Publishing.

Kippen, C. *The history of shoes: Shoe making.* Curtin University of Technology, Perth, WA.
Retrieved April 19, 2005 from http://podiatry.curtin.edu.au/shoo.html.

National Fashion Accessories Association, Inc. 1997. *History of the handbag.* Retrieved April 19,
2005, from www.accessoryweb.com/history.html.

Northhampton Borough Council. *History of shoes.* Retrieved April 18, 2005, from
www.northampton.gov.uk/site/scripts/documents_info.php?categoryID=1482&document
ID=142-30k.

O'Keeffe, L. (1996). *Shoes: A celebration of pumps, sandals, slippers, & more.* New York: Workman
Publishing.

Shoes on the Net. *Anatomy of a shoe.* Retrieved April 18, 2005, from
www.shoesonthenet.com/anatomy.html.

Chapter 10

Allen, K. R. (2003). *Bringing new technology to market.* New.York.: McGraw-Hill.

Chu, J., & Pike, T. (2002). What top-performing retailers know about satisfying customers: Experience is key. *IBM Institute for Business Value.* Retrieved November 1, 2007, from
www.304.ibm.com/jct03004c/tools/cpeportal/fileserve/download3/14265/ibm_retail
crm.pdf?contentid=14265.

Hawkins, D. I., Mothersbaugh, D. L., & Best, R. J. (2007). *Consumer behavior building marketing strategy* (10th ed.). New York: McGraw-Hill Irwin.

Hurlbut, T. (2007a). Retail strategy: Building brand equity. Retrieved October 10, 2007, from www.hurlbutassociates.com/BuildingBrandEquity.html.

Hurlbut, T. (2007b). Competitive shopping: Studying your competitors. Retrieved October 10, 2007, from www.hurlbutassociates.com/StudyingYourCompetitors.html.

Kaufman, S. (2007, August 22). Knock it off—at your peril. *Visual Merchandising and Store Design*. Retrieved October 10, 2007, from www.visualstore.com/index.php/channel/21/id/12375.

Levy, M., & Weitz, B. A. (2004). *Retailing management* (5th ed.). New York: McGraw-Hill Irwin.

Paglucia-Morrison, G. M. (2005). The customer-centric store: Delivering the total Experience, *Retailing Issues Letter, Center for Retailing Studies, Mays Business School, Texas A&M University,* 17(2), 1–4.

Solomon, M. R., & Rabolt, N. J. (2004). *Consumer behavior in fashion*. Upper Saddle River, NJ: Prentice Hall.

Chapter 11

AMA Board Approves New Marketing Definition. (1985. March 1). *Marketing News,* p. 1.

American Marketing Association. (2007a). *Dictionary of marketing terms*. Retrieved March 28, 2007, from www.marketingpower.com/mg-dictionary-view69.php.

American Marketing Association. (2007b). *Dictionary of marketing terms*. Retrieved March 28, 2007, from www.marketingpower.com/mg-dictionary-view1862.php.

Blackwell, R. D., Miniard, P. W., & Engel, J. F. (2006). *Consumer behavior* (10th ed.). Mason, OH: Thomson South-Western.

Brass, K. (2007, October 2). Luxury takes flight in cyberspace. *International Herald Tribune*. Retrieved October 10, 2007, from www.iht.com/articles/2007/10/02/style/rweb.php.

Hauser, J. (2005). *Introduction to marketing, Spring 2005*. Retrieved September 23, 2006, from Massachusetts Institute of Technology, Sloan School of Management Web site: http://ocw.mit.edu/OcwWeb/Sloan-School-of-Management/15-810Spring-2005/CourseHome/index.htm.

Office of Textiles and Apparel, U.S. Department of Commerce. (2007a). Major shipper's report: U.S. imports by country. Retrieved October 31, 2007, from http://otexa.ita.doc.gov/MSRCTRV.htm.

Office of Textiles and Apparel, U.S. Department of Commerce. (2007b). U.S general imports in U.S. dollars. Retrieved October 31, 2007, from http://otexa.ita.doc.gov/scrits/tquads1.exe/catdata.

Textile/Clothing Technology Corporation. (2007). Turning research into reality. Retrieved October 30, 2007, from www.tc2.com.

TradeStats Express. (2007). HS 62 – Apparel articles and accessories, not knit. Retrieved October 31, 2007, from http://tse.export.gov/NTDChartDisplay.aspxUniqueURL=rqpeq5550xjkcblss0z455-2007-10-31-0-18-24&Flow=Balance.

United States International Trade Commission. (2007). Tariff information center. Retrieved October 31, 2007, from www.usitc.gov/tata/index.htm.

U.S. Census. (2007b). Estimated annual retail and food services sales by kind of business: 1992 through 2005. Retrieved October 14, 2007, from www.census.gov/svsd/retlann/pdf/sales.pdf.

Vargas, M. (2007). The value of friendship. Retrieved January 6, 2008, from http://retailindustry.about.com/od/crm_relationships/a/loyalty1friends.htm.

World Trade Organization. (2007). What is the WTO? Retrieved October 31, 2007, from
www.wto.org/english/thewto_e/whatis_ehtm.

Chapter 12

Bag Borrow or Steal. (2007, October 10). *How it works*. Retrieved October 10, 2007, from
www.bagborroworsteal.com/ui/hoitworks.

Blackwell, R. D., Miniard, P. W., & Engel, J. F. (2006). *Consumer behavior* (10th ed.). Mason, OH:
Thomson SouthWestern.

Fishbein, M., & Ajzen, I. (1975). *Belief, attitude, intention and behavior,* Reading, MA: Addison-
Wesley.

Hawkins, D. I., Mothersbaugh, D. L., & Best, R. J. (2007). *Consumer behavior Building marketing
strategy* (10th ed.). New York: McGraw-Hill.

Kermond, C. (2007, September 19). The world wide op shop. *The Age,* p. Metro 16.

Loudon, D., & Della Bitta, A. J. (1988). *Consumer behavior concepts and applications* (3rd ed.).
New York: McGraw-Hill.

Tauber, E. M. (1972). Why do people shop? *Advertising Age, 36,* 47–48.

U.S. Census. (2007a). Estimated per capita retail sales by selected kind of business: 1992 through
2005. Retrieved October 14, 2007, from www.census.gov/svsd/retlann/pdf/percap.pdf.

Wells, W. D. (1961). Measuring readiness to buy, *Harvard Business Review, 39,* 81–87.

Chapter 13

Business Week. (September 4, 2006). *Fashion conquistadore*. Retrieved January 6, 2008, from
http://www.businessweek.com/magazine/content/06_36/b3999063.htm?chan=search

CNN.com. (2001, June 15). *Zara, a Spanish success story*. CNN.com Europe/Business. Retrieved October 10, 2007, from http://edition.cnn.com/BUSINESS/programs/yourbusiness/stories2001/zara/.

Eddie Bauer. (2007). *Global labor practices*. Retrieved October 10, 2007, from http://investore.eddiebauer.com/responsibility/global_labor.cfm.

Fair Labor Association. (2007). *Companies, suppliers, licensees*. Retrieved October 14, 2007, from www.fairlabor.org/participants/companies.

Frings, G. S. (2005). *Fashion from Concept to Consumer* (8th ed). Upper Saddle River, NJ: Pearson Prentice Hall.

Gap Inc. (2007). *Improving factory conditions*. Retrieved October 10, 2007, from http://www.gapinc.com/public/SocialResponsibility/sr_factories.shtnml.

Global Purchasing Companies. (2007). *Global purchasing companies: Strategic planning for the retail industry*. Retrieved October 10, 2007, from www.globalpurchasinggroup.com.

Hawkins, D. I., Mothersbaugh, D. L., & Best, R. J. (2007). *Consumer Behavior Building Marketing Strategy* (10th ed.). New York: McGraw-Hill.

KMA Global Solutions. (2007). *KMA global solutions advancing loss prevention through innovation*. Retrieved October 14, 2007 from www.kmaglobalsolutions.com/index.php?option=com_content&task=view&id=15&Itemid=37.

Levy, M., & Weitz, B. A. (2004). *Retailing Management* (5th ed.). New York: McGraw-Hill Irwin.

Loudon, D., & Della Bitta, A. J. (1988). *Consumer Behavior* (3rd ed.). NY: McGraw-Hill.

National Retail Federation. (2007). NRF *Foundation retail careers and advancement*. Retrieved October 17, 2007, from http://www.nrf.com/RetailCareers/.

PrimeNewswire. (2007, October 10). *KMA Global International announces expansion of source tag supply agreement with major international brand to 50 million units*. Retrieved October 10, 2007, from www.primenewswire.com/newsroom/news.html?d=125624.

Smykay, E.W., & Breibart, J. (1971). *Introductory Marketing*. New York: Macmillan.

The Neiman Marcus Group. (2007). Careers at the Neiman Marcus Group. Retrieved October 10, 2007, from www.neimanmarcuscareers.com/edp/career.shtml.

The Wall Street Journal. (2007, September 27). Heard on the runway. *The Wall Street Journal Online*. Retrieved October 10, 2007, from http://blogs.wsj.com/runway/2007/09/27/dgs-distinguising-details

U.S. Department of Labor. (2007). Appendix: Employment by occupation, 2004 and projected 2014. Retrieved October 17, 2007, from www.bls.gov/emptab1.htm.

Vargas, M. (2007). Retail industry profile. Retrieved September 13, 2007, from http://retailindustryl.about.com/od/abouttheretailindustry/p/retailindustry.htm.

Zara.com. (2007, October 12). Zara. Retrieved October 12, 2007, from www.zara.com.

credits

index